S0-FQO-436

Medieval and Renaissance Series
Number 9

MEDIEVAL

AND

RENAISSANCE STUDIES

Proceedings of the Southeastern Institute
of Medieval and Renaissance Studies
Summer, 1978

Edited by Frank Tirro

Duke University Press, Durham, N.C.

In memoriam

Myron Piper Gilmore

Foreword

During the academic year 1962–63, faculty members and administrative officials of Duke University and the University of North Carolina at Chapel Hill discussed cooperative plans aimed at expanding and improving activities in the humanities. A grant from the Ford Foundation in October, 1963, resulted in the creation of the Cooperative Program in the Humanities, a venture planned and managed by a Joint Central Committee from the two universities. The program quickly improved and expanded, stimulating humanistic studies first in the Carolinas and Virginia and later in the South as a whole. The value of the Cooperative Program was soon recognized in academic communities both regional and national, and many stimulating gatherings of distinguished scholars and eager young researchers and teachers led to productive activities in wide-ranging interdisciplinary programs.

Eventually, the Cooperative Program metamorphosed into a new organization of national and international scope, the Southeastern Institute of Medieval and Renaissance Studies. The first Summer Institute took place on the campus of the University of North Carolina in 1965, and the succeeding Institutes, funded by grants from the National Endowment for the Humanities, the Duke Endowment, the Mary Babcock Reynolds Foundation, the Donner Foundation, and the two universities themselves, alternated between the two campuses every summer for which funding was available.

The essays in this volume were originally presented as public lectures during the ninth session of the Southeastern Institute of Medieval and Renaissance Studies, held on the campus of Duke University from July 3 to August 11, 1978. The breadth of their subject matter, the span of their chronology, and the penetrating thought of each exemplifies the work of this Institute. They are offered here to permit their wider circulation and as a record of the activities of the Institute. A description of the aims of the Institute and a list of seminars and participants are included in the Appendix.

Many individuals contributed generously their invaluable guidance, energy, and time. Their help in nurturing a successful ninth Summer Institute and a volume of Proceedings deserves special attention. Sincere thanks are due the dedicated faculty members of the joint UNC-Duke Committee of the Southeastern Institute: Jaroslav T. Folda, III, John M. Headley, G. Mallary Masters (co-chairman), Aldo Scaglione, Petrus Tax, and Joseph S. Wittig of the University of North Carolina; Edward P. Mahoney, Dale B. J. Randall, Bruce Wardropper, George W. Williams, and Ronald G. Witt of Duke. Gratitude is due all the Senior Fellows who extended themselves far beyond the preparation of seminars and lectures, but especially we are grateful to Professor Arthur B. Ferguson who accepted the challenge of Professor Gilmore's Erasmus seminar at the last possible moment. Frederic N. Cleaveland, then Duke Provost, was deeply involved in the affairs of the Southeastern Institute, and our present Provost, William Bevan, has underwritten the cost of the volume you hold in your hands. The Summer Institute could not have functioned without the aid of hardworking secretaries who arranged housing, receptions, posters, and numerous important details—Robert Baker, Terry Hamlin, Dora Polichek, Janet Whitehead, and Suzanne Wood. No book is complete without an adequate index, and for this we have J. Samuel Hammond to thank.

Holbein's woodcut from the *Dance of Death* served as logo for the ninth Summer Institute, and this emblem seemed particulary appropriate for its combination of artistic, musical, sacred, secular, and philosophical motifs. In retrospect, it pointedly reminds us now, as it did our humanist counterparts in the sixteenth century, that death profanes the temples of life. The one event that clouded the proceedings of the ninth session of the Institute was the absence of Myron Piper Gilmore, Gurney Professor of History and Political Science at Harvard University. Illness prevented his coming, and after a few short months, death took him from us. All those who knew him feel his loss poignantly, and it is to him that the present volume is dedicated.

Beatus homo qui invenit sapientiam,
   Et qui affluit prudentia.
Melior est acquistio eius negotiatione argenti,
   Et auri primi et purissimi fructus eius.

Proverbs 3:13–14

Frank Tirro
Chairman, 1977–1980

February, 1980
Durham, N.C.

Contents

MEDIEVAL

AND

RENAISSANCE STUDIES

I

An Apocalypse Panel on the Ruthwell Cross

Paul Meyvaert

The Mediæval Academy of America

William Camden (1551–1623) had, on his own admission, been interested in the past since his schoolboy days. Before becoming schoolmaster at Westminster at the age of twenty-four, he had already visited the "antiquities" of many parts of Britain and taken notes on them. In 1577 he met the geographer Abraham Ortelius, then on a visit to England, and received the advice "to restore Britain to Antiquity and Antiquity to Britain" by producing an antiquarian survey of the whole country based on his topographical notes. The result was a small octavo volume, issued in 1586, under the title *Britannia*.[1] It proved to be a great success and went through several editions, passing from octavo through quarto to folio size within the author's own lifetime. The work won him a group of ardent admirers, eager to supply new material for future editions. Most of the material sent to Camden is now lost, but some fragments survive, for example, in British Library MS Cotton Julius F. VI. A few of the notes in this miscellany are in Camden's own hand, others in the hands of some of his correspondents. On a page now numbered folio 352 is a Latin note of one of Camden's admirers, Reginald Bainbrigg of Appleby (in Westmorland), which reads:

This past winter, moved by a great desire for enquiry, I wandered over the hills and valleys and into the ancient churches of Scotland—where did I not go? what place did I not approach? to find something new—when unexpectedly I encountered a cross of wonderful height which is in the church at Ruthwell. It has on it beautiful images telling the story of Christ. It is wonderfully decorated with vines and animals, and on the two sides, ascending from the base to the top, and then opposite, descending from the top to the base, it is incised with strange and unknown letters. The inscription runs thus [here follow a few of the runes, as copied by Bainbrigg].[2]

Other information in the Cotton manuscript shows that Bainbrigg made journeys to Scotland in 1599 and 1601. It remains uncertain which of these journeys produced the note just quoted.[3] But Bainbrigg's brief lines appear to be the earliest reference extant to the Ruthwell Cross.

Another of Camden's correspondents, Nicholas Roscarrock, provides (in a letter of August 1607) the first written reference to the Bewcastle Cross, a monument recognized to have close iconographical affinities with the cross at Ruthwell.[4] Camden mentioned the Bewcastle Cross in the sixth edition of *Britannia*, published in the same year, 1607.[5] But the information sent to him by Bainbrigg about the Ruthwell Cross was never printed.[6]

The era of rediscovery was obviously fired with enthusiasm and admiration for these notable antiquities, but unfortunately it was followed by the darkest chapter in the history of the Ruthwell monument, when the esteem of antiquarians gave way to the animosity of zealots and iconoclasts. The General Assembly of the Church of Scotland, held at Aberdeen in 1640, passed an "Act anent the demolishing of Idolatrous Monuments" (Session 2, held on 29 July) which reads:

Forasmuch as the Assembly is informed, that in divers places of this Kingdome, and specially in the North parts of the same, many Idolatrous Monuments, erected and made for Religious worship, are yet extant, Such as Crucifixes, Images of Christ, Mary, and Saints departed, ordaines the saids Monuments to be taken down, demolished, and destroyed, and that with all convenient diligence: And that the care of this work shall be incumbent to the Presbyteries and Provinciall Assemblies within this Kingdome; and their Commissioners to report their diligence herein to the next Generall Assembly.[7]

(The printed acts of the next General Assembly, of 1641, however, make no mention of this subject.) In the following year, 1642, when the Assembly was held at St. Andrews, the matter was again raised, in the fourth session, on 30 July, this time in connection with "Idolatrous Monuments in Ruthwell." The act was a short one: "Anent the report of idolatrous monuments in the Kirk of Ruthwell the Assemblie finds that the monument therin mentioned is idolatrous, and therefore recommends to the Presbyterie that they carefully urge the order prescrived by the Act of Parliament anent the abolishing of these monuments, to be put to execution."[8] It should be noted that the reference here is to a single monument, which must be the Ruthwell Cross. One may regret that minutes of the deliberations were not kept, since these might have informed us which specific iconographic features of the cross were considered most objectionable. We must assume that there were no passionate antiquarians among those who passed the act, or among those who were commissioned to carry out its main provision, namely, the breaking up and defacement of the monument that had excited Bainbrigg's admiration. That this provision of the act was zealously carried out is only too evident from the subsequent record of events.

The fact that there is a subsequent record is again mainly due to the interest in antiquity and especially in monuments containing strange and unusual inscriptions which continued to animate the learned men of the following century. It is not my intention here to cite every allusion to the cross that can be traced, but only those which allow us to see how the shattered fragments of the cross were gradually recovered and reunited to form a whole.[9]

In September 1690 William Nicolson, canon and later bishop of Carlisle, was first informed of the existence of a stone with runic inscriptions at Ruthwell.[10] But it was only in April of 1697 that he was able to visit Dumfriesshire and make a transcription.[11] This he sent to George Hickes, the English divine and scholar who published it in the section on Islandic writing of his *Linguarum Vett. Septentrionalium Thesaurus Grammaticocriticus et Archaeologicus* (1703).[12] In 1704 Nicolson revisited Ruthwell to check his earlier transcription and made some further notes in his diary:

Besides these [inscriptions] there are some little Fragments of them on the heavy pedestal of this Cross which lyes in Murray's Quire [choir], the antient burial place of the Murrays Earls of Annan now extinct. This was so clumsy and unwieldy that we could not (without Crows and Levers) remove it. But on the side which lay to view were these words—ET INGRESSUS ANGELUS . . . Some lesser pieces which seem to have been in the middle, we found thrown under Throughstones in the Church-yard.[13]

The section of the cross whose four sides were described by Nicolson and whose inscriptions were printed in Hickes' work is the same section that was illustrated by Alexander Gordon in his *Itinerarium Septentrionale*, published in 1726. Concerning the piece which Nicolson calls "the pedestal of the cross" Gordon comments, "This obelisk, some think, was originally of one entire stone, but is now broke into three parts. . . . On the lowest of its three divisions is a representation of our Saviour upon the cross with two figures, one on each side, much defaced."[14] Since the Annunciation and Crucifixion are on the same side, this statement implies that when Gordon saw it the lower part still lay imbedded in the floor of the church, as in Nicolson's day. It was only extracted from the floor towards the end of the eighteenth century, as we learn from the description of the monument which Richard Gough wrote to accompany the engraving by A. de Cardonnel published in volume II of *Vetusta Monumenta* (1789). Gough writes: "The lower half of the two figures with the inscription has been lately recovered from the filth and dirt which covered them."[15] This made possible for the first time a description of the other three sides of the lower section.

In 1772 Thomas Pennant had made a tour of Scotland and visited Ruthwell. In describing the various fragments of what he terms the Ruthwell "obelisk" he remarks:

The pedestal lies buried beneath the floor of the church: I found some fragments of the capital [he means the uppermost portion], with letters similar to the others; and on each opposite side an eagle, neatly cut in relief. There was also a piece of another, with Saxon [he means non-runic] letters round *the lower part of a human figure, in long vestments, with his foot* [sic] *on a pair of small globes*; this too seemed to have been the top of a cross.[16]

Pennant believed that this last fragment belonged to another monument, but by 1789 (as can be seen from Cardonnel's drawing and Gough's description), the connection of this piece with the other fragments had been made:

The upper part of the stone on this side contains another compartment, having in relief *a half figure standing on two balls or globes*, and this imperfect inscription on the border round it DORAMUS T NONEUM. (Plate I)[17]

At a date between 1799 and 1802—we are not sure of the exact year—a singular discovery was made:

A poor man and his wife having died within a day or two of each other, it was resolved that they should both be buried in the same grave, which, on that account, required to be made unusually deep. The gravedigger in the course of his labour came to a fragment of sandstone of considerable bulk, which was found, on one of its sides, to contain the upper part of the image of the Supreme Being, with the *Agnus Dei* in his bosom, and, on the reverse, a representation of the upper part of two human figures in the act of embracing. On applying this fragment to the monument, it was found to coincide with that portion of it which Pennant mistook for the top of a cross, the limbs and flowing robes of the image of the Deity being that which he describes as "the lower part of a human figure in long vestments, with his feet on a pair of small globes." It had probably been surreptitiously buried along with the body of some votary of the Church of Rome . . . from a superstitious belief in its supernatural virtues.

This account was written by the Reverend Henry Duncan, minister of the Ruthwell church for forty-four years (1799–1843), whose name will always remain honorably associated with the Ruthwell Cross.[18] After the imperfect notices of earlier observers, Duncan brings to the Ruthwell monument a discerning eye, and—as will appear—a helping hand. He recognized that this important fragment (which he rightly associated with those surviving aboveground) had been intentionally buried, at some depth, and sought to explain this remarkable circumstance by suggesting that adherents of the Roman Church had been the agents of the burial. We may ask, however, whether this major fragment could not have been buried by enemies rather than friends, in order to remove it forever from the light of day and the sight of their fellow men. If so, we should bear in mind the further question: why should this particular fragment be so much more obnoxious than the others left aboveground? What (or whom) did the iconoclasts see on this part of the cross before they defaced it?

Henry Duncan was concerned not only about the buried fragment but also about those that lay on the ground of the unenclosed churchyard,[19] and decided in the summer of 1802 to assemble the various fragments and re-erect the monument in a garden which he had laid out next to the churchyard. It would seem that in this year all the surviving pieces were set up in the form of a single column, the missing pieces being replaced by other pieces of stone (see Plates II, III, IV). At that time Duncan evidently entertained hopes that some day he might recover the lost transom, but by 1823 he had concluded that this part was irretrievably lost, and in that year, basing his design on the shape of the uppermost fragment or "capital" and also on "drawings of similar Popish relics," he produced, with the aid of a country mason, the transom still seen today at Ruthwell.[20] No one would now claim that this reconstruction bears any real relation to what must have been the original design. Whether the original transom still lies buried, waiting to be discovered, is an open question as far as I am concerned. But we have some right, I believe, to assume that the disappearance of this piece may likewise be connected with its specific iconographic content.

Duncan was the first to establish that the cross had originally been made from two separate blocks of sandstone. This led him to surmise that the stones had been cut at different times, and that the upper stone was later, and of less perfect workmanship than the lower one.[21] He also had this further observation to make about the figure standing on the globes:

The lower compartment of the upper stone . . . contains the image of the Father standing on two globes or worlds (indicating probably the world which now is and that which is to come), with the Agnus Dei in his bosom. The only letters of the legend which can be deciphered are D O R A M U S, being doubtless part of the word *adoramus*.[22]

The Ruthwell Cross was declared to be an "ancient monument" under the provisions of the Ancient Monuments Protection Act of 1882. It had then stood in the open for close to a century, and to prevent further damage and deterioration through weathering, it was decided to place it under cover once more. A special apse was constructed on the north side of the church, and the cross was moved there in 1887, while the Reverend James McFarlan was minister of the church.[23] The cross today still stands in this special apse.

Some wild hypotheses were at first developed about the meaning of the runic inscription on the cross. John Kemble was the first, in 1840, to identify the runes as Anglo-Saxon[24] and, in 1844, to point out their connection with the poem called the "Dream of the Rood," found in the Vercelli manuscript.[25] This last discovery was also made independently, in 1865, by F. E. C. Dietrich.[26] The problems of the cross and the poem have remained intertwined ever since, the cross being used to date the poem, and the poem to interpret the cross. I believe it can be shown that the runic verses are a later addition, and that for this reason the dates of the cross and of the poem must be dissociated.[27]

The iconographic links between the Ruthwell and Bewcastle Crosses remained unknown for a long time. Since the Bewcastle Cross lacked any identifying Latin inscriptions around its panels, and also since it was in far worse condition (due to having always stood out in the open), the identification of the panels presented more difficulties. William Nicolson (mentioned above), in a letter of 1865 to Obadiah Walker, identified at the top of the Bewcastle Cross "the Effigies of the B[lessed] V[irgin] with the Babe in her Arms," in the middle zone "the Picture of some Apostle, Saint or other Holy man, in a sacerdotal Habit," and at the bottom "the Pourtraicture of a Layman; with a Hawk, or Eagle, perch'd on his Arm."[28] Daniel and Samuel Lysons in volume IV of their *Magna Britannia* (on Cumberland), published in 1816, identified the middle figure as Christ. They had this to say about the uppermost figure, described by Bishop Nicolson as "the Blessed Virgin with the Babe in her Arms": "This description, which several succeeding writers appear to have copied, without inspecting the original, is very erroneous. The female figure is so defaced that nothing more than a general outline can be distinguished; what she holds in her left arm is much better preserved, and is evidently the holy lamb."[29]

D. H. Haigh, in a paper published in 1857, seems to have been the first to assert an iconographic link between the Bewcastle and Ruthwell Crosses. Although he was familiar with Duncan's paper, Haigh nowhere discusses Duncan's explanation of the figure standing on the globes, but unhesitatingly asserts that this figure on both crosses represents John the Baptist with the Holy Lamb.[30] George Stephens, in his monumental *The Old-Northern Runic Monuments of Scandinavia and England*, which appeared in 1866, does quote Duncan on one page (p. 407), but in his description of the panel (p. 413), without further discussion, adopts Haigh's identification of the figure as John the Baptist. With the single exception of James McFarlan's little pamphlet,[31] all the works I have consulted right down to the most recent ones state that the panel containing the lamb represents John the Baptist. An alternative explanation like that proposed by Duncan is never mentioned, not even to be dismissed. Most accounts, on the contrary, seem to assume that the traditional iconography of John the Baptist puts the identification of the figure on the Ruthwell panel beyond the limits of doubt.[32]

A few writers have sought to go beyond iconography and integrate the figure of the Baptist within an overall theological interpretation that links all the panels together into a unified theme. Thus Fritz Saxl writes: "The Jews had sacrificed the paschal lamb, and obtained salvation from Egyptian servitude; Christ is the paschal lamb, which taketh away the sin of the world. . . . St. John, the "voice of one crying in the wilderness," is therefore shown on the Cross above Christ in Majesty whom the beasts and dragons adore in the desert."[33] Meyer Schapiro, who interprets the cross as a celebration by recalcitrant British or Celtic monks of the eremitical ideal, in defiance of Rome, is able neatly to fit the figure of St. John the Baptist, "prototype of Christian asceticism," into this general argument.[34]

I would like, however, to raise a basic question: Was the panel we are dealing with conceived originally to represent John the Baptist, as everyone now assumes? Henry Duncan had felt no hesitation whatever in stating that the figure represented the "Supreme Being," "the Father," and this because the figure was standing on "a pair of globes."[35] Most scholars who have dealt with the cross overlook this feature entirely, or do not consider that it merits comment. A few, however, have felt the need to make some observations, and these are worth examining. Fritz Saxl, in a footnote to his study of 1943, has this to say: "the strange globes under St. John's feet are probably a kind of suppedaneum [footstool]." Saxl does admit the oddness of this feature, and thought it could be explained by some kind of oval or circular (or semicircular) design present in a footstool. It is unlikely that anyone who examines the examples he provides (see Plates V and VI) will be convinced that they offer an adequate explanation.[36] Saxl seems to have been unaware of the earlier discussion of this feature in the official report on the Ruthwell Cross, by G. Baldwin Brown and A. Blyth Webster.[37] These authors make no mention of Duncan's hypothesis, and take it for granted that the panel represents John the Baptist. However their comment about the globes is interesting:

The two feet of the Baptist are generally described as supported on round globes, but others have seen in these supposed "globes" merely a pair of wooden "sabots" seen in front view. The "sabot" ... is the footgear of Mary and Elizabeth in the "Visitation" [on the reverse side of the cross], but in this case of the Baptist the old view is really the correct one, for on a close inspection the two feet are seen fully modelled outside and on the top of the two globe-like objects, and not *in* them, as would be the case were they "sabots." The probability is that there was some miscalculation about the height of the figure. . . .[38]

"Miscalculation" is, of course, a convenient method for disposing of an awkward problem. It should be stressed that the conclusion of Brown and Webster, that the feet were on a pair of globes, fully agrees with the earliest descriptions, which, as we saw above,[39] were made before the monument was erected in the open where it then stood for almost a century, exposed to the elements (see also Plate I). At this point no help can be obtained from the Bewcastle Cross, which had always stood out of doors, and whose surfaces had much deteriorated over the centuries. It is certainly not possible to say that the figure on the Bewcastle Cross did not also stand originally on a pair of globes.

It would seem appropriate to me that we should now try to rethink this identification, starting afresh, and basing our thinking on what can actually be seen on the cross today, or deduced from descriptions of competent witnesses who saw it in a less deteriorated condition. I would suggest that we start with the Latin inscription. The only sequence of letters that can be read with certainty is the one on the lower half of the vertical border on the right side of the figure: D O R A M U S (see Plates II and III). There has never been any doubt about this sequence, nor that it represents the word *adoramus*. There are traces of incisions in the horizontal border below the figure, and these have been read differently by different authors. In the 1787 publication by Cardonnel and Gough a sequence T N O N E V M is given.[40] A glance at Plate II may suggest how Gough's reading could have been thought possible,[41] but it presumes forms of N and O that occur in none of the other inscriptions.[42] After carefully examining the cast of the cross at the Victoria and Albert Museum, and projecting lights over the surface from every angle, I concluded that only two letters could be discerned with any degree of certainty, namely a V followed by an M (V ᚻ) directly under the globe on which the left foot rests.[43] But it is impossible to see what word these letters were part of. A sequence like *adoramus in eternum. amen* cannot be ruled out. It remains, however, that Henry Duncan and other writers were quite correct in stating that *adoramus* was the only word of this inscription about which we can have any certainty.

In 1974 D. R. Howlett proposed a way to complete the inscription around the panel.[44] Accepting the sequence of letters in Cardonnel-Gough as authentic, he proposed a stanza:

> Agnum Dei aDORAMUS eT NON EUM
> singilatim totam vero Trinitatem,

and suggested that this could have been laid out around the panel:

(a) descend left border
(b) lower border
(c) upper border
(d) descend right border

or

(a) descend left border
(b) lower border
(c) ascend right border
(d) upper border

Neither of these arrangements is acceptable. Since the Latin inscriptions on the other panels—which Howlett did not consider—are laid out in a consistent manner, we have no ground for assuming that this panel departed from the norm.[45] Here is a survey of the other panels:

(1)   †IHS XPS / IVDEX AEQVITATIS
      BESTIAE ET DRACONES COGNOVERVNT IN DESERTO SALVATOREM MVNDI (cf. Is. 43:20)

The inscription consists of two distinct statements. The first was begun in the upper border and continued on the right. The second statement was begun in the left border and then continued in the remaining space of the right border.

(2)   †SCS PAVLVS / ET A[ntonius——] / FREGERVNT
        PANEM IN DESERTO

The inscription, in all probability a single statement, begins in the upper border, continues on the right, and gets completed on the left.

(3)   †MARIA ET IO[s] / [eph——in Aegyp] / TV[m——] (cf. Matt. 2:14)

The inscription begins in the upper border and like (2) probably continued on the right, to finish on the left.

(4)   †A[ttulit alaba] / STRVM VNGVENTI ET STANS RETRO
        SECVS PEDES / EIVS LACRIMIS COEPIT RIGARE
        PEDES EIVS ET CAPILLIS / CAPITIS SVI TERGEBAT
        (cf. Luke 7:37–38)

This, the longest of the inscriptions, begins again in the upper border, continues on the right, then on the left, and finishes in the lower border.

(5)   †ET PRAETERIENS VIDI[t hominem caecum] /
        A NATIVITATE ET SA[navit eum a]B INFIRMITA[te]
        (cf. John 9:1)

Since the upper border of this panel was already filled by the concluding words of the previous long text, the inscription was put on the left and then continued on the right.

(6)   [† et] INGRESSUS ANGEL[us] / [ad eam dixit ave
        gratia plena dominus] / TECVM BEN[edicta tu in
        mulieribus] (cf. Luke 1:28)

This inscription begins in the upper border, continues on the right, and ends on the left.

On the basis of this evidence we are therefore justified in assuming that the word *adoramus* came towards the end of the inscription. The inscription, in fact, ended with a call to adoration.

It is the presence of this one word, *adoramus*, that singles this panel out from all the others. It should be noted that the other inscriptions are all descriptive in nature. Making use of wording taken for the most part from the Scriptures, they explain the contents of the panel to the beholder. While it is true that our panel does contain the figure of a lamb, no onlooker would be in doubt that the figure behind the lamb is the one that dominates the panel. The inscription must also have alluded to this figure.

Can this figure be John the Baptist? The scriptural basis for representing the Baptist with a lamb is well known. In the Gospel of John, on two occasions (1:29,36), John points to Jesus with the words "Ecce Agnus Dei." The characteristic later medieval iconography of the Baptist holding a lamb might incline us to believe— as indeed it persuaded D. H. Haigh—that the Ruthwell panel must belong to this tradition.[46] But some caution is necessary here. We know that in the East, from an early date, the Baptist was represented with a lamb. The Quinisext Council (known as the Council in Trullo) in 692 took note of the fact that scenes in which the Baptist pointed to a lamb as an image of Christ had become common, and prohibited the depiction of Christ in this manner.[47] Since the decree speaks only of the Baptist pointing to a lamb, it offers no clear evidence for a figure carrying a lamb.

However such a figure does occur in one panel of the famous Maximian chair at Ravenna (see Plate VII). Here the Baptist, identifiable by his camel-hair cloak, carries a medallion containing the lamb. This ivory chair apparently reached Ravenna in the middle of the sixth century, but most art historians believe that it was made either in Alexandria or at Constantinople.[48] In any case it shows us the kind of iconography that was current in the East before 692.

It is by no means clear how the iconography of the Baptist developed in the West. The *Liber Pontificalis* states that Pope Sylvester (314–335) caused a baptismal font to be made which displayed "in labio fontis baptisterii agnum aureum fundentem aquam . . . ad dexteram agni, Salvatorem . . . in leva agni, beatum Iohannem Baptistam."[49] The Baptist was therefore represented here, together with Christ, close to the figure of a lamb, but clearly not carrying the lamb in his arms. When did the figure of the Baptist holding a lamb become popular in the West? A search through the Princeton Index of Christian Art fails to turn up any undeniably Western example that predates the year 900. Those who accept the identification of the Ruthwell figure as the Baptist might point to it as such an example, with a possible parallel in the Baptist panel of the Ravenna throne. But there are many points of difference between these two depictions—at Ruthwell there is no suggestion of a camel-hair cloak, there is no medallion, and the lamb faces in the opposite direction; on the Ravenna chair it turns its head back to look at the Baptist; at Ruthwell a much more intimate relationship is shown, with the lamb's head resting on the breast of the standing figure. All these features suggest a quite different tradition, and this is only reinforced when we add the presence of the two globes under the figure's feet. It is also difficult to imagine how the rather short inscription around the panel could have referred to the Baptist as the main subject, and yet ended in a call to adoration (*adoramus*). We must therefore seek the solution to this problem in another direction.

Having noticed how many of the other Latin inscriptions on the cross borrow the words of Scripture, we can begin by asking what texts link together the word *adorare* with images of a lamb and another figure. A glance at a Latin concordance of the Bible shows that there is only one possible source, the Book of Revelation. Here we encounter numerous allusions to "the one seated on the throne." and to "the lamb," linked with references to the adoration paid to the Deity. For example: "et clamabant voce magna dicentes salus *Deo nostro qui sedet super thronum et agno . . .* et ceciderunt in conspectu throni in facies suas *et adoraverunt* Deum dicentes: Amen" (Apoc. 7:10–12). These are the elements we need to explain the mysterious figure on the Ruthwell Cross, and I believe that we have here the main key for understanding this crucial panel. It now remains for us to see whether the panel can be fitted into a recognizable tradition of Apocalypse imagery, or at least to see whether sufficient evidence survives to persuade us that the Ruthwell panel was designed as a *maiestas* scene based on the Apocalypse.

Art historians recognize that the Ruthwell Cross is a unique monument in that we know of no obvious and immediate prototypes that can account for the iconography of the cross as a whole. Nor indeed do there seem to be any immediate models for the individual panels. As Saxl explains it, we can assume that Mediterranean models do underlie the panels, but these have all been given a peculiar Northumbrian cast. It would, of course, be interesting to know what sort of models were used—ivories, painted panels, illuminated manuscripts. Since the manuscript tradition is our main source for knowledge of Apocalypse illustrations, we have the added problem of passing from one medium (monumental sculpture) to another (illuminated manuscripts). This has immediate implications concerning the layout of a *maiestas* scene. In the manuscript tradition the central figure—whether it be God the Father, Christ, the Lamb, or the Throne—is always shown surrounded by the four animals that are mentioned in the text of the Apocalypse. On a page in a book these animals can be neatly arranged around the central figure. But the obligatory shape of any cross makes such a disposition difficult. It is therefore important to note that immediately above our panel we find the four animals (as evangelist symbols) forming the four arms of the cross-head.[50] We do not know, unfortunately, what figure was represented in the central panel of the cross-head. It could well have been another Apocalypse lamb, standing on the sealed book, such as we find on two of the cross-heads discovered in 1891 in the foundations of the post-Conquest Chapter House at Durham, and now preserved there in the Chapter Library.[51]

Our problematical panel is dominated by the male figure standing on two globes. As we saw above, it was the presence of these globes which led Henry Duncan to conclude that the figure represented "the Father" or "the Deity." His explanation of the globes as signifying "the present world" and "the world to come" can now no doubt be disregarded, but his suspicion that the globes were intended to be symbols of divinity was a shrewd one, and it is unfortunate that this significant feature has been so constantly overlooked by later writers. Anyone who has studied the works of Gisinger,[52] Alföldi,[53] Schramm,[54] Cook[55] and others[56] will find it difficult to doubt that the globe is, indeed, an attribute of divinity or sovereignty—one which Christian artists borrowed from pre-Christian classical art. It is interesting, for example, to compare a painting at Dura-Europas, which shows five little divinities standing on their quartered globes,[57] with a gold glass in the Vatican Museum, where Christ is shown seated with an identical globe at his feet.[58] In antiquity both the heavens and the earth were represented in the form of spheres. Christian artists could therefore illustrate a text like Isaias 66:1 ("the heaven is my seat and the earth is my footstool") by showing God the Father or Christ seated on a globe with another globe beneath the feet. Globes abound in the surviving art works, single globes serving as seats or footstools, and double ones as seat and footstool, or one as seat with the other held as an orb in the hand. The uniqueness of the Ruthwell panel lies in the fact that the two globes are placed under the two feet.

I suggested above, when alluding to the animals that usually surround *maiestas* scenes in Apocalypse illustrations, that the shape of the cross presented an obstacle to their being depicted in similar fashion on the stone. It could likewise be asked whether the problem of depicting a globe as seat on such a panel caused it to migrate to a different position, resulting in double globes under the feet. Or were the two globes intended to show that the figure should be considered as a seated figure, even though he is represented as standing? It must be remembered that one of the conventions of the insular art of the period was the representa-

tion of standing evangelists with the suggestion of a chair behind
them (see Plate V), to indicate that they were in fact meant to be
considered as seated. This would therefore be a somewhat parallel convention.[59]

Although I have been unable to find any other clear examples
of two globes beneath the feet, there are two medieval art works
that deserve consideration in this connection. One is an ivory gospel cover at Darmstadt dated from the early tenth century (Plate
VIII). A. Goldschmidt describes the central figure thus: "Christus
thront auf dem Regenbogen, die Füsse auf der Weltkugel, in der
wiederum kleinere, Kreise unterschieden sind."[60] Here we do
have the suggestion of a circle under each foot, and the text presented by the open book is a significant one: "Data est mihi omnis
potestas in celo et in terra." The Apocalypse makes no mention of
a figure seated on the rainbow (*iris*) but it does speak of the rainbow surrounding the throne (Apoc. 4:3 "et iris erat in circuitu
sedis"). If the large circle around the lower portion of the seated
Christ is meant as a rainbow, this would establish this image within
the Apocalypse tradition. We might then ask whether the two
circles under the feet were originally globes meant to represent
"heaven" and "earth" over which all power is given to Christ.[61]
The Darmstadt ivory should be related to one of the paintings in
the famous St. Sever Apocalypse where, on folio 199, Christ is
shown seated, holding an open book, again with similar circles
under each foot.[62] The inscription here reads: "ubi quatuor ani-
malia et viginti quatuor seniores adorant tronum" (see Plate IX).
The link between this image and the Darmstadt ivory (where the
four animals also occur) is striking, and suggests the existence of
a tradition within which the Ruthwell panel could be placed.

We come finally to the juxtaposition of the lamb and the male
figure. An attentive reader of the Book of Revelation soon becomes aware that a certain ambiguity permeates the great *maiestas*
scenes that are presented to him. The central images are those of
"a throne" or "seat," of "one seated on the throne," of "a lamb"
who is "in the middle of the throne," or who is positioned in such
close proximity to "the one seated on the throne" that both together are the single object of adoration; thus the throne can be
referred to as the single "seat of God and of the lamb." This ambiguity—on the level of verbal images—is reflected in the surviv-

ing works of art. Translating the Deity—and especially a Deity that was also a Trinity, hemmed about with dogmatic formulations—into visual terms presented problems to Christian artists. Although by no means frequent, the attempt was occasionally made to represent the Apocalypse imagery of "the one seated on the throne" and "the lamb" together, in close proximity, so that "the throne" could be considered to hold both together.

The St. Sever Apocalypse has an example in the large *maiestas* scene on fols. 121v-122 (Plate X). A male figure seated on a globe occupies its center, with his feet resting on the segment of another globe. In his right hand he holds over his breast a medallion in which a lamb is standing. The left hand holds a staff which terminates in another medallion which contains a dove.[63] This is therefore an attempt to represent the Deity as Trinity—with the addition of one element, the dove, not mentioned in the Apocalypse text.

We can also find the representation of a male figure, with cruciform halo, holding a large medallion in which a lamb is shown, on fol. 88r of the famous *Liber Floridus* (see Plate XI). The table of contents (fol. 4r, n. LXXVIII) gives as title for this page "De IIII[or] elementis" and, indeed, on the folio in question we now find texts about fire, air, earth, and water.[64] But a close look at this folio reveals that the whole layout of the design was originally intended to represent a scene from the Apocalypse. Some of the inscriptions meant for this purpose are still plainly legible. Close to the two upper medallions, to the right and left of the mandorla, we read the names of Matthew and John—to which no doubt corresponded the names of Mark and Luke near the lower medallions. On the left-hand side of the page we read "Angelus fortis," and on the level of the base of the altar "Iohannes unus de senioribus dixit ei," and "Senior dixit dignus est agnus aperire." Since none of these inscriptions have any connection with the theme of the four elements, they were omitted in the Wolfenbüttel copy of the *Liber Floridus*.[65] The inscriptions surrounding the mandorla and the circle at the bottom of the page are liturgical texts based on the Apocalypse. The lamb in the medallion faces in the same direction as the lamb in the Ruthwell panel; one foot is raised to touch the book, but the damage done to the Ruthwell monument prevents us from knowing if this feature was also repeated there.

Hanns Swarzenski has remarked that Lambert of St. Omer, the compiler of the *Liber Floridus*, rarely invented anything; instead he constantly copied from earlier models.[66] We can therefore conclude from folio 88r the existence of an iconographic tradition representing the lamb and seated figure together in an Apocalypse cycle that must not be confused with the "Apocalypse depictus" contained in another section of the *Liber Floridus*.[67] The same basic iconography—lamb in medallion held by seated Lord, with lamb touching book—is also found on fol. 113v of Berlin, Kupferstichkabinett MS 78 A 1, a North-German Gospel Book of about the year 1050. The illustration here precedes the Gospel of John.[68]

Of even greater interest for our present purpose is the cycle of illustrations to which the name of the English Apocalypse has been given. This tradition is known to us through a fairly large group of manuscripts. There is still debate among art historians about the various families that constitute the group and their interrelationship, and much of the manuscript material still remains unpublished.[69] There is agreement, however, that the cycle had its origin in England, although it gained much popularity also on the other side of the Channel. None of the surviving manuscripts appears to be the archetype of the group as a whole, and none predates the thirteenth century.

Since there was a considerable amount of borrowing in the course of the transmission, a full-scale genealogical study of each separate illustration will be needed to determine what was, in each case, the earliest form.[70] Only when this investigation is complete will we have an idea of what the manuscript looked like from which the cycle descends, and only at that stage will it be possible to say something useful about the much earlier model which underlies the thirteenth-century group.

While keeping this caution in mind, we may nevertheless point to one feature distinguishing the English Apocalypse cycle; that is the manner in which, in the *maiestas* scenes, the figure of "the one seated on the throne" and "the lamb" are represented in close proximity, the lamb in these instances not being contained in a medallion (see Plates XII and XIII). This juxtaposition is, of course, what we find on the Ruthwell panel.[71] There is also frequently a globe at the feet of the seated figure, and he is often

PLATES

I. Detail of engraving by Cardonnel (1789)

II. Figure standing on globes (front view)

Courtesy of the Warburg Institute

III. Figure standing on globes (side view)

IV. Figure standing on globes (side view)

Courtesy of the Warburg Institute

V. E. H. Zimmermann, "Plate 275" (see note 36)

VI. Cover of Sancta Sanctorum Cross (see note 36)

VII. Chair of Maximian, Ravenna (John the Baptist)

VIII. Darmstadt Gospel Cover

IX. St. Sever Apocalypse, fol. 199

X. St. Sever Apocalypse, fols. 121v–122

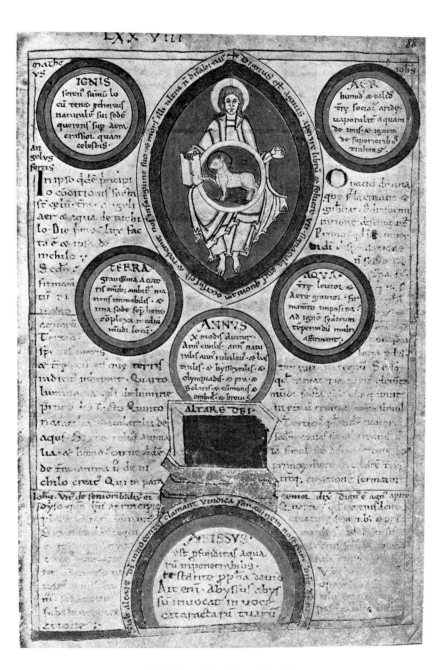

XI. Liber Floridus, fol. 88

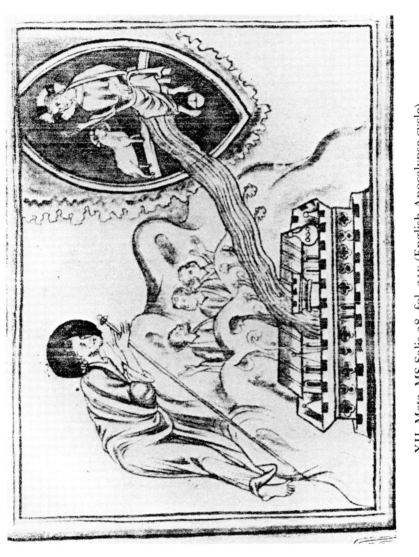

XII. Metz, MS Salis 38, fol. 31v (English Apocalypse cycle)

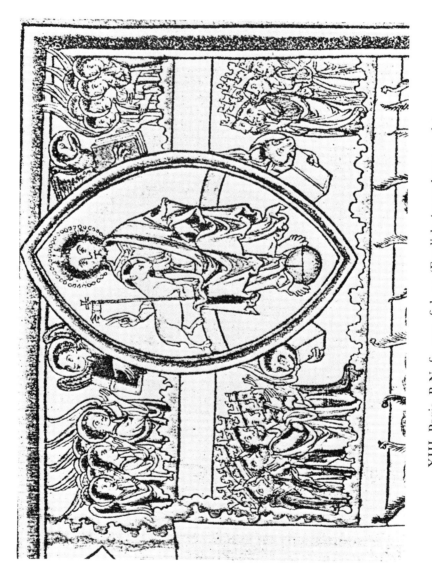

XIII. Paris, B.N. fr. 403, fol. 11 (English Apocalypse cycle)

XIV. Ruthwell Cross (vinescroll and runic verses)

Courtesy of the Warburg Institute

shown seated on the segment of an arc. It appears, therefore, that the English Apocalypse cycle must have had a much earlier model which is in some way connected with the iconography of the Ruthwell panel. In other words, the panel seems to bear witness in the eighth century—if that is when the cross was made—to the existence of an iconographic tradition for which evidence is lacking in the intervening period, but which gains wide currency and considerable popularity in the thirteenth century.

As Henry Duncan related in his account of 1833, the fragment of the cross that contains the lamb was unearthed at the end of the eighteenth century, after having lain buried underground for a long time. It is remarkable that a block of stone that had been thus protected by a deep layer of earth should appear so heavily defaced, far more so in fact than the pieces that had remained aboveground. It has the appearance of having been severly mutilated in an attempt to obliterate the face of the figure and the lamb, as well as the inscription surrounding the panel. At this point we should recall that this fragment had evidently been intentionally buried, perhaps by friends (as Duncan thought), otherwise more likely by foes, but in any case for reasons that must have been related in some way to the understanding at the time of what the panel represented. There can be no doubt that a figure representing the Deity would have been considered more "idolatrous" than would one of John the Baptist. There are traces of halos around the heads of both the figure and the lamb, but it is impossible to determine whether these were originally cruciform, like the ones around the head of Christ in the other panels, and also in the Apocalypse illustrations of the English cycle.

I believe that a reasonable case has now been made for considering the panel we are dealing with as a representation, not of John the Baptist, but of a *maiestas* scene from the Apocalypse. Does this mean that we are now in a position to interpret its meaning, and to explain how it fits into the overall theological scheme that inspired the cross? Is it, in fact, legitimate to think in terms of a unified conceptual synthesis at this period? Anyone who has begun to read through the Apocalypse commentaries that could have been circulating at the time—Victorinus as modified by Jerome, Tyconius, Primasius, Caesarius of Arles, and Bede—and who has noticed how this or that particular verse was treated, will soon come to realize that the Apocalypse imagery lent itself to a wealth of interpretations. Which text are we going to choose, and which particular interpretation, as the key to the Ruthwell monument? According to Caesarius of Arles "the one seated on the throne" stands for "the Father and the Son," and the lamb for "the Church, together with its head, which dies for Christ so that it may live for Christ."[72] Tyconius—whom Caesarius and Bede admire, despite his Donatist background—opts for the equation of the lamb with the Church.[73] Thus Henry Duncan's spontaneous identification of the Deity and the Agnus Dei, which I take to be well-founded in his personal observation, seems far less firm and straightforward in the light of these other possibilities.

Is there anything, then, that we can assert with confidence? All that we know of the ancient monument at Ruthwell, in its sadly battered condition, recommends us to treat it with caution as well as respect. Its very uniqueness compounds our difficulties. For comparison we have a few other old crosses, but nothing so elaborate; the nearest parallel, the Bewcastle Cross, is much less complex in conception, and even more dilapidated. There are no written sources with specific relevance to the iconography of crosses, and the Scripture commentaries in circulation at the time disagree in their interpretation of this or that image. Manuscript illuminations, ivories, metalwork, and the like, give us little guidance for the early period that produced the cross.

In this situation we cannot hope to recapture the full significance of the Ruthwell monument. But in recognizing the Apocalypse panel for what it is, we have altered such understanding as we do possess, I believe for the better. We now have a scene that fully justifies the *adoramus* of the inscription, and explains the particular animosity of the later iconoclasts. The implications of the panel are also altered in a subtle but significant way. In replacing a depiction of John the Baptist with a *maiestas* scene we have exchanged an element of anticipation, as expressed by the Precursor, for an element of completion and fulfillment. In this connection it is perhaps worth noting that the scenes at the bottom of the shaft on this side of the cross are related to the infancy of Christ; there may be a sense of temporal progression from the beginning of Christ's earthly life at the bottom to his appearance in glory at the top. I would hesitate, however, to place much weight on such a suggestion, since the logic of the cross's decoration (if indeed there is any logic) so consistently eludes us. We have no choice, I believe, but to concede that a full comprehension of the meaning intended by those who erected the cross is now beyond our reach. Nevertheless, in restoring the *maiestas* scene, we have added a note of profundity to our own understanding. The meaning of the cross, as we now perceive it, is a little deeper than before.

Appendix: The Date of the Runic Verses

Since there is no general study, as far as I know, that deals with the way inscriptions were laid out in medieval times around square or rectangular panels, it may be useful for me to offer here my own set of diagrams, which will also facilitate discussion of the Ruthwell inscriptions.

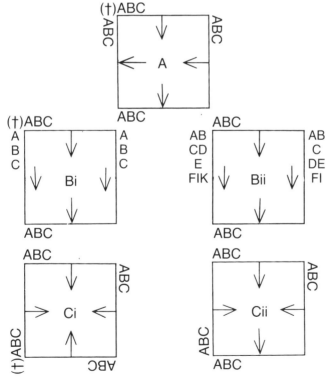

(†) A cross usually marks the starting point of the inscription.

The diagrams are, in fact, self-explanatory. The noticeable feature of A is that the letters in both the right and left vertical borders are oriented toward the left. In the B variations the letters in these borders have the same orientation as those in the upper border. The only difference between Bi and Bii is that in the former the letters descend in single file, whereas in Bii several letters are crowded together on each level of the descending file. In Ci the letters are oriented toward the center; this allows for a continuous and unbroken inscription, but it means that in order to read what is inscribed in the bottom border the image (or object) has to be turned upside down. The variant Cii tries to eliminate this difficulty, but in doing so is obliged to break the continuity. Another way to overcome the difficulty is to complete the inscription in the other borders, leaving the bottom one blank.

The layout most commonly found is C, in one or another of its forms. The starting point is usually in the lower corner of the left vertical border, although it may occur at another point on this border, or even in the top border. A thorough study of all the variations to be found in the abundant surviving material may one day help to throw new light on the practice of this or that individual medieval scriptorium. Thus, for example, the early Fulda scriptorium seems to have had a fondness for Bi.[74]

The Latin inscriptions on the Ruthwell Cross follow pattern A. This particular layout is by no means common. The only other examples I have come across are the inscriptions around (1) the plan of the Tabernacle on fols. IIv-III of Codex Amiatinus,[75] (2) the Crucifixion image in Durham Cathedral Library, MS A II 17, fol. 38v,[76] and (3) the image of the scribe Eadwine in Cambridge, Trinity College, MS R.17.1, fol. 283v (the Eadwine Psalter).[77] Since the Ruthwell Cross and the first two of these other examples are from the North of England, I wonder whether Eadwine was inspired by some early model, also from the North, particularly since I have not been able to discover other examples of A in the twelfth century. I am hardly conversant, however, with all the available material, and others may be able to contribute further evidence on this matter.

It is the runic inscriptions on the Ruthwell Cross that present the most interesting problem. Only traces of these inscriptions now remain on the upper stone. The letters most clearly visible are G I S G (X I Ͷ X), close to the ADORAMUS on the Apocalypse panel (see Plate III). From this remnant as well as from the traces of runes visible on the opposite side, it appears that the runes on the upper stone follow the same pattern as the Latin inscriptions (= A), with the letters of both left and right vertical borders oriented toward the left.[78]

The most famous runic inscription on the cross is that found surrounding the inhabited vinescroll on the two sides of the lower stone
(see Plate XIV). This inscription contains poetic verses closely related to
those of the "Dream of the Rood" in Codex CXVII of the Vercelli Cathedral Library, a manuscript which Neil Ker dates to the second half
of the tenth century.[79] The layout of this long inscription follows pattern Bii.

The immediate question that poses itself is why this inscription does
not follow pattern A, which prevails elsewhere on the cross. Careful
measurement shows that Bii is not a more economical layout than A, so
exigencies of space cannot have been the determining factor. Considerations of legibility cannot have played much part, since everyone recognizes that the way the verses are cut makes for very difficult reading. In
the opinion of R. I. Page, our authority on English runic inscriptions,

> the runes of the top stone were cut sensibly, so as to run in fairly long text
> lengths along the borders they filled. Not so those of the lower stone, for where
> these occupy the vertical borders . . . they are set, not along the length of the
> border, but in a succession of short horizontal lines of two, three, or four letters
> each. Thus that section of the text which fills the top and then the right-hand
> vertical border of the east face is divided up "[.]gere / dae / hi / nae / go / da /
> lm / eʒ / tti / gþ /. . . ." This looks absurd and is maddeningly hard to read. So
> odd does is appear that I incline to think it may not be part of the original design
> for the Cross, and to wonder if these runes were added by a later carver who
> had less command over the space he had to fill. But this is a heretical view and
> not shared by art historians.[80]

The orthodox view of these runic verses as an integral and original
feature of the cross has found support in two sorts of reasoning, theological and aesthetic. It has been argued that the content of the poem is
intrinsically linked with the conceptual theme of the cross as it emerges
from the sculptured panels. I admit that while the runic verses appear
very suitable for *any* cross, I can discern no compelling link between
their content (and that of the "Dream of the Rood") and the iconographic schema presented by the Ruthwell panels.[81] The aesthetic argument contends that there is "a commonsense improbability" that the
"ugly wide margins" surrounding the vinescroll would have been left
blank and devoid of any inscription.[82] Since, unlike the other panels,
the vinescroll does not require identification or explanation, this argument has the appearance of being rather subjective. Who is to decide
what looked "ugly" to an Anglo-Saxon of the eighth century? But even
if we grant some validity to this view, the fact remains that it cannot
provide us with any guarantee that an inscription was actually planned
and executed in these spaces when the cross was originally made. Many
incomplete manuscripts have come down to us from the Middle Ages—

manuscripts where the rubricator, the illuminator, and sometimes the scribe himself has failed to complete his task. Why should sculptured monuments not be subject to the same vicissitudes?

The most stubborn of our difficulties in dealing with these runic verses is still the peculiar way they are laid out, illustrated as pattern Bii. After wading through volumes of runic material in Harvard's Widener Library (relating to England, the Isle of Man, and Scandinavia), I can say with certainty that *no* form of pattern B is normal for runes. By and large runic inscriptions follow the same patterns as Latin ones. The inscriptions around the panels of the Franks Casket, for example, follow pattern C—with the lower border sometimes left blank. Some special reason must therefore be found to explain the anomalies of arrangement displayed by the runic verses on the Ruthwell Cross.

The explanation that most readily suggests itself is the following. It is legitimate to assume that the two pieces of sandstone which form the cross received their original decoration while they were lying in a horizontal position on the ground. At this stage it would have been possible to move them about, so that a carver could have easy access to all the surfaces—cutting letters along the "vertical" borders would have presented no problems, since they did not assume their vertical position until the cross was erected. Once the cross was standing in an upright position, however, this would no longer be the case, and a pattern like Bii might indeed present itself as the most obvious solution to a craftsman contemplating the standing monument.[83] This explanation implies, of course, that the borders around the vinescroll on the lower stone were devoid of inscriptions when the monument was first set up. It also implies that some time must have elapsed between the erection of the cross and the addition of the verses. In other words, if this explanation is correct, the date of the cross can no longer be used to date the inscription, and the date of the inscription must be determined on other grounds, like the shape of the runes, or the linguistic elements of the language used. These are questions for specialists in the field, who have the necessary expertise.[84] One does not have to be an expert, however, to see the point of the observations I have offered here. The explanation I am proposing is, I believe, the simplest and most logical one available, and it does not require us to assume any untypical or anomalous procedures (or any incompetence) on the part of the original creators of the Ruthwell Cross.

Notes

1. See T. D. Kendrick, *British Antiquity* (London, 1950; reprint ed., New York, 1970), chap. 8, "Britannia," pp. 134–167.

2. For the Latin text see F. Haverfield, "Cotton Iulius F. VI. Notes on Reginald Bainbrigg of Appleby, on William Camden and on some Roman Inscriptions," *Transactions of the Cumberland and Westmoreland Antiquarian Society*, n.s. 11 (1911), 373–374, and R. I. Page, "An Early Drawing of the Ruthwell Cross," *Mediaeval Archaeology*, 3 (1959), 287.

3. Michael Swanton, *The Dream of the Rood* (Manchester, 1970), p. 9, speaks of Bainbrigg's journey to Scotland as occurring "between 1599 and 1601." Haverfield, in the article cited in the previous note, makes it clear that there were several journeys.

4. See A. S. Cook, *Some Accounts of the Bewcastle Cross between the years 1607 and 1861* (Yale Studies in English, n. 50), reprinted in *The Anglo-Saxon Cross* (Archon Books: Hamden, Conn., 1977), pp. 131–258; see p. 131.

5. *The Anglo-Saxon Cross*, p. 132.

6. The information about the Ruthwell Cross found in later editions of the *Britannia*—postdating Camden—was drawn from printed sources.

7. I quote from *The Acts of the General Assemblies of the Church of Scotland from the year 1638 to the year 1649. Inclusive. Printed in the year 1682. To which are now added the Index of the unprinted Acts of these Assemblies* . . . (George Mosman: [Edinburgh], 1691), pp. 92–93.

8. The Acts of the Assemblies of 1642–1646 are contained in a manuscript volume (CH 1/1/9) now in the Scottish Record Office at Edinburgh. The text quoted is from page 15. I owe this information and a copy of the act to the kindness of Dr. B. L. H. Horn, Assistant Keeper at the Record Office. The index of unprinted acts (see note 7) listed for the Assembly of 1642 an "Act anent Idolatrous monuments in Ruthwall." This has led many scholars to believe that the act itself was not preserved. It was not printed, but it has indeed survived in manuscript form.

9. There is an excellent bibliography in F. Willett, "The Ruthwell and Bewcastle Crosses," *Memoirs and Proceedings of the Manchester Literary and Philosophical Society*, 98 (1957), 122–136. A few items, however, have escaped Willett's attention, including those mentioned in notes 2 (Haverfield), 7, and 41 (Collingwood) of the present article.

10. Henry Ware, "Bishop Nicolson's Diaries," *Transactions of the Cumberland and Westmorland Antiquarian and Archaeological Society*, n.s. 1 (1901), 35: "Aug 19 [1690]. Mr. Lason inform'd me of two Runic Inscriptions to be mett with in Scotland. . . . 2. In ye Church at Rothwald (alias Revel) in ye road from Annan to Dumfrese."

11. Letter of Nicolson to Mr. Lhwyd, 22 April 1697: "I took a progress (last week) into Scotland to view a famous cross in a church near Dumfries. I was surprised with the inscriptions, very fair and legible on all its four sides. They were Latin and Runic intermixed. . . ." *Letters on Various Subjects . . . to and from William Nicolson D.D.*, ed. J. Nichols, vol. I (London, 1809), p. 62.

12. See Nicolson's letter to Hickes, *op. cit.*, pp. 158–161.

13. Henry Ware, "Bishop Nicolson's Diaries: Part II", *Transactions of the Cumberland and Westmorland Antiquarian and Archaeological Society*, n.s. 2 (1902), 196.

14. *Itinerarium Septentrionale* (London, 1726), pp. 160–161.

15. (London, 1789), Plates 54–55; Gough's remark is on p. 1 of the commentary.

16. *A Tour in Scotland and Voyage to the Hebrides, 1772* (2nd ed., London, 1776), Part I, p. 98 (emphasis mine).

17. *Vetusta Monumenta*, II, p. 2 of commentary of Plates 54–55 (emphasis mine). A comparison of Gough's transcriptions of the Latin inscriptions with what is actually found on the monument does not inspire much confidence in his ability to record the letters correctly; for example, STANS RETRO SECUS PEDES is rendered as SIAN EIR SELV-SIIDES (see Plate I)!

18. "An Account of a Remarkable Monument in the shape of a Cross, inscribed with Roman and Runic Letters, preserved in the Garden of Ruthwell Manse, Dumfriesshire," *Archaeologia Scotica*, 4 (1833), 318–319.

19. The transfer of the main fragments from within the church to the graveyard outside occurred sometime between 1789 (when Gough wrote his account), and 1794 when John Craig, then minister at Ruthwell (1783–1798), in volume 10 of the *Statistical Account of Scotland* (pp. 226–227) wrote of them as lying outside in the open.

20. Duncan gives an account of his actions in "An Account of a Remarkable Monument . . .," *Archaeologia Scotica*, 4 (1833), 318–319.

21. *Ibid.*, 315.

22. *Ibid.*, 326.

23. McFarlan gives an account of these events in his small pamphlet *The Ruthwell Cross* (2nd ed., Dumfries, 1896), pp. 25–26. The first edition was printed in 1885 before the transfer of the cross.

24. "On Anglo-Saxon Runes," *Archaeologia*, 28 (1840), 327–372.

25. "Additional observations on the Runic Obelisk at Ruthwell, the Poem of the Dream of the Holy Rood . . .," *Archaeologia*, 30 (1844), 31–46.

26. *De Cruce Ruthwellensi et de auctore versuum in illa inscrirtorum qui ad Passionem Domini pertinent* (Marburg, 1865).

27. See the Appendix to this essay.

28. Nicolson's letter is quoted on p. 134 of the volume referred to above in note 4.

29. Vol. IV (London, 1816), p. cc.

30. "The Saxon Cross at Bewcastle," *Archaeologia Aeliana*, n.s. 1 (1857), 151–152 [on Bewcastle] "the effigy of St. John the Baptist, pointing with his right hand to the Holy Lamb, which rests on his left arm. This figure had been supposed to be the Blessed Virgin with the Infant Jesus. Mr. Lysons, however, corrected this error in part, representing as a lamb what had been supposed to be the Holy Child, but the figure which holds it, has in his engraving the appearance of a female. It is, though in flowing robes, decidedly a male figure, and the face is bearded. . . ." pp. 167–168 [on Ruthwell] "St. John the Baptist, with the Holy Lamb, to which he points with his right hand, resting on his left arm. Around it are the remains of an inscription—ADORAMUS."

31. See above, note 23. A later minister at Ruthwell, John L. Dinwiddie, also published a pamphlet, *The Ruthwell Cross and Its Story* (Dumfries, 1927). This author (on p. 103) takes care to conceal that Duncan, whom he greatly admires, had ever entertained other notions about the panel: "The largest piece—showing the figure of 'John the Baptist with the Agnus Dei' . . . was discovered in the digging of a grave which had to be made unusually deep. It was at once identified by Dr. Duncan as a highly important section of the upper shaft of the Cross." One has the impression that Dinwiddie is trying to cover up a faux pas made by his predecessor!

32. I discuss this point in detail later in the essay.

33. "The Ruthwell Cross," *Journal of the Warburg and Courtauld Institutes*, 6 (1943), 4.

34. "The Religious Meaning of the Ruthwell Cross," *Art Bulletin*, 26 (1944), 236.

35. See above for fuller reference.

36. Saxl sends his readers to the following illustrations: "cf. E. H. Zimmermann, *Vorkarolingische Miniaturen*, 1916, pl. 275. Besides cf. the Anholt Gospels, Sotheby Sale, 31st May, 1927, and the cover of the Sancta Sanctorum Cross, *Monuments Piot*, 15 (1906), pl. 7." I have been unable to consult the Anholt Gospels plate, but I reproduce one of the evangelists from plate 275 of Zimmermann as Plate V since this has a bearing on a remark made below about the standing position of the figure on the cross. Plate VI shows the cover of the Sancta Sanctorum Cross.

37. Printed as an appendix (pp. 219–286) to volume VII of *The Royal Commission on Ancient and Historical Monuments and Constructions of Scotland; Seventh Report with Inventory of Monuments and Constructions in the County of Dumfries* (Edinburgh, 1920). [Much of this report is repeated verbatim in G. Baldwin Brown, *The Arts in Early England*, vol. 5 (London, 1921).]

38. See the appendix mentioned in the previous note pp. 225–226. The authors try to support their view of a miscalculation by adding that "it will be seen that on the corresponding panel on the southern side of the cross the height of the two figures of the

"'Visitation' [panel] has been similarly made up with a plain block of stone under their feet." The "plain block," however, represents the lower border of this panel—situated at the base of the upper stone of the cross—which is devoid of any inscription. This panel—whose content is still a matter of debate (Visitation? Martha and Mary?)—is distinguished from the others by this feature, the absence of any Latin lettering similar to that found on all the other panels (including the one that is the subject of this paper). The runic inscription (Latin words in runic lettering) found on this panel is laid out in a fashion that suggests it is not the work of the original craftsman. (The lay-out of the Latin inscriptions is provided later.)

39. See in particular the comment by Thomas Pennant cited above.

40. See my discussion and note 17 above on the unreliability of Gough's transcriptions.

41. G. B. Brown and A. B. Webster in their official report (see n. 37) state that "on the bottom margin letters are to be made out, but form no intelligible words. T N D N . . . V can be read from the dexter end of this margin, but no interpretation has been suggested" (p. 226). Brown must have been somewhat unsure of the T N D N sequence since he omits to mention it on p. 127 of *The Arts in Early England* (vol. 5). It is not clear why F. Willett ("The Ruthwell and Bewcastle Crosses," *Memoirs and Proceedings of the Manchester Literary and Philosophical Society*, 98 [1957] 103), states that T N D N . . . V are in runes, a suggestion repeated by M. Swanton, *The Dream of the Rood* (Manchester, 1970), p. 14. W. G. Collingwood in "The Ruthwell Cross in its Relation to other Monuments of the Early Christian Age," *Transactions of the Dumfriesshire and Galloway Natural History and Antiquarian Society*, ser. III, vol. 5 (1916–1918), p. 44, writes "under the St. John I think we can read ADORAMUS IN (initium) ET F(ine)M, recalling the formula of the lately discovered stone at Kirkmadrine and others." There is not enough space, however, for the three additional words in the bottom margin.

42. We still lack a thorough up-to-date palaeographical study of the Latin lettering. For a table giving the different forms of the letters see W. R. Lethaby, "The Ruthwell Cross," *Burlington Magazine*, 21 (1912), 145; Brown and Webster, p. 243 of their official report (see n. 37 above), repeated in Brown, *The Arts in Early England*, vol. 5, p. 176.

43. This V and M are of the same shape and size as the MV in the word *adoramus*. We are dealing with Latin letters and *not* with runes. I am very grateful to the Victoria and Albert Museum authorities for allowing me to examine the cast at a time when it was not on public display.

44. "Two Panels on the Ruthwell Cross," *Journal of the Warburg and Courtauld Institutes*, 37 (1974), 333–336.

45. See the Appendix for some further comments on the layout of inscriptions. Many of the Latin inscriptions on the cross survive only in fragmentary form, indicated here by the use of capital letters.

46. There is no satisfactory modern scholarly study of the iconography of John the Baptist. For some useful pointers and a bibliography, see the article "Jean le Baptiste" in the *Dictionnaire de Spiritualité*, vol. 8, cols. 189–192. The article "Johannes der Täufer" in the *Lexikon der Christlichen Ikonographie*, vol. 7, is not very helpful, since it does not allow one to discern the historical development in the iconography.

47. G. Mansi, *Sacrorum Conciliorum Nova et Amplissima Collectio*, vol. 11, cols. 977–980, n. 82: "In nonnullis venerabilium imaginum picturis, agnus qui digito praecursoris monstratur, depingitur. . . ."

48. See G. Bovini, *Ravenna, Città d'Arte* (Ravenna, 1967), p. 82: "Nonostante questa varietà e queste diverse influenze, tuttavia la cattedra—che alcuni studiosi pensano sia stata eseguita ad Alessandria d'Egitto (Ajanalov, Diehl, Cecchelli) ed altri invece a Costantinopoli (A. Venturi, Weigand, Bettini, Morath) ed alcuni infine a Ravenna stessa (Stuhlfant, Volbach)—forma un complesso unitario ed organico." E. Kitzinger, *Byzantine Art in the Making* (Cambridge, Mass., 1977), p. 94 opts for Constantinople.

49. Ed. L. Duchesne (Paris, 1886–1892), vol. 1, p. 174.

50. The panel immediately above contains Matthew and his symbol. It is recognized that the uppermost stone, containing John and his symbol on one side, and an eagle on the

opposite side, was misplaced by Duncan when he erected the monument in 1823. To be correctly placed this stone would have to be rotated right around, so that John and his symbol would stand above the Matthew panel. The missing transom, containing Luke and Mark with their symbols, together with the central panel, may well still lie buried somewhere in the vicinity of the church.

51. These cross-heads are now numbered 20 and 23. See Elizabeth Coatsworth, "The Four Cross-Heads from the Chapter House, Durham," in *Anglo-Saxon and Viking Age Sculpture and its Context: Papers from the Collingwood Symposium on Insular Sculpture from 800 to 1066* [ed. James Lang], (Oxford, British Archaeological Reports: British Series, 49, 1978), pp. 85–92, figures 1A and B.

52. F. Gisinger, ed., *Der Globus, seine Entstehung und Verwendung in der Antike*, (Leipzig, 1927).

53. A. Alföldi, "Insignien und Tracht der römischen Kaiser," *Mitteilungen des Deutschen Archaeologischen Instituts. Römische Abteilung* 50 (1935), 117–120.

54. P. E. Schramm, *Sphaira, Globus, Reichsapfel: Wanderung und Wandlung eines Herrschaftszeichens* (Stuttgart, 1958).

55. W. S. Cook, "The Earliest Painted Panels of Catalonia, II," *Art Bulletin*, 6 (1922–1923); see especially sec. 4, pp. 38–60, "The Iconography of the Globe-Mandorla," with numerous illustrations.

56. For further literature consult the *Lexikon der Christlichen Ikonographie*, s.v. "Kugel," "Himmel," etc.

57. See F. Cumont, *Fouilles de Doura-Europos: 1922–1923* (Paris, 1926), tableau XVII, planche LV.

58. See E. H. Kantorowicz, "The Quinity of Winchester," *Art Bulletin*, 29 (1947), p. 78 and fig. 26d.

59. I am very grateful to Professor E. Kitzinger for making this suggestion to me.

60. A. Goldschmidt, *Die Elfenbeinskulpturen aus der Zeit der karolingischen und sächsischen Kaiser* (Berlin, 1914–1926; reprint ed., 1969), vol. 1, 79–80, n. 162 and plate LXXIV.

61. In Paris, B.N. lat 13,336, fol. 1, there is a drawing (s.xi-xii) depicting Christ, in mandorla, seated on an arc, with another arc under his feet. The image is entitled "Deus maiestatis." Within the arc under the feet are the words "omnia ei subiciuntur." This agrees with the Darmstadt ivory inscription "data est mihi omnis potestas in celo et in terra," and almost certainly represents the idea implicit in the double globes under the figure on the Ruthwell Cross, namely the subjection of the created universe (heaven and earth) to Christ and the Godhead.

62. Paris, B.N. lat. 8878. This particular illustration, from fol. 199, is reproduced in G. Vezin, *L'Apocalypse et la fin des temps* (Paris, 1973), fig. 30.

63. This image is also reproduced in W. Neuss, *Die Apokalypse des hl. Johannes in der altspanischen und altchristlichen Bibel-illustration* (Münster in W., 1931) vol. 2, pl. 36, fig. 126, and in Emile A. van Moé, *L'Apocalypse de Saint-Sever, manuscrit Latin 8878 de la Bibliothèque nationale* (xie s.) (Paris, 1943) pl. 12.

64. *Lamberti S. Audomari canonici Liber Floridus*, ed. A. Strubbe and A. Derolez (Ghent, 1968), p. 179. Fol. 88 is the first leaf of a binion (ff. 88–91), the rest of which contains astronomical material under the title (in the index) "Beda de astrologia."

65. Fol. 58v of Wolfenbüttel, Herzog August Bibliothek, Cod. Guelff. 1 Gud. lat., reproduced in *Monumenta Annonis: Köln und Siegburg, Weltbild und Kunst im hohen Mittelalter* (Cologne, 1975), p. 90. I have not been able to check the other six copies of the *Liber Floridus* listed by Swarzenski in the article mentioned in the next note. One must assume that Lambert of St. Omer, the author of the compilation, did not want this page—already begun as an Apocalypse scene—to go unused, and decided to fill the space available with texts on the four elements.

66. In "Comments on the Figural Illustrations," *Liber Floridus Colloquium (1967)*, ed. A. Derolez (Ghent, 1973), pp. 21–30. See, for instance, p. 24.

67. This illustrated Apocalypse has disappeared from the Ghent manuscript but survives in the copies; see Swarzenski, (*op. cit.*, pp. 27–30), who points out (p. 28) that this particular cycle stands apart from the other known families of medieval Apocalypses. He even ends

(p. 30) with the suggestion that this cycle may be connected with the Apocalypse cycle at Wearmouth-Jarrow mentioned by Bede! (See also note 71, below.)

68. See the Exhibition Catalogue *Zimelien Abendländische Handschriften des Mittelalters aus den Sammlungen der Stiftung Preussischer Kulturbesitz Berlin* (Weisbaden, 1970), p. 62, illustr. 43. For yet another example see Hildesheim, codex 18, fol. 174, reproduced in P. Bloch and H. Schnitzler, *Die Ottonische Kölner Malerschule* (Düsseldorf, 1967) fig. 440.

69. Reiner Haussherr, "Eine Verspätete Apocalypsen-Handschrift und ihre Vorlage," in *Studies in Late Medieval and Renaissance Painting in Honor of Millard Meiss* (New York, 1977), vol. 1, pp. 219–240, has made a fascinating study of the relationship between two of the manuscripts (Düsseldorf, Kunstakademie MS A.B. 143 and Metz, Bibl. munic. MS Salis 38, now destroyed). He underlines the difficulties of studying the cycle as a whole at the present juncture. For further bibliography on the English cycle see note 1 of Haussherr's study.

70. For example, if one compares the illustration for Apoc. 22:1 ("et ostendit mihi fluvium aquae vitae . . . procedentem de sede Dei et agni . . . ") in (a) Metz, MS Salis 38, fol. 31v, (b) New York, The Cloisters Apocalypse, fol. 37, (c) London, B.L. Add. 17333, fol. 46, (d) Paris, B.N. fr. 403, fol. 42, and (e) Cambridge, Trinity College, MS R. 16. 2, fol. 25v, it immediately becomes obvious that (a), (b), and (c) transmit the earliest form of the *maiestas* image, showing the male figure (with the lamb) seated on the arc, with a globe at his feet, and *a stream of water issuing from where he is seated*. In (d) the arc has been replaced by a real throne, and *the globe at the feet has been turned into a waterspout* from which the stream issues forth. In (e), the *maiestas* scene of (d), with throne and waterspout, has been set within the "heavenly Jerusalem" plan taken from a manuscript of the Beatus tradition. The progression from (a) to (e) is intelligible, but the reverse is not. Salis 38—at least for the particular image—probably brings us close to the ancient model which underlies the English Apocalypse cycle, and thus helps to show how the lamb and seated figure were a feature of this model.

71. One does not find this particular feature in some of the other early cycles like those of Trier-Cambrai, Valenciennes-Paris, Bamberg, and the Beatus group. Its absence from Valenciennes, MS 99 should perhaps be noted, since it has been argued that a Northumbrian exemplar underlies this manuscript, and attempts have also been made to link Valenciennes 99 with the Apocalypse paintings at Monkwearmouth mentioned by Bede. It could be that the real link is between the Jarrow paintings and the English Apocalypse cycle through the witness of the Ruthwell panel. Rosemary Cramp has argued that the Ruthwell Cross owed something, directly, to Wearmouth-Jarrow workmanship; see her Jarrow Lecture of 1965, *Early Northumbrian Sculpture*, pp. 10–11.

72. *Expositio in Apocalypsim* (ed. G. Morin, *Opera omnia*, vol. 2 [Maredsous, 1942], p. 22, ll. 20–21, and 26–27).

73. Bede, *In Apocalypsim* (*P.L.* 93, 145D): "Tychonius agnum ecclesiam dicit, quae in Christo accepit omnem potestatem."

74. The inscription that surrounds the image of Rabanus Maurus presenting his *De laude S. Crucis* to Gregory IV is laid out in this fashion; see Vienna, Nationalbibl. MS 652, fol. 2v, a ninth-century manuscript from Fulda (reproduced in F. Heer, *Charlemagne and His World* [London, 1975], p. 193). The inscription also occurs in a tenth-century English copy of the same work, Cambridge, Trinity College, MS B.16.3, fol. 1v (reproduced in M. Rickert, *Painting in Britain: The Middle Ages* [Baltimore, 1954], plate 19). The same inscription is likewise found in Valenciennes, Bibl. munic. MS 186, fol. a—a twelfth-century manuscript containing the homilies of Peter Lombard. For another Fulda example, see the Calendar leaf (10th c.) in Berlin, Staatsbibl. MS theol. lat. fol. 192 (reproduced in L. Grodecki et al., *Le Siècle de l'An Mil* [Paris, 1973], fig. 104). Bi also represents the normal layout for inscriptions in Byzantine manuscripts.

75. The plan of the Tabernacle in the Wilderness—often erroneously described as the Tabernacle in the Temple—has been reproduced in many publications. I list here only one, since it contains a good bibliography: J. J. G. Alexander, *Insular Manuscripts: 6th to the 9th Century* (London, 1978), illustration 23 and pp. 32–35. Codex Amiatinus was certainly produced before 716 and very probably before 700.

76. See R. A. B. Mynors, *Durham Cathedral Manuscripts to the End of the Twelfth Century* (Oxford, 1939), plate 3. E. A. Lowe (*C. L. A.* II, n. 149) gives the date of this portion of the manuscript as eighth century.

77. See M. Rickert, *Painting in Britain: The Middle Ages* (Baltimore, 1954), plate 71. The Eadwine Psalter is dated c. 1150.

78. The inscriptions that surrounded the four panels forming the cross-head may have been laid out according to pattern C, if one can judge correctly from the "In principio / erat / verbum" that now surrounds John and his symbol (an eagle) on the uppermost stone.

79. On the relationship between the two sets of verses see M. Swanton, *The Dream of the Rood* (Manchester, 1970).

80. R. I. Page, *An Introduction to English Runes* (London, 1973), p. 150.

81. I believe there are a number of new things to be said, on the level of theological interpretation, about several of the panels, and I hope to return to this matter in another paper.

82. This is the opinion of Rosemary Cramp, "The Anglian Sculptured Crosses of Dumfriesshire," *Transactions of the Dumfries and Galloway Antiquarian Society*, ser. 3, 38 (1959–1960), 12.

83. I have so far come across only one other instance of pattern Bii. The Greek verses that occupy the margins of the Limburg *stauroteca*, a Byzantine art work of the tenth century, are laid out in this fashion—with a single line of letters on the top and bottom borders, and rows of one, two, or three letters descending the two vertical borders. For good reproductions see the articles by J. Rauch and others in *Das Münster*, 8 (1955), 201–240. For the problem of how the verses are to be read, see E. Follieri, "L'ordine dei versi in alcuni epigrammi Bizantini," *Byzantion*, 34 (1964), 447–467. In a recent article ("*Lignum Domini* and the Opening Vision of *The Dream of the Rood*: a Viable Hypothesis?" *Speculum*, 53 [1978], 441–459), Annemarie Mahler has argued that it was the fashioning of a reliquary cross for a relic of the True Cross that provided the inspiration for the "Dream of the Rood." If the relic had reached England originally in a Byzantine *stauroteca* similar to the one now at Limburg, could this have provided an additional model for the layout of the runic verses on the Ruthwell Cross? The relationship between the layout of the runes and the Limburg *stauroteca* has also been pointed out in a recent article by Ute Schwabb, "Das Traumgeschicht vom Kreuzesbaum," *Philologische Studien Gedenschrift für Richard Kienast* (Heidelberg, 1978), pp. 131–192.

84. It is unfortunate that more runic letters have not been preserved on the top stone of the cross, since a comparison of their shape with those on the lower stone might have provided clues to the date, particularly if it could be shown that the runic inscription at the top (laid out like the Latin ones) preserves an earlier form of the runes.

Poetry and Lexicography in the Translation of Piers Plowman

George Kane
University of North Carolina at Chapel Hill

That a poem is essentially not translatable will be evident to literary critics simply from consideration of the inseparability of form and content in poetry. The abstractions by which we define those concepts appear as intellectual exercises or critical expediencies when we attempt translation. The translator immediately discovers how the external form of his poem as a complex of linguistic norms implies classes of meaning both beyond the lexicographical and totally peculiar to the language in which it was composed: namely the physical effect of significant form, that is of organized sound expressing organized sense; and the emotional experience insofar as this is developed by connotation. Neither of those classes of meaning is authentically transferable into another language; the translation will either lack them or, more probably, offer substitutes. Its form in that other language will create more or less appreciable new meanings of those classes.

Theoretical discussion of translation by linguisticians reaches the same conclusions more laboriously. One reads, for instance, "the greater the significance of the form for the comprehension and appreciation of the message, the more difficult it is to find appropriate formal equivalences in the receptor language,"[1] or, "the degree of difficulty in approximating the content of the original increases with the relative importance that connotative meaning properties possess in the text to be translated."[2] The implication of the expressions "more difficult" and "degree of difficulty" in those quotations, that there is a possibility of full success, appears not intended; the almost invariable conclusion of any theoretical discussion is that wholly satisfactory translation of anything but purely utilitarian prose is impossible. Any translation describable as a "self-contained literary work of art" must to the extent of the justice of that description differ existentially from and imperfectly represent its original.[3] By axiom, moreover, no translation is wholly satisfactory to anyone competent in the language of its original. What does in theory appear to be reproducible in translation is the form of event and thought in a poem, its abstractable prose meaning.[4] Even this can be difficult in practice.[5]

The nature of the problem makes theoretical discussion of translation, especially by linguisticians with evidently little experience of the activity or of poetry, unenlightening. It is also repetitive; the approaches to the predictable negative conclusion tend to differ mainly in the variety of jargon employed. Even in the liveliest discussion, things seem new which have been forgotten: Steiner in *After Babel*,[6] dismissing, without naming him, Dryden's division of translation into variously "metaphrase, paraphrase and imitation"[7] as "the sterile triadic model," the "perennial distinction between literalism, paraphrase and free imitation," because it is "wholly contingent," without "precision or philosophic basis," offers as if something novel, "the key fact that a fourfold *hermeneia*, Aristotle's term for discourse which signifies because it interprets, is conceptually and practically inherent in even the rudiments of translation."[8] But that is not new: without the gratuitous multiplication of categories it will be old hat to anyone who has ever had to translate an English author into Latin, and it was expressed forty years ago, in language endearingly free of jargon, as "that thinking things out again which is the foundation of translation as a fine art."[9]

What matters in Steiner's sentence is the statement that the threefold classification "has no precision or philosophic basis," in other words is arbitrary. That is true of any categorization of translation, never mind how manifold. For any translation is at best a second-best, not a liberation from "the need for learning a language"[10] but a makeshift to supply a deficiency of linguistic knowledge. And the management of detail in any translation will be governed by the unique relation between the character of the text being attempted and that of the recipient language and culture at the moment of translation. From both these considerations every translation worth taking seriously is an event of wholly casual origin and a pragmatic solution of a particular problem.[11]

This applies a fortiori to translating *Piers Plowman*, by which I understand producing an authentic modern English version of the work. The added force comes from the poem being itself in a form of English, differentiated only historically and only partly so differentiated. The English of 1978, directly descended from that of 1378, has changed and continues to change in many particulars of grammar and lexicography but not uniformly or systematically and not always (to the untrained eye) visibly. So the Jakobson definition of what he calls "intralingual translation or *rewording*," as "an interpretation of verbal signs by means of other signs of the same language,"[12] applies only if one adds the qualifier "where necessary."

For both psychological and linguistic reasons intralingual translation is very difficult.[13] The historical identity of the two forms of the language, evident to anyone from their extensive similarity of appearance, introduces an emotional element, subconscious resentment of the need for translation, such as expresses itself in the indestructible illusion that Chaucer's English, if its spelling is modernized, is pretty directly accessible. A word which looks the same in modern as in early English ought, after all, to mean the same. In fact there is a double semantic variable: of contextual aptness, as in an ordinary lexicographical situation; and of historical aptness: is there evidence that the word was actually used in a particular sense at a particular period? So in theory a fourteenth-century word and its twentieth-century descendant identifiable visually as such can have totally different sets of semantic values, or approximately identical sets, or some approximately identical and some chronologically differentiated values. Elementary generalizations, of course, for any reader of Middle English, but if he is honest he will agree that while the first and second possibilities give him little trouble, the third, by far the most often instanced, is easy to overlook. It bedevils the interpretative, the analytic function of translation from Middle English (as of course also from other early languages into their descendants).[14] And it haunts the expert translator from the early to the modern form of his language, who can find himself in a state of mind analogous to that of the genuine bilingual, who finds it difficult to translate at all closely from one of his languages into the other.

Here then is our predicament: in the first instance poetry is not susceptible of perfect translation; in the second, the greater a poem the less chance there is of a translation doing it even poor justice—and then, in the third, translating from early to modern English involves special, initially lexicographical hazards. In that situation what is the best pragmatic solution? What compromise is right, when some effects cannot be transferred, between what can be sacrificed and what must be preserved? The answer may emerge from consideration of the extent to which some of the various formal elements of the poem can genuinely be rendered accessible today. The essential beginning must be interpretation. Then, on the presumption that the desideratum is to create not a modern approximation to *Piers Plowman*[15] but the most accurate possible representation of those features of it which are realizable in modern English, the translation acquires the character of an open act of historical cognition in which, prima facie at least, the form of event and thought, the "conceptual framework" of the poem will be a factor. How correct that presumption may be will now be my concern.

The first and most important single element of external form to be lost in producing the kind of translation I have just described is the verse. Reasons for translating *Piers Plowman* into prose could be multiplied,[16] beginning with the fact that no verse system equivalent to the alliterative long line is in use today, but the main reason must be the impossibility of reproducing together in modern English even a remote correspondence to the intricate and subtle music of Langland's verse and the intricate and subtle argument of his sense. That is a categorical assertion, but much of the rest of this essay will incidentally demonstrate its correctness.

It goes without saying that the loss by translation into prose is immense. Its scale can be gauged from the critical proposition that there are in the poem many passages of doctrinal or homiletic substance now largely destitute of any but historical interest which still read enjoyably in the original because of the technical brilliance of the verse that expresses them, a brilliance in which Langland's often highly ingenious satisfaction of the formal requirements of the alliterative long line can seem the least re-markable element. Ironically with the loss comes a hazard: the translator into prose will often want to reduce alliteration with lexicographically unnecessary synonyms, or redistribute alliterating terms, in order to avoid uncomfortable effects like those in Malory's transprosing of *The Alliterative Morte Arthur*.

Another salient quality of external form lost in translation of *Piers Plowman* is concision and with concision poetic energy. That loss could, for what it is worth, be measured: the Penguin translation of the B version runs to 1,000 lines more than its original. What actually matters, of course, is the greater diffuseness of individual statements. There are various linguistic reasons for this.

One is loss of meaning in the verbs *shall, will* and *may*. We today use the first two pretty indiscriminately as future auxiliaries. But in Middle English *shall*, among other senses, signified certainty of outcome:[17] *no dynt shal hym dere as in deitate patris* (XVIII, 26),[18] "it is certain that no blow will injure him in his godhead" (the reason why Christ jousts with Death in his human nature); or else necessity, compulsion:[19] a master who holds back the pay of his servants says *Ruþe is to here rekenyng whan we shul rede acountes*, "it is pathetic to hear what I owe when we are obliged to make up the accounts" (V, 427); or else imposed obligation:[20] *Thow shalt seye I am þi Suster*, says a whore to a pardoner (V, 642). And *will* in *Piers Plowman* more often than otherwise signifies some aspect of volition. Such meaning is, for example, evident in *if þow wilt be gracious to god to do as þe gospel techeþ* (VI, 227),[21] or where Avarice lends money to *folk þat lese wol*, "people who are willing to lose"[22] a clipping from every coin (V, 247); and Envy expresses his change of heart, *I wole amende þis if I may*, "I am resolved to correct this if I am able" (V, 134).[23] As for *may*, which along with its preterite *might* we generally use to express possibility, permission or sanction, in Middle English its primary sense was "having the ability or power to carry out an action,"[24] as in the last example, or in Envy's description of the effect of his gastric ulcer, *I myȝte noȝt ete many yeres as a man ouȝte*, "I have been unable to eat normally for many years" (V, 121). These verbs are very common; their Middle English meanings are seldom clearly conveyed by the modern forms and often call for more extended paraphrase.

Another reason is the disuse of subjunctive forms in modern

English. Where Middle English can by the subjunctive express, for instance, uncertainty: *What man of þis world þat hire were leuest*, "the man who might be dearest to her" (III, 6); or hypothesis: *This were a wikkede weye*, "This would be a cruel road" (VI, 1); or condition: *founde I þat his pardoun Miȝte lechen a man*, "if I found that his pardon was able to cure a person" (XIII, 252, 253), almost invariably modern English needs several words to transmit the full meaning.

Similarly the obscuring of the dative function adds to the prolixity of translation. To give just one instance: *This were a wikkede weye*, the converted people of the field complain, except if one had a guide *That myȝte folwen vs ech foot*, "who would be able to trace each foot (of the road) for us" (VI, 2). Subjective and objective genitive uses are frequent in Middle English. It is said to the man who makes ostentatious benefactions, *god knoweþ . . . þi cost and þi coueitise*, "what it cost you and how avaricious you are in fact" (III, 67, 68). They can seldom be translated without expansion.

A feature of Middle English syntax and particularly of Langland's usage is the infinitive construction where now a finite clause is customary. There are, for instance, infinitives of purpose with unsignalled change of subject. Avarice lends money *to legge a wed and lese it*, "on such terms that the borrower puts down collateral and forfeits it" (v, 241); or of prescription in a legal document: *And þei to haue and to holde . . . a dwellynge*, "And it is further specified that they shall own and retain ownership of" (II, 102, 103); or of injunction: *Preestes and persons wiþ Placebo to hunte*, "Parish clergy are not to hunt, but to recite prayers such as the Office of the Dead" (III, 311). In every such instance an accurate translation will be longer than its original.

That will also be the case where, as is common Middle English usage, personal and relative pronouns are unexpressed and modern English requires them. It will be the case where the style is paratactic and the logical relation of the parts of sentences is not indicated. That is a characteristic of Langlandian style: I give one notable instance which has tricked editor[25] and translator. In the third line of the poem the Dreamer tells how he dressed himself in sheep's clothing, *In habite as an heremite, vnholy of workes*, literally, "in a hermit's habit, unsanctified of conduct." This appears in a current translation as "in the garb of an easy-living hermit," as if there were a distinctive dress for the less pious hermits.[26] But the whole point of the statement is the Dreamer's admission of the discrepancy between his appearance of pious living and actual un-regeneracy, possibly to be read as a kind of act of humility by the poet, and this must be made explicit in translation at whatever cost of compression. The need becomes extreme where the text instances a stylistic mannerism that goes beyond parataxis to the point of illogical ellipsis. A small illustration: a speaker says of a woman under accusation, "I shall put her to the test myself, and *soopliche appose*" (III, 5); the last two words, literally "question truthfully" or "truly," can mean only "question in such a way as to get a true answer."[27] There are larger ones. The personification Sloth resolves to attend church regularly: *Shal noon ale after mete holde me þennes Til I haue euensong herd* (V, 453, 454), literally, "Drinking after dinner will certainly not keep me from church until I have heard vespers," which is meaningless unless we supply "I shall not drink" before *Til*.[28] And to illustrate another grade of ellipsis, a speaker tells how Jesus Christ allowed himself to be be-trayed *to se þe sorwe of deying*, "to experience what mankind suffers in death"; then she goes on, *The which vnknytteþ alle care and com-synge is of reste*, "which casts off all grief and is the beginning of repose" (XVIII, 214, 215). That rider seems to diminish the di-vine benevolence[29] and translation must properly supply the doc-trinal connection.[30]

The qualities of concision and diffuseness of style can appear as characteristics of the external form of a poem, but because they are determinants of the intensity of its effect they are also neces-sarily factors in its feeling. An analogous generalization, of some-what greater complexity, applies to the classifiable figures of Langland's style in their relation to the emotional meaning of *Piers Plowman*. To the extent that this is abstractable, the emotional meaning, the feeling of *Piers Plowman*, exists also as form. That form varies serially to constitute an incremental whole from situa-tions of particular emotional quality. In diversity of stylistic effects it corresponds to the mixed style of religious writing, varying with pastoral admonition, high doctrinal explication, simple spiritual movements like penitence, religious exaltation, estates criticism, or apocalyptic anxiety. As we read we sense the changes of effect in large emotional movements, as if particular passages were definable units with integral capacity to evoke special responses. But in fact those movements relate to often gradual variation of texture, specifically to the classes of figures combined in a passage and their ordinal collocation, the figures existing by intellectual definition, but effective as language charged with feeling.[31] The possibility of reproducing their effects in translation is then at the outset a matter of the extent to which both the individual figures and their effectiveness in combination survive or can be reproduced in modern English. Let us look at some.

I begin with allegory, the most immediately striking, although actually by no means most distinctive, element in Langland's style. The more elementary uses readily survive translation thanks to their establishment in the modern English tradition in the seventeenth and eighteenth centuries. More special uses are harder to preserve. There is for instance momentary personification, sometimes accompanied by lexicographical difficulty. For instance, a prayer for the king runs, "May God grant you to govern your country *so leaute þee louye*" (Prol. 126). The verb *louye*, "may love," establishes *leaute*, the fourteenth-century form equivalent to modern English *loyalty*, as a personification. But precisely as a personification it is untranslatable by "Loyalty"; it seems to mean either "your loyal subjects" or, in my view more probably, "law-abiding people."[32] Whichever meaning one opts for, some of the tension of the original is lost along with the personification. Local personification can generate considerable meaning. For instance, goes a homily, it is easier for a poor man than a rich one to avoid the capital sins. If he wrestles with Anger he is bound to lose; against Gluttony his indigence protects him; his bed is too cold and uncomfortable to encourage him in Sloth. As for Avarice, and here the figure of wrestling recurs, but this time the poor man is allegorized as Poverty, the latter is *but a petit þyng, apereþ noȝt to his nauele*, "only a tiny creature, doesn't even come up to Avarice's navel, and it was never much of a bout between a big and a small opponent" (XIV, 243, 244). The abrupt personification is not casual. It evidently enables the homely index of height, and appears pointed by the gallicism *petit*, which may be a Langlandian first use, and if so suggests affectation. These features between them draw attention to the assumed tone of sardonic humor in the passage—it is, after all, preposterous to commend poverty—and as for a poor man being free of the desire for possessions, his innocence is likely to be only relative, a matter of scale. So we are forced to consider the real, the spiritual reasons for the commendation of poverty. How much of that will come over in translation? Then there is double allegorization: *"Now repente," quod Repentance,* "'Now repent!' said Repentance" to Anger (V, 182); if a starving man steals a loaf or a naked man a shirt, *Nede anoon righte nymeþ hym vnder maynprise,* "Necessity straightaway stands surety for him," says Necessity himself to the Dreamer (XX, 17); in the collapse of the Church at the end of the poem Contrition abandons contrition because of the "comfortable words" of his confessor (XX, 369–71). The double allegorization looks like a demand by the poet for thoughtful attention; this is not likely to survive translation. Allegorization is not constant. In one place Patience is a guest at a dinner (XIII, 29), in another a garment (XVIII, 168); the gold coins called florins are variously retainers of a powerful woman so crowding the streets as to obstruct the free movement of personified integrity (III, 157)[33] and an illness with which a clever lawyer is afflicted, which makes him speak hypocritically (IV, 156).[34] In these and many similar, more complex instances[35] allegory has become a figure of thought, simultaneously a personification and a metaphor.

The texture is even more intricate when the allegory occurs in a macaronic context. Not that macaronic verse is itself necessarily hard to translate. For instance to use *"Contra!"* in a scholastic dispute (X, 349), or to qualify a statement with "That is *in extremis*" (X, 352), or even to make a bilingual pun, *Fy on faitours and in fautores suos,* "Shame on those who beg needlessly and those who support them" (XV, 215), are transmittable professional mannerisms. And when the Dreamer reports, *I drow me in þat derknesse to descendit ad inferna,* "I made my way in that darkness . . . " (XVIII, 111), the Latin is the poet's invocation of the Creed for authority in an apocryphal matter. The right course would seem to be to keep the Latin here. But other macaronic puns are more dynamic. For instance a cynical friar, able from the proceeds of the confessional to eat well, nevertheless gets a very sour sauce unwholesomely ground *In a morter, Post mortem* (XIII, 44); the pun in collocation with the verb confers a minatory tone. And there is another grade of difficulty in, for instance, a reference to the parable of the wedding feast: *Multi to a mangerie and to þe mete were sompned* goes the text, "Many were summoned to a feast and a meal"; when they had all arrived the porter unlocked the gate *And plukked in Pauci pryueliche*, "snatched in a few without giving a reason for his choice" (XI 112, 114). Here *Multi* and *Pauci* give the scriptural reference;[36] the complicating elements are *maungerie*, a pretentious or ceremonious term, and *plukked*, used for sharp, abrupt, or violent action, instead of the ordinary words *feste* and *nom*; they signify the special nature of the occasion and the apparent arbitrariness of the selection, and charge the passage with the Dreamer's anxiety about predestination at this point.

How serviceable Langland found the macaronic device, especially in combination with allegory, appears from his use of it at two high climaxes of the poem, meticulously prepared occasions of intense religious as well as poetic emotion. The first is the moment of spiritual transformation of the people of the field after the confession of the sins and Repentance's prayer:

> Thanne hente hope an horn of *Deus tu conuersus viuificabis nos*
> And blew it with *Beati quorum remisse sunt iniquitates.* (V, 506, 507)

The second comes after the defeat of Death and the devil, when Mercy, Truth, Righteousness, and Peace are brought into accord by Love and there has been, in Christ's speech of victory, implication of his ultimate mercy to all mankind:

> Truþe trumpede þo and song *Te deum laudamus*,
> And þanne lutede loue in a loud note,
> *Ecce quam bonum & quam iocundum.* (XVIII, 422–423)

In both passages the effective elements are: satisfaction of the yearning for freedom from guilt and for assurance of salvation, figured in the reconciliation of the opposed abstractions of divine justice and divine mercy; physical realization of the abstractions through the archetypally moving activity of music; and then the expression of these in the resonant Latin of the Psalms and the great hymn, evocative from a lifetime of religious observance. Each element is bound to lose some effect in translation, the combinations much more.

The problem set the translator by such striking, complex uses of relatively simple figures, whereby rhetorical form generates feeling that enters the abstractable meaning as an assertion of its force, must be evident. That of producing the finer texture of Langland's style, the detailed economy of language by which he controls response, is just as severe.

A markedly distinctive feature of his style is wit. One of his means of creating wit is incongruity, through use of a term of a grade one would not, prima facie, have expected in the context. It is possible that in some instances the device may be merely self-gratifying, playful, or else a generation of stylistic energy to sustain attention: the poet once refers to language as *a game of heuene* (IX, 104), a celestial diversion, so to speak. Sometimes the incongruous terms, commonly in alliterating positions and often finite verbs, have a look of being intellectual replications to the auditory form. So Lady Meed (here personifying the expectation of loot) claims that in the French campaigns she *batred* the King's soldiers on the back and made them *hoppe for hope* of having her at will (III, 199, 200); Christ made Lazarus *rise and rome* before the Jews (XV, 595); he *knokked on* the moneychangers in the temple with a cord (XVI, 128). And verbs denoting physical actions by personifications, as when Repentence *ran* to give out the theme of the sermon (V, 60: for the theme see 182), or Do Better *is ronne*, "has run" to the religious life, (VIII, 91) or where Truth sees Righteousness "come running" (XVIII, 165) may be primarily inducements to acceptance of the personifications by imputing to them visualizable physical activity.

But elsewhere similarly incongruous verbs develop ultralexical meaning, which cannot be translated succinctly and moreover may need explication. Intelligence nowadays is ineffectual unless it *be carded* by Covetousness (X, 18), dragged out slowly and laboriously into a usable state like matted wool with a carding comb. Scripture *skipte an heiʒ*, "skipped aloft"(hardly appropriate of a preacher), into a pulpit and preached on the uncomfortable text "many are called but few are chosen" (XI, 107); the unexpected verb can suggest how readily and easily the concept of predestination might become an anxious preoccupation. Not all the learning in Christendom could *cracche*, "scratch, scrape, grab" the just, pagan Trajan from hell (XI, 144): the difference of grade between subject and predicate has adverbial force. Lazarus is *Lollynge* in

Abraham's bosom (XVI, 269); his posture of helplessness, as of a baby too young to hold its head up, suggests the condition of dependency of "our forefathers in darkness" upon divine grace. Hope *cam hippynge*, that is "followed hopping along," after Abraham and the Samaritan (XVII, 62), carefree (for the moment) as a child at play. Covetousness *Iogged*, "trotted unhurriedly," to a judge and "jousted" in his ear, thus suborning him (XX, 134); the leisurely verb implies that no great effort such as getting into a gallop was needed.[37]

When this ironic use is of other parts of speech than the finite verb it can extend meaning even farther. In an ideal world *Bisshopes Bayardes* will be *beggeris Chaumbres* (IV, 124): literally the fine mounts which bishops ride (but for a few notable journeys Christ travelled on foot, we recall) will be accommodation for paupers; the meaning extends to all prelates who live in the style of lords temporal. Corrupt parochial clergy are blind buzzards (X, 272); the criticism—the context is of the beam in one's own eye—is pointed by the nature of the buzzard (in British English the hawk *buteo buteo*), despised as useless for falconry,[38] and remarkable only for its keen vision. In his first epiphany, as a peasant farmer, Piers Plowman speaks of the fall of Adam and Eve as eating *apples vnrosted*, that is raw, or unbaked apples (V, 603). He is talking in the language of his class at this point, a part of establishing his initial character. Baked apples were a main item of peasant diet in the poor season of a bad year, namely late summer before new grain came to market (VI, 292–299); at that time they would be windfalls or still green on the tree, and pain would come to those who ill-advisedly ate them raw. The great commandment of love is described as a "charm" (XVII, 20, 23). The unusual application of that term directly and extensively evokes contrast between the efficacy of a central doctrine of Christianity and the delusion of belief in magic like that of Hawkin earlier in the poem:

> goddes word ne grace gaf me neuere boote,
> But þoruȝ a charme hadde I chaunce and my chief heele.
>
> (XIII, 340, 341)

"God's word and his grace were never any good to me; I had my luck and my main success from a charm." In those examples the irony, an index of the discrepancy between, variously, actual and right conduct, or Piers's character early and later in the poem, or of the scale of difference between temporal and eternal values, is implicit in the incongruity of language. It is easily enough explained, but what does the translator use to render Bayard and buzzard and unroasted apples? There are many such instances. The problem is as hard when the device of irony consists in using concrete terms for abstract, particularly doctrinal and spiritual concepts. Hell is the *poukes pondfold*, the devil's "pen" or "pound" (XVI, 264); the Dreamer has *þouȝtes a þreve*, "twelve sheaves" or "two stooks"[39] of thoughts about the Trinity (XVI, 55). In the Middle English such expressions make us think of errant man as like a strayed farm animal, and of how perplexing to the plain man is the most immense doctrine of Christianity; in translation they will merely appear eccentric.

Another practically untranslatable feature of Langland's style is the pun,[40] whether homeophonic or perfectly ambiguous. As the reader will know, in the Middle Ages as in classical times the pun was neither a social misdemeanor nor a device for amusing theatre audiences with sexual innuendo, but a valued and commended figure of thought.[41] For an instance of the echoic kind: it is said of a sinful man, *Moore to good þan to god þe gome his loue caste* (XIII, 356), "The man loved property more than God." The echo, differentiated only in the vowel, evokes the doctrine of the true and false good, which condemns him. A mismatched couple married for money have *no children but cheeste*, "strife" (IX, 172), again differentiated only in the vowel from *cheste*, a "strongbox." And Glutton, once he was got home from the tavern, *after all þis excesse he had an Accidie* (V, 359), "after all this excess succumbed to sloth"; here the pun operates by *excesse* and *Accidie* in collocation evoking *accesse*, "a seizure, an onset of fever,"[42] and the sloth consequent on his sin appears a sickness of the soul. In a trial for robbery with violence a clever defending lawyer argues,

> Bettre is þat boote bale adoun brynge
> Than bale be ybet and boote neuer þe bettre. (IV, 93, 94)

"It is better that injury should be made good by compensation than that wrongdoing be punished and no compensation paid." His glibness, to the impression of which the puns (incidentally also personifications) contribute, suggests how legal brilliance can obscure issues and obstruct the right course of law.

And puns by ambiguity: on Judgement Day a bishop will be accountable to Christians, the preacher tells them, for

> What he lerned yow in lente . . .
> And what he lente yow of oure lordes good to lette yow fro synne,
> (V, 294, 295)

that is, for "What he taught you in Lent and what he gave to you from our Lord's treasure to hinder you from sin." The exact rhyme of *lente*, "gave, bestowed on" with the name of the penitential season suggests that the gift of our Lord's treasure might be comfort and guidance in the longer penitential exercise of preparing for another life. A wealthy man concerned for the state of his soul should be entertained not by minstrels but by the poor and sick; these will at his death comfort the man who in his lifetime *liþed hem* (XIII, 451), that is either "listened to them" as minstrels, or "improved their condition" as objects of charity.[43] At a dinner party the Dreamer is infuriated by the conduct of an important guest, a friar theologian, and says "I shall dispute with this *Iurdan wiþ his Iuste wombe*" (XIII, 84). *Iurdan* was the name of a contemporary theological controversialist;[44] it also means "chamber pot" or "glass vessel with a bulb-like body;"[45] and *Iuste* can mean "just, righteous," or "vessel with a narrow, long neck and a large bottom."[46] In those cruel puns the poet has made the Dreamer express the bitterness and anger of simple Christians at what they saw as the cynicism and failure of dedication of the clergy. They are untranslatable.

Poetic form, concision and along with this force of statement, the energy expressed through feeling generated in a highly figurative style, and extensive ultralexical meaning: a dismal list of probable loss in the translation of *Piers Plowman*, and it is by no means complete, for my demonstration was restricted to a few differences between the early and present language and some figures characteristic variously of religious dream visions or of Langland's personal style.

There will also be loss of tonal effect, the quality of utterance which, as of an historical voice, is part of the experience of any significant poem. The tone of this one is simply not reproduceable in today's English. There is space to illustrate this only in respect of some altered usage; the matter of the Dreamer's tone of voice as an individual, a main factor in our impression of him as a dramatic personality,[47] is too large a subject for this occasion. As to the historical authenticity, our language has no longer any usage corresponding to the pious oaths that lard the speech of even the most innocent characters, or to violent but unobscene terms of abuse like *sherewe* or *feloun* or *lorel* or *losel* or *ribaud* or *harlot*[48] or *boie*.[49] For the imaginative numeral usages of Middle English we substitute colorless adverbs: *hewe fir at a flynt foure hundred wynter*, "strike fire from a flint four hundred winters" says the poem of an unavailing activity (XVII, 248); "for ever" is the translator's attempt.[50] Our criteria of value are less vivid: we no longer gauge worthlessness by a sop or a pea or a piecrust[51] or a rush or a stalk of cress. Our food habits have changed: the expensive dishes relished by Friar Jordan (XIII, 41) we would think of as sloppy messes, and the bacon rejected by the peasants when times are good (VI, 309) has become dear. A poor man in those days dressed in *russet* (VIII, 1), the tweed that we buy when we can afford it. As for money, supposing it were possible to assess the value in 1378 of *a pound of nobles*, "a pound weight of gold coins of a particular kind first minted by Edward III" (X, 295), still the visual effect of the original correlative would be unreproduceable. And how can we equate *two pens*, evidently more than enough, which the Samaritan gave for the keep of the man set upon by thieves (XVII, 79)?

The questions multiply. Why, for instance, is a priest called Sir Piers *of Pridie* (V, 312)? Why is Plato twice described as a poet (X, 178; XI, 37)? How can breaking wind be a form of entertainment (XIII, 231)? Why does Friar Jordan use the name *dido* to dismiss a statement as fanciful nonsense (XIII, 172)? What were Folville's laws (XIX, 247)? Countless such details of information which the poet and his creation the Dreamer and their contemporary audience took for granted have had laboriously to be recovered or await recovery. The expressions embodying them require annotation, not translation. To that extent again the character of the translation as a source of literary and dramatic experience is diminished.

The conclusion is in sight that an authentic poetic equivalent to

Piers Plowman is not reproduceable in modern English: the particular instance substantiates the generalization. And so lexicography can appear the least of the translator's problems. The impossibility has to do with feeling, from the nature of the external form, and because language changes make the modern lexical equivalent more diffuse than the original; or with the inseparable compound of feeling and ultralexical meaning generated in figures of speech and thought, to describe which, let alone reproduce it, would need a sustained commentary; or with tone, if only because of the linguistic and cultural remoteness of the poem. It should, however, also have become evident that there is compensation for the loss of the poetry in the understanding of the reasons which impose the loss. That is how *Piers Plowman* is available as an act of historical cognition. And also, once we acquiesce in the sacrifice of its poetry (to possess which we need, after all, only to learn Middle English) it is available as a form of event and thought.

But that availability depends on a translation which accurately reproduces the abstractable prose content of the poem, and so lexicography regains its true appearance of primary importance. Such a translation is theoretically feasible; the dictionaries available are, in general, good or adequate. It is also practically difficult. The translator will be well advised to adopt as a working principle that historical differentiation of meaning between a fourteenth-century word and its twentieth-century descendant is as likely as not, and never guess.[52] So for instance in the fable of belling the cat he will translate *venyson* (Prol., 190) unspecifically as "game" in its primary historical sense, and avoid the absurd suggestion of a domestic cat pulling down a deer.[53] He will not be misled by *yonge men* (III, 214) when the expression means "yeomen, personal attendants,"[54] or by *stokkes* (V, 576) where it means "idols, graven images,"[55] or by *vnderstonde* (XIV, 279) where it means "be receptive to instruction, pay attention."[56] The dictionary is there to protect him against mistaking historical descent, so that where the text says of the slothful ways of a reprehensible couple that they *breden as Burgh swyn* (II, 98) his translation will read not "breed like" but "get fat like town pigs."[57] He must believe that his poet is intelligent and that accordingly where his translation makes poor sense it is probably wrong. If then he uses the dictionary intelligently he will not write of eminent lawyers with an eye out for lucrative cases (Prol., 211) that they "stood swaying from side to side" when the verb in question also affords the contextually appropriate sense "wait in readiness or expectation."[58] And when a sinful man confesses that he is generous in charitable gifts *losse þere-by to cacche*,[59] apparently "in order to incur loss by that means," the nonsense must direct him to the lexicography of *losse*, which, he will find, can mean "praise, admiration."[60]

He must read his text with vigilant understanding. Then, where it says that Charity is not found *at Ancres þere a box hange* (XV, 214), remembering that anchorites were walled up in their cells and unlikely to "carry almsboxes"[61] around like modern charity workers, he will understand that *þere* means "outside whose cells." And when Christ proclaims after his descent into hell, *lede I wole fro hennes Tho ledes þat I loue, and leued in my comynge* (XVIII, 400, 401), he will recognize the violence of the occasion and not translate *I wole* by "I shall."[62]

His respect for his poet's language and its meaning ought to check him from setting up, so to speak, his own meaning. So where the text says of the lawyers profiting from the crime of Wrong, *Tho wan Wisdom and sire waryn þe witty* (IV, 67) the fact that he finds *wan* difficult[63] will not induce him to leave it out of his translation.[64] And similarly he will not suppress the Dreamer's challenge to his audience, *ye men þat ben murye* (Prol., 209), "you people who are laughing," at the fable, of course, because he does not perceive how the poet is signalling the important bivalent analogy between ludicrous and serious in his immediate subject.[65]

There will be a wide variety of instances of what theorists call "emic" concepts, "culture specific"[66] in the historical sense, which he will find it not just impossible to translate perfectly but even difficult to annotate; one such is *curteisie* with its adjective *curteis* used in religious connections.[67] He will find some distinctively Langlandian uses awaiting their lexicographer: for instance *bidders and beggeres*, which looks like a doublet but may have a complicated sense relating to the immorality of begging, or the opposites *winner* and *wastour*, apparently relating to a combination of notions of morality and economics with no modern equivalent. He will need to be continually vigilant in translating the general term *clergie*, with a range of meanings between "the second estate" and "learning,"[68] not to mention its particular, *clerk*, with a comparable variety. The prima facie easy terms *truth* and *loue* and *charite* will test his theology.

Prose translation notwithstanding he will need a sensitive ear. If the connotation of an original term survives, he must keep the term. In the catastrophe at the end, where the text tells how in a wild attack Death *to duste passhed* (XX, 100), "beat into dust" kings, knights, emperors, and so on, he must know better than to substitute "powder" for "dust" because the dust-mortality association is still strong.[69] Correspondingly he must command the tonal values of modern English and not represent the words of a proud woman forswearing her besetting sin who says in effect, "I shall never again succumb to pride, but keep myself humble" (V, 67), as "Here's an end to all my swaggering airs."[70]

With all these cautions his translations will at best be jejune, a melancholy event.[71] His concern must be that, by working as knowledgeably, seriously and respectfully as he is able, and giving himself no airs, he will keep the inevitable disparagement of his poet to the unavoidable minimum.

Notes

1. E. A. Nida, "A Framework for the Analysis and Evaluation of Theories of Translation," in R. W. Brislin, ed., *Translation: Applications and Research* (New York, 1976), pp. 51–52.

2. W. Winter, "Impossibilities of Translation," in W. Arrowsmith and R. Shattuck, eds., *The Craft and Context of Translation* (Austin, Tex., 1961), p. 73.

3. J. Mathews, "Third Thoughts on Translating Poetry," in R. A. Brower, ed., *On Translation* (New York, 1966), p. 67: "One thing seems clear: to translate a poem whole is to compose another poem."

4. Compare W. V. Quine, "Meaning and Translation," in Brower, *On Translation*, p. 148: "Empirical meaning is what remains when, given discourse together with all its stimulatory conditions, we peel away the verbiage. It is what the sentences of one language and their firm translations in a completely alien language have in common."

5. *"There is no completely exact translation."* W. Winter, "Impossibilities of Translation," p. 69. Compare J. C. Catford, *A Linguistic Theory of Translation* (London, 1965), pp. 93–103, and H. C. Triandis, "Approaches toward Minimizing Translation," in Brislin, *Translation*, pp. 229–230.

6. George Steiner, *After Babel* (London, 1975).

7. Quoted by E. S. Bates, *Modern Translation* (London, 1936), p. 107. For a modern equivalent, see Catford, *A Linguistic Theory*, p. 25.

8. Steiner, *After Babel*, p. 303.

9. Bates, *Modern Translation*, p. 124. Compare D. S. Carne-Ross, "Translation and Transposition," in Arrowsmith and Shattuck, *The Craft and Context*, p. 6: "True translation is much more a commentary on the original than a substitute for it. Like criticism, to which it is closely allied, its role is interpretative."

10. For that notion see L. Ray, "Multidimensional Translation: Poetry," in Brislin, *Translation*, p. 262.

11. Compare Georges Mounin, *Les Problèmes Théoriques de la Traduction* (Paris, 1963), pp. 278–279.

12. R. Jakobson, "On Linguistic Aspects of Translation," in Brower, *On Translation*, p. 233.

13. Compare Steiner, *After Babel*, p. 28.

14. F. L. Saran, *Das Übersetzen aus dem Mittelhochdeutschen* [now in at least its fifth impression], revised, B. Nagel (Tübingen, 1967), instances some of the difficulties of translating that language into modern German.

15. A corresponding approximation would be Nevill Coghill's Chaucer translations, *A Choice of Chaucer's Verse* (London, 1972) and *The Canterbury Tales* (London, 1977). Like their originals they are lively and readable, and being in verse they have in a sense a corresponding external form. They also reproduce with fair accuracy the abstractable content of their originals. But the verse is twentieth-century, and the feeling is more Coghill's than Chaucer's.

16. Several important ones are given in J. F. Goodridge, *Piers the Plowman: William Langland: Translated into Modern English with an Introduction* (reprint ed: London, 1975), p. 21.

17. *A New English Dictionary on Historical Principles* [hereafter *N.E.D.*], ed. James A. H. Murray (Oxford, 1888–1928), s.v. "Shall" 8.a.

18. *Piers Plowman* references are to G. Kane and E. T. Donaldson, *Piers Plowman: the B Version* (London, 1975).

19. *N.E.D.*, s.v. "Shall" 3.

20. *N.E.D.*, s.v. "Shall" 5.a.

21. *N.E.D.*, s.v. "Will" v.[1] or "Will" v.[2]1.

22. *N.E.D.*, s.v. "Will" v.[1]6.

23. *N.E.D.*, s.v. "Will" v.[1]10. The dictionary gives no instance of this sense, "expressing

determination, persistence and the like," before Caxton, but it is clearly present here and in the other resolutions of amendment at V, 69, 226, 301, 455.

24. *N.E.D.*, s.v. "May" v.¹1, 2; *Middle English Dictionary* [hereafter *M.E.D.*], ed. Hans Kurath (Ann Arbor, Mich., 1954), s.v. "mouen" v. (3) 1, 2.

25. See E. Salter and D. Pearsall, eds., *Piers Plowman* (London, 1967), p. 61, note to ll. 2, 3: "I dressed myself in rough clothes, like a shepherd, in the garb of a hermit of secular life." Failure to value the contrast led these editors to mistranslate the preceding line where *shepe / shep* however spelled means "sheep," not "shepherd." This is an old error, found in one family of C manuscripts, and hallowed in Skeat's note to the line. Elsewhere, however, the Dreamer specifically describes his customary dress as clerical habit, *longe clothes* (Salter and Pearsall, *Piers Plowman*, p. 78, l. 41).

26. So Goodridge, *Piers the Plowman*, p. 262: "*In the garb of an easy-living hermit*, i.e., one who did not keep to his cell. . . . Shepherds and hermits were dressed alike." How Goodridge knows this he does not reveal, but the poet appears not to have thought so: he presently writes of "easy-living" hermits that they *Cloþed hem in copes to ben knowen from opere* (Prol., 56), "to look distinctive." The *copes* here are clerical dress (*M.E.D.* s.v. 2): see C revision (*The Visions of William concerning Piers the Plowman: Text C* [London, 1873], X, 210, 211, *clothed hem in copes clerkus as hit were, Other on of som ordre*.

27. To judge by examples in *N.E.D.* and *M.E.D.*, use of *appose* with an adverb of manner is not very common. When this does occur (see *M.E.D.*, s.v. "ap(p)osen" 1.(a) for examples) the adverb (*with wordes strongue . . . streite, sad & sar, weel*) most often implies an effect on the person interrogated. If, however, *sooþliche* here is an extension of such modification it is so extreme as to appear a trope.

28. It is intriguing to speculate whether the slovenly expression was designed to contribute to the impression of the speaker's main trait. But this may just be colloquial syntax: compare, *May no peny ale hem paie ne no pece of bacoun, But if it be fressh flessh ouþer fissh yfryed* (VI, 309, 310).

29. *his goode wille* (XVIII, 212).

30. Compare also *Tho was he Iesus of Iewes called, gentile prophete, And kyng of hir kyngdom and croune bar of þornes* (XIX, 48, 49) and *Ther nede haþ ynome me þat I moot nede abide And suffre sorwes ful soure, þat shal to Ioye torne* (XX, 46, 47).

31. How subtly the poet is able to vary this might be illustrated from the difference of response to Haukyn's account of his sinful state in Passus XIII of the B version, which evokes compassion in the spirit of XIV, 325, "*So hard it is*," quod haukyn, "*to lyue and to do synne*," and to the same passages, incorporated with relatively little modification, into the confessions of the sins in the C revision.

32. *M.E.D.*, s.v. "leaute" n. assigns the first meaning "Uprightness, honorableness, honesty; truth; justice, fairness" to this word. It is often used in contexts of public behavior such as government and courts of law. There is another, lexicographically very problematic personification of *lewte* at XI, 84. In XX, 348, the problem is of another kind: the need to translate *Hende speche* as "the natural instinct not to disoblige," or "the desire to be agreeable," neither of which will do as the name of a personification.

33. *feiþ may noȝt haue his forþ, hire floryns go so þikke*. The translation is authorized by either *M.E.D.*, s.v. "forth" adv. 1, in which case the expression is elliptical (sc. *haue his wei forþ*), or *N.E.D.*, s.v. "forth" adv., prep., and sb. C, "to have outlet; fig. to have free course."

34. *'I falle in floryns', quod þat freke, 'and faile speche ofte.'* See *M.E.D.* s.v. "fallen" v. 24c.

35. Thus "Lady Meed," Mede, the central figure of Passus II–IV, signifying various aspects of the social change to a monetary society which Langland found generally destructive of integrity, would strictly need several modern names to match the development of her representation. The personifications *Conscience* and *Ymaginatif* have even more complicated identities deriving from medieval notions of psychology and not reproduceable by single terms.

36. Matthew 22:14, *Multi enim sunt vocati, pauci vero electi.*

37. One such expression, *dyngen vpon Dauid* (III, 312) where *dyngen* is a verb used of threshing with a flail (*dyngen vpon sheues*, VI, 141) is strikingly instanced in an apparently earlier poem. The slack parson in *The Papelard Priest* complains that he is obliged to leave

a good party to *dyngen opon dauyd wyt a dirige* (*London Mediaeval Studies*, II, i [1951], pp. 34 and 44, l. 56).

38. Compare *my buzard love* in *Loves Diet*, l. 25 (*The Poems of John Donne*, ed. H. J. Grierson [reprint ed.: London, 1958], I, p. 56).

39. See *N.E.D.*, s.v. "Thrave, Threave." This would have been a fully live metaphor in the fourteenth century.

40. The problem of translating puns is solemnly discussed in Catford, *A Linguistic Theory of Translation*, pp. 94ff.

41. See for example H. Lausberg, *Handbuch der Literarischen Rhetorik* (Munich, 1973), p. 322: "Die *annominatio* (Paronomasie) ist ein (pseudo-)etymologisches Spiel mit der Geringfügigkeit der lautlichen Änderung einerseits und der interessanten Bedeutungsspanne, die durch die lautliche Änderung hergestellt wird, andererseits. Hierbei kann die Bedeutungsspanne bis ins Paradoxe gesteigert werden. Die so hergestellte Etymologie . . . zwischen den beiden Wörtern wird dem Publikum als eigene Arbeitsleistung vom Autor zugemutet."

42. *M.E.D.* s.v. "acces(s)e," n. 1. This ingenious *annominatio*, incorporating metaphor, is a refinement of the earlier form of the line, *aftir al þis surfet an axesse he hadde* (*Piers Plowman: the A Version*, V, 201). The pun-evoking word *excesse* was apparently a new importation; Langland's B-text use of it probably antedates all the dictionary examples. One C scribe apparently did not believe in it and substituted *excessus*; at least two scribes in the B tradition wrote *accesse* in its place. None of this makes translation any easier.

43. See *M.E.D.* s.v. "lithen" v. (2), v. (3), and *N.E.D.* s.v. "Lithe" v.², v.³

44. See M. Marcett, *Uhtred de Boldon, Friar William Jordan, and Piers Plowman* (New York, 1938).

45. See *M.E.D.* s.v. "jordan" n.

46. See *M.E.D.* s.v. "juste" n. The two meanings derive ultimately from the same Latin etymon. Langland could have known this.

47. How much of this most careful creation of the poet comes across in translation it is hard for anyone who knows the original poem to judge; for him the Dreamer has a vital existence of which he is bound to be aware even when reading a translation.

48. See *M.E.D.* s.v. "harlot" n. 3b for the fifteenth-century and apparently earliest recorded uses of the word to mean female prostitute. Its primary fourteenth-century sense was abusive of the male sex, as in Old French.

49. See *M.E.D.* s.v. "boie" n. (1) 4 for the fifteenth-century development of the meaning "male child, boy, youth."

50. Goodridge, *Piers the Plowman*, p. 213. The usage is emotional, not perfunctory: the feeling can be observed in children striving to form and formulate conceptions of magnitude or scope. Compare for example Prologue 211, 212, *an hundred . . . Sergeantz . . . at þe barre*; III, 123, *She makeþ men mysdo many score tymes*; III, 145, 146, *She may neiȝ as muche do in a Monþe ones As youre secret seel in sixe score dayes*; III, 181, *Thow hast hanged on myn half elleuene tymes*, V, 368–370 *I haue . . . Sworen. . . . There no nede was nyne hundred tymes*; V, 425, *þus tene I trewe men ten hundred tymes*. The numbers are both arbitrary and conveniently alliterative, but they become poetically significant once selected; we recognize their "rightness after the event." Compare Kenneth Burke, "*Lexicon Rhetoricae*," in R. W. Stallman, *Critiques and Essays in Criticism: 1920–1948* (New York, 1949), p. 235.

51. Strictly speaking the "heel" of a meat pie, the bottom crust. Anyone with experience of the commercial British product will know that this part of it is, to say the least, unpalatable.

52. Bates, *Modern Translation*, p. 99: "Translators may be divided into four kinds: those who neither use nor need dictionaries; those who need them and use them; those who need them but don't use them; those who would like them but have to do the best they can without. Sixteenth-century translators belonged to the last class; our contemporaries to one or other of the other three classes." There is probably no Middle English scholar in the first of those classes, and there should not be any in the third.

53. Goodridge, *Piers the Plowman*, p. 30. The word embarrasses him, and he puts it in quotation marks.

54. *N.E.D.* s.v. "Young Man, Youngman" 2b. Compare Goodridge, *Piers the Plowman*, p. 50.

55. *N.E.D.* s.v. "Stock" sb. 1d; Goodridge, *Piers the Plowman*, p. 78, "pairs of stocks." With *stokkes* correctly translated *loke noʒt þerafter* assumes its correct sense, "do not look back at them in longing."

56 *N.E.D.* s.v. "understand" v. 6a; Goodridge, *Piers the Plowman*, p. 175. His mistranslation of the verb extends to *by so*, which must mean "provided that."

57. *M.E.D.* s.v. "breden" v. (2) b, "spread out," here "become broad" from O. E. *brǣdan*. The activity of *M.E.D.* "breden" v. (3) "breed," is not shown by its Middle English lexicography to be reprehensible, and anyway town pigs breed like country pigs. The reference is to the consequence of gluttonous feeding, made possible by abundantly available pigswill, not to mention the content of the medieval town gutter. Compare Goodridge, *Piers the Plowman*, p. 41.

58. *M.E.D.* s.v. "hoven" v. (1) 2; compare also *N.E.D.* s.v. "Hove" v.¹2; Goodridge, *Piers the Plowman*, p. 31.

59. This is the form of the half line in Skeat's B text (W. W. Skeat, *Piers the Plowman* [reprint ed.: London, 1930], XIII, 299), and its spelling *losse*, historically better as *los* or *loos*, might seem misleading. But *M.E.D.* under "los" n. (2) cites *losse* among variant spellings.

60. Compare Goodridge, *Piers the Plowman*, p. 160, where mistranslation of *losse* leads to further error: translation of the purpose clause signalled in *þere-by to* as one of result.

61. Goodridge, *Piers the Plowman*, p. 185.

62. Goodridge, *Piers the Plowman*, p. 228.

63. It means "profited." See *N.E.D.* s.v. "Win" v.¹6c, "to get gain, make profit."

64. As does Goodridge, *Piers the Plowman*, p. 57.

65. As does Goodridge, *Piers the Plowman*, p. 31.

66. "In any translation one has to face the problem of the extent to which what he is to translate is culture-specific (emic) or universal (etic). It is easy to see that etic concepts, such as fire, moon and sun, produce fewer translation difficulties than emic concepts, such as the Greek concept of *philotimo* or the Anglo-American concept of *fairness*." H. C. Triandis, "Approaches toward Minimizing Translation," p. 229.

67. See I, 20; XII, 77; XIV, 147; XV, 557; XVII, 245; XIX, 449; XIII, 15; XV, 104.

68. Compare the meanings of *clergie* in Prol. 116 and III, 165, and XII, 85, where the suggestion is of not much more than the literacy needed to read the Mass-book.

69. Goodridge, *Piers the Plowman*, p. 248.

70. Goodridge, *Piers the Plowman*, p. 63.

71. Steiner, *After Babel*, p. 269.

Mode and Voice in Seventeenth-Century Meditative Verse: A Discussion of Five Newly Discovered Poems by Dudley North

Dale B. J. Randall

Duke University

The discovery of a cache of poems by Dudley North, fourth Lord North (1602–1677), provides us with a set of fresh opportunities and problems.[1] Faced with an array of fifty new seventeenth-century sonnets, satires, pastorals, epigrams, and elegies, we soon see that one problem is the need to decide how much or how little these poems resemble others of their time. A reader who turns to North's meditative verse, for instance, as we shall be doing here, is likely to find that a knowledge of the meditative tradition is valuable. More striking is the fact that an empirical knowledge of these new meditative poems proves to be an opportune motive for reconsidering our abstract sense of just what meditative verse really is. Therefore my aim here is to suggest the mutual illumination of the meditative mode and some newly discovered meditative poems by Dudley North.

I

Multiplicity of meaning in the term "meditative verse" might be thought sufficient to turn the wary from its use. As Professor Martz long ago suggested, however, the phrase has particular relevance to the seventeenth-century English poetry which grew out of devotional practices of the time.[2] Such practices stretched back well before the *Spiritual Exercises* of St. Ignatius, back before his medieval predecessors, back at least to St. Augustine.[3] It is little wonder that when they manifested themselves in written form, they took on a bewildering variety of shapes. Indeed, when all his evidence was gathered, Professor Martz was moved to write that the meditative tradition was manifested in the seventeenth century in the *Holy Sonnets* of John Donne, the soliloquies of Hamlet, and certain passages in *Paradise Lost.*[4] We have here a term, therefore, which applies to a literary mode that runs through the lyric, the dramatic, and the epic.

One's instinct may be to look for a term that will let us classify with more refinement. After all, the history of poetics is grounded on classification. If one turns to the word "contemplative" for clarity, however, one must face the consequences of twisting a term traditionally reserved for a process superior to meditation, namely, beholding the divine.[5] One might also seek escape through such labels as "speculative" or "deliberative," but the fact remains that the seventeenth century spoke most commonly of "meditation," and that term or some form of it retains its central pertinence for seventeenth-century studies today.

For a glimpse of English concepts regarding meditation in the century of Donne and Dryden, let us begin with James Cleland's little handbook called *Heropaideia* (Oxford, 1607). Cleland writes that

as the *Persians* alwaies meditated vpon everie matter of importance, as in making of warrs, peace or truces, in marrying their daughters or any such like thinge, a daie before they speake of it: so I councell you to meditate well after yee haue *Hard*, or *Read* any lesson. For *meditation is the fountaine of algood councell and wisdome, the rule of al affaiers, the mother of al learning,* and in a word, the *engenderer of al vertue.* (pp. 160–161)

Despite its fine results, "meditation" for Cleland turns out to be simply "serious thought."

At the other extreme—and here we turn back gratefully to Martz—"by the beginning of the seventeenth century all the most important spiritual writers are agreed upon the place and significance of 'meditation' as describing a particular stage and process in the spiritual life."[6] More particularly, the aim of this meditative process is the state of "devotion."[7] Here is some firm ground. But even here there is room for great variety. As Alonso Rodríguez put it, "There is a great deale of difference betweene *Meditating* and *Meditating.* . . ."[8] One might engage, for example, in the elaborate methods of the Jesuit Edward Dawson, as explained in his paraphrase of Ignatius called *The Practical Methode of Meditation* (1614).[9] These involved preparatory prayers and preludes—the best-known prelude being the "composition of place," whereby one was supposed to visualize as vividly as possible some event in the life of Jesus or a saint. A second kind of prelude, and one that is more important for our present study, was composition through comparison, through "similitude." During the course of these and subsequent steps the meditation was supposed to exercise all three powers of the soul (memory, understanding, and will), leading finally to resolutions of the now-aroused will—this latter step involving some sort of colloquy between the meditator, on the one hand, and God or a saint, on the other.

Not all Englishmen could be expected to be enamored of any such fancy system. On the other hand, Richard Baxter, one of the greatest of Protestant spokesmen, observed in 1650 that meditation was "confessed to be a Duty by all."[10] The result is that in the same years in which we find translators of Continental Roman Catholic devotional writers we find also a number of English writers working to create a somewhat simpler and more characteristically Protestant theory and literature of meditation. And these men frequently take the word "meditation" to refer to "general reflections upon doctrinal or devotional topics in the form of short, informal essays or soliloquies."[11] That a written form is implied here is probably only one of several reasons why the goals and methods of meditation sometimes came to be conceived as similar to those of a sermon.[12]

Of particular interest with regard to the poems that we shall be considering is *The Arte of Divine Meditation* (1606) by Joseph Hall, who soon was to become a prominent figure at the court of James. Hall distinguished two basic kinds of meditation. First there was the "deliberate" meditation, meditation on a topic that was consciously selected and "wrought out of our owne heart."[13] For such meditation Hall had in mind not the usual old topics—the mysteries of Christ and the four last things—but a wide variety of generally religious subjects. Second, Hall described a type of meditation that he termed "extemporall," meditation "occasioned by outward occurrences offred to the mind"—because God constantly provides us with occasions that are pregnant with spiritual meaning.[14] For instance, one may be struck by the fact that no tree bears fruit in autumn unless it has blossomed in the spring.[15] Hall backed off somewhat from Ignatian cultivation of the imagination and senses, and spoke for a simple, two-step method that started with analysis of a subject by the understanding, then moved toward the affections. And whether we choose "deliberate" or "extemporall" meditation, according to Hall, "It begins in the vnderstãding, ends in the affections; It begins in the braine, descends to the heart; Begins on earth, ascends to eauen. . . ."[16]

Of course we cannot fill in here the whole spectrum of meditative possibilities in seventeenth-century England. We have made progress, however, if we can agree that we are concerned not with meditation on just any serious subject, à la Cleland's Persians, but meditation as it relates to feelings of religious devotion. We have made progress if we recognize that sometimes meditation was reconstructed or imitated in verse, and, furthermore, that we are concerned with verse which tends to move from earth to heaven, from temporal to eternal. Meditative poems of the sort that I wish to discuss, in brief, share a basic subject matter, a basic aim, and a basic structure.

It is necessary to recall, however, that all these characteristics may manifest themselves in different kinds of verse. Here is the rub. And here is the reason why the subject matter, aim, and structure that I have in view may be better regarded as elements of a mode than of a genre. The practical question of which particular works to include in any literary genre is, sad to say, often answered differently by different people. One calls to mind, for instance, the enormously different circumferences that different critics have drawn in order to speak of the picaresque novel. As for seventeenth-century English verse, it is fairly clear that Donne's "Satire III" is a satire, and his *Holy Sonnets* sonnets, and yet Martz published both in an anthology of meditative poems. Is, then, all coherence gone? I am inclined to think that "Satire III" is best regarded as a satire with meditative qualities rather than as a meditation with satiric qualities, but this problematic example and others like it are much less important in themselves than in pointing the way to the usefulness of the concept of mode. Some genres, to be sure, may be defined at least fairly accurately—for example, the epithalamion or the funeral elegy. But the literary forms which in some way are related to the extra-literary devotional practice of meditation are much too varied to justify calling them a genre.[17] Turning to the term "mode," on the other hand, gives us a means of discussing a cluster of characteristics in a given work without necessitating that we lock them into a single genre. It is to provide some essential flexibility, then, that I shall be discussing here not verse meditations but meditative verse. Putting this another way, I should like to proceed with the understanding that we are considering here how a widespread, highly varied, and largely nonliterary religious practice manifested itself in one of the more significant, interesting, and varied of seventeenth-century literary modes.

II

As we approach the particular poems in our present discussion, it should be said at once that they are not major works of art. On the other hand, they are interesting for a variety of reasons, including, at least for the time being, the fact that they have been brought to light only recently.

Literary historians with an eye for detail may recall that Dudley North, fourth Lord North, was the writer of several prose works.[18] His *Narrative of Some Passages in or Relating to the Long Parliament* (1670) is a latter-day rationalization of why North remained so long in the most famous of English Parliaments. Thinking that men of good will should try to temper the wind, he kept his seat in the Commons until he was expelled in 1648, in Pride's Purge, shortly before Parliament had the King beheaded.[19] His *Observations and Advices Oeconomical* (1669) is a little handbook that North wrote on how to run a great house without extravagance. Here he observes, for instance, that "I have thought it strange, that Servants are now worse then in former ages," and that "it is far from necessary" for one's "Houshold-stuff" to be "*a la mode*, as they call it."[20] It is perhaps especially significant to us here that he also offers the opinion that "Of Countrey delights, Study may deserve the first place"[21] and that the head of the house, not the resident chaplain, should lead the household in "the external and publick Service of God there twice a day. . . ."[22] Posthumously, North's family published his *Light in the Way to Paradise* (1682). This book contains a small handful of miscellaneous pieces in prose, but, as the title indicates, it is given over mainly to offering some illumination for a Christian's earthly progress. The journey's course is common enough for a religious handbook, but perhaps one should pause to note that it moves from earth to heaven, from temporal to eternal.

The other works in this volume include a short biography of Edward North, first Lord North, founder of the family fortunes in the time of Henry VIII; a number of short compositions which North calls—appropriately, in view of Joseph Hall's words—"occasionals"; and, of particular interest here, a 473-word paragraph entitled "A Sundays Meditation upon Eternity, June 17. 1666." North begins his meditation as follows: "HAVING set my self to meditate upon Eternity, in the everlasting part whereof all the hope of a good Christian consisteth, I soon perceived that I went about to fathom a bottomless depth, with the bounded line of Reason . . . " (p. 117). He tells how he followed reason as far as possible, then had to call on faith, which is "above reason," and he concludes, inevitably perhaps, but after expending some efforts, "Oh the infinite wisdom of God," who satisfies His own justice and demonstrates His mercy "even to the putting of Mankind into a condition of blessedness far beyond his first estate in Paradise. . . ."[23] As we shall be able to see later, this prose piece, called a meditation by North himself, has some interesting parallels to his meditative poems. All three of North's published books, it turns out, throw light on both his life and his verse.

Descended from a family which gained wealth and favor under Henry and, rather remarkably, retained both under Edward, Mary, and Elizabeth, North himself was at first something of a courtier, but finally retired to the country. Though I do not know that he ever did so, he could have claimed literary distinction in his heritage in the person of Sir Thomas North, and perhaps even in his own father, Dudley, third Lord North, who was a colorful figure at the court of James and, in particular, among the followers of the ill-fated Prince Henry.[24]

The Dudley North who concerns us here was created Knight of the Bath in 1616; made a brief, gentlemanly appearance at St. John's College, Cambridge; went soldiering abroad as a young man; toured a bit on the Continent; married a rich coheiress, Anne Montagu, in 1632, and thence proceeded to become the father of fourteen children. North spent his remaining years in three places: London, the family seat in Cambridgeshire, and a second seat which he bought in Suffolk.

So far as I have been able to determine, only three of North's poems have been published thus far—one in Latin in 1619, one in his *Light in the Way to Paradise*, and one in an obscure anthology that appeared about two hundred years after his death.[25] The explanation is not simply that gentlemen were supposed to be reluctant to appear in print. After all, North published two volumes of prose. More likely the reason that his verse remained in manuscript is that he meant what he told his wife in the little foreword he wrote for his poems: "as hee was noe wayes by nature designed to Appollo his lawrell, soe hee never affected the honor to attayne it. . . ."[26]

Fortunately, North's poems were recorded and preserved in the calligraphic hand of his wife, who transcribed them late in the lives of both, apparently in the 1670's. Unfortunately, they are in no perceivable order, and to think about them clearly it is helpful, perhaps necessary, to arrange them in categories of some sort. Once the task of ordering is attempted, North's interest in varieties of literary form becomes obvious. Of course one cannot be sure in every instance what he had in mind. When he entitles a poem "Riddle," it is reasonably clear that he is attempting a riddle. It is a characteristic of literary kinds in every age, however, that forms and modes interinanimate one another—epigram and satire, satire and pastoral, pastoral and novel. My earlier example to illustrate this point was Donne's "Satire III." Turning specifically to Dudley North, we soon see that certain of his meditative poems have strong affinities with others of his works that appear to be more specifically "sacred" or "divine."[27] They also overlap with some of his poems that are perhaps better regarded as epigrams. To picture the complexity caused by the intersecting of genres in the poems by North (and, indeed, elsewhere), perhaps we might call to mind the overlapping circles that all of us have seen made by raindrops falling into a pond. The evidence is so complex and admits of such a variety of interpretation in both pond and poetry that I wish merely to suggest a label for certain poems by Dudley North—the label of "meditative verse"—and not to insist upon it. If I may venture yet further into metaphor, I would say that my goal is not to build a stone wall to enclose some ground, but to pencil a line on the map.

Despite the need for such caution, I am glad to add at once that the works we shall be considering here really do share some qualities with one another that they do not share with North's other poems. For instance, all begin on earth and move toward heaven; and, although all concern spiritual matters, none is built directly on a biblical event.[28] To put a somewhat finer point on the matter, we may identify two of the five as fair examples of Joseph Hall's "deliberative" meditative technique, and two of the others (maybe three) as samples of his "extemporall" or occasional variety. It is perhaps not coincidental that the poems in this group of five evince still other kinds of similarity. For instance, all are moderately extended pieces, ranging from thirty-six to eighty-three lines; all are stichic rather than strophic; and all are composed in iambic pentameter—four out of five of them in couplets.[29] On such grounds these poems seem to me to constitute a reasonably self-consistent cluster.

Analyzing them in a broad sort of way, one sees that two are examples of composition by similitude—and, indeed, move no great distance beyond similitude. Each of these two is devoted mainly to exploring a single, complex, and highly conventional metaphor. The other three grow out of problems and events in North's own life. Each of the five, wherever it has begun, leads to an acknowledgment of God.

Thus far we have been concerned mainly with problems of genre and mode. As we move closer to North's individual poems, it will be useful to introduce a subject that is related to both modal and generic questions, though the fact is sometimes overlooked. The subject of voice in literature is a concern to writers of all times, whether or not they think about it consciously. Cicero, for instance, wrote of it specifically, as did Shakespeare, Donne, and Milton, Robert Frost and William Butler Yeats, and, of course, countless others.[30] Voice is a variable that is operative in every poem. Sometimes, as in Milton's "Lycidas" or Herbert's "The Collar," it varies widely within a single work. Sometimes, on the other hand, voice holds fairly steady in a given poem—as, for example, in Southwell's "Looke Home."

The point I should like to make at the moment, however, is that certain literary genres typically appear to call for certain kinds of voices. That is, voice may be an aspect of genre. Dudley North, in his "Satyre. 1636," recognizes that when he assumes the stance of satirist he is expected to convey some degree of detestation. He tells us so in the poem.[31] Two of the questions we might ask of a poem, therefore, are whether it blends voice and verse in a conventional way (as in North's "Satyre. 1636") or plays voice against form (as Southwell does in "What Joy to Live?"). A third question, and one that applies to far more poems than at first we might imagine, is perhaps the most challenging of the three: to what extent does a given poem draw upon multiple voices that typically might be found in *different* genres?

Still another question worth asking (and clearly I am raising more questions than I can answer in any detail here) is to what extent any one of these three techniques conveys or obscures the poet's real voice or (probably better) his real voices. Speaking of the Renaissance, Jerome Mazzaro observes that "A writer's success depended upon his sounding like his model, not, as critics seem to suggest, by his sounding like himself."[32] Hence we find Aston Cokayne offering his poems with a flippant "protest to all censorious men, / They flow not from my heart, but from my Pen."[33] On the other hand, we are concerned here with meditative verse, which seriously involves both the mortal and the divine and the relations between the two. More particularly, it encourages introspection. The conflict that such facts imply between general voice and personal voice forms an important part of the seventeenth-century background against which we must place Dudley North's meditative poems.

III

The first of North's poems to be considered here—and it should be noted that their numbering is my own—is a thirty-six-line work entitled "A Description of Man."[34] Here North explores the ubiquitous old concept of the microcosm. In fact the term "microcosm" itself turns up in the poem (l. 13). North's specific approach involves the comparison (it antedates Plato) of a man to a city.[35] As we proceed we shall see North drawing repeatedly on that joint savings account of images to which all Renaissance poets unhesitatingly laid claim, images which, in a very important way,

mark North as a writer of his time. Possibly the best-known Jacobean poem using the man / city image is Donne's Holy Sonnet
XIV ("Batter my heart"). For an example farther down the scale
of excellence one might cite John Hagthorpe's poem beginning,
"Thus man is like a Towne. . . ."[36]

   North's treatment of the subject begins,

> Man is a structure fayre, compos'd of all
> The choysest goods in Natures Arcenall,
> A Citye fram'd for goverment, and state. . . .

If the military or naval flavor of the word "Arcenall" is at all puzzling, one might suggest that it is partly explicable in terms of
North's years as a soldier. Furthermore, it is in keeping with such
later words here as "magazin" (l. 8), "informers" (l. 11), and "sentinells" (l. 18), all of which help to prepare us for the conflict that
surfaces toward the end of the poem. North offers a number of
comparisons here: man's face is a "frontispice": that is, a façade
(l. 14). Man's head provides "counsell" to the city (l. 15); and his
"fow'r noblest senses" are "sentinells" (ll. 17–18). Although this is
the simplest of North's meditative poems, it has such points of
interest as his assumption that the nobility are born to rule (one
doubts that he ever wavered in the matter) and his assertion (despite the verse context) that fancy is to be ruled by judgment. The
poem goes on to argue for the need of the soul to comport herself
as a good tenant, her failure to do so resulting in a loss "of all
fayre harmonye" (l. 26). In speaking of the importance of harmony, of order and degree, of course North alludes to concepts
that pervaded every phase of life in his time, and manifested
themselves everywhere in literature. In light of the military and
civil strife of the seventeenth century, however, and especially
North's involvement in it, his imagery has its own special interest.
Writing of man's inner conflicts, he observes that

> Nought's there but mutinye, all order dyes,
> Th'affections they in fierce rebellion ryse. . . .(ll. 27–28)

This from the man who bought books to make himself a better
soldier abroad,[37] but never was at ease, I believe, raising money
for parliamentary troops in Cambridgeshire.[38] The poem draws
to a close by saying that God, if won over by man's repentance,

may rectify all. And the final couplet, beginning with a logical "Thus," comments rather neatly on all of the preceding lines by offering the paradox that man, whether he governs himself well or ill, is a living demonstration of the glory of God.

In short, the poem delivers the speaker's musing upon a deliberately selected commonplace, man as city, and it does, indeed, lead to God. The entire little piece, a warning against insubordination in man, is cast in the form of a meditative *descriptio*. And, to illustrate one of my earlier points, I would suggest that the modal adjective "meditative" has a greater appropriateness here than the generic word "meditation" on account of such factors as the vigorously impinging circles in the poem of an emblematic nature.

Throughout the poem, it might be observed, the speaker's voice is sober, clear, controlled, and matter-of-fact. The speaker appears to be concerned but not very vitally engaged. We may conclude on various biographical grounds that the poem is faithful enough to the poet's own thinking, and yet there is a certain dryness to it—perhaps, we might sense at this point, owing to the poet's limited skill. But of course we need more evidence.

The second poem to be considered here is untitled but opens with a line that appears to tell nearly all: "Our Lyfe vnto a Garden I compare."[39] At once we have the writer's central "similitude," and again it is drawn from the Renaissance and ancient arsenal of images.[40] The widespread use of the garden in literature need not be argued here. I would suggest only that it is to be explained in three major ways: by the natural appeal of a real garden, by the multiple kinds of meaning that may be derived from a symbolic one, and by the convergence of these two in the belief that the elements of nature are all part of God's hieroglyphics. As Henry King observed in a book that North acquired for his library, "euerie *Species* is a line . . . , euerie peculiar work a character for Man, to read his Maker."[41] In North's work, as so often in the verse of his time, one who seeks some of the sensuous appeal of a real garden is doomed to disappointment, and this despite the poet's many years in the country. Only once does North achieve something notably sensuous in his garden verse, and that is in his paraphrase based on the fourth chapter of Canticles, in which case his own lines are obviously lifted on the wings of Solomon's song. The poem at hand, as the opening line suggests, is not intended as a garden lyric. It is, rather, a meditative poem that partakes of the tradition of the garden allegory.

Forty-two lines long (and I give the length of each poem to suggest something about the scope it allows for the poet's work), the poem introduces very early a conventional image we already have seen North use in the first poem, but it closes with a touch of relative freshness, suggesting overall that this work has engaged the writer's imaginative interest a bit more fully. The early and almost predictable repetition of image is that just as man's soul is God's tenant in the city, so is man God's tenant in the garden. The two symbols, city and garden, are somehow opposite and equal. Each is a place where nature must be subdued, order established. It would almost seem that North was constructing a pair of poems. In any case, they have interesting parallels, and the completeness they suggest about God's omnipotence and omnipresence is appropriate.

Early in the poem North observes that man's entry into the garden of life yields bitter aloes, plants known to have "a greuous sauour," says the herbalist William Turner.[42] It is no Eden that North has in mind. On the contrary, man in his passage is bound to be wounded by the "bryars" of affliction here (l. 6). The passage calls to mind Genesis 3:17–18:

... Because thou hast hearkened vnto the voyce of thy wife, and hast eaten of the tree, . . . cursed is the ground for thy sake. . . . Thornes also and thistles shall it bring forth to thee: and thou shalt eate the herbe of the field.

Although man's safety is threatened yet further by a "wyly serpent" (l. 7), he is not defenseless. He has protection in the plant called herbgrace (l. 8)—an apparent symbol of the grace of God.[43] North's allegorical or symbolic conjunction of serpent and herbgrace is perhaps enhanced for us if we know that one of the medicinal properties of the plant, again according to William Turner, is its efficacy "agaynst serpentes."[44]

Having noted that a tenant of this garden must pay rent (i.e., give constant praise) and also render service (i.e., labor), because this is a post-Adamic age, the poet is in position to name another crucial plant. Its name is a pun. "Right vse of tyme," writes North, "must ever bee affected" (l. 14).[45] It helps to know that Sir Francis Bacon recommends planting whole alleys of thyme because of the delight of treading upon these fragrant plants, and also that they were proverbial symbols of sweetness.[46] But durational time was another matter altogether, and recent studies have shown us that the sixteenth and seventeenth centuries became almost obsessed with it.[47] In this poem the point is simply that time may be either wasted or applied toward fruitful ends. North becomes quite involved here. The garden of our life, he writes, is capable of bearing happy fruit, its "active Father" being "th'Eternall Sunn" (l. 18)—which is both a paradox and a common pun of the day.[48] The part of midwife is taken by "show'rs of grace" (l. 19), and the part of nurse, by labor. Obviously each phrase in a poem like this might be glossed at some length. For instance, one might cite here a parallel to Nowell's *Catechisme* (1570), which was long required reading for loyal Englishmen. God, writes Nowell, "will with the diuine dew of hys grace so water & make frutefull the drynesse and barrennesse of my hart, that I may bring forth plentifull frutes of godlinesse. . . ."[49]

North's most original touch in the poem comes with his introduction of the subject of weeds. The weeds are descended from New Testament tares, I suppose, but, be that as it may, these products of "Nature"—nature which is operative beneath the beneficent "Sunn"—these weeds are potent enough to impress the most sanguine of gardeners:

> Theyr rootes with earth soe intermixed lye,
> Noe art, or pow'r in man can make them dye. . . . (ll. 30–31)

If one knows the English gardener's plague of couchgrass, one knows the kind of problem North has in mind.[50] At the metaphorical level, at any rate, God's assistance is required to root out "natural" vice. The neatest touch in the poem is that God's assistance takes the form of holy fire. "Is not my word like as a fire, saith the Lord?" (Jeremiah 23:29).[51] Not only is fire appropriate for North's poem at a symbolic level; it is appropriate also at the level of what a farmer really could do in an era before man had experimented much with poisons for plants. The horticultural books of the time frequently advise burning patches of land.[52] And of course, as with so many other beliefs, the Renaissance Englishman could find good precedent among the ancients. Virgil had written of the benefits of burning in his *Georgics*.[53]

The purpose of purifying our life's ground is achieved if the earth is enabled to fulfill God's will by bearing fruit. Jesus said, "He that abideth in me . . . bringeth forth much fruit" (John 15:5). North then concludes, as he did his first meditative poem, with another summarizing couplet, this time beginning with a "Soe" (instead of a "Thus"), directing our final attention not merely to the "pretious flowers" which life may afford (l. 41), but also to the eternal reward which is available to all laboring, prayerful men who manage to submit their will to God's; "endlesse blisse," writes North, "shall crown our latest [i.e., final] howers" (l. 42). At this point we might call to mind Hall's observation, in his *Arte of Divine Meditation*, that "A man is a man by his vnderstanding part: but he is a Christian by his will and affections."[54]

A certain distance that we are likely to sense about the voice in this poem may be partially explained if we look at its somewhat misleadingly personal first line and compare it with the final line. The first line—"Our Lyfe vnto a Garden I compare"—is indeed cast in the first person singular and so, it would appear, is the rest of the poem. From the outset, however, the subject matter catches up the speaker *among others* so as to produce a series of first-person plural references, leading the reader at last to the line, "And endlesse blisse shall crown our latest howers." The stated concern is more with *us* than *me*. The focus is on a shared situation, and at the end there is a shared reward. The realm of literary meditation is certainly broad enough to accommodate many kinds of approach, but a rather impersonal voice is the result here. In addition to traditional allegory the poem may well call to mind—as our first poem does—the emblem verse of North's day, not merely because of its subject matter and prosy level of competence, but also because of its rather objectively monitory tone of voice. Perhaps we may go so far as to call the result a meditative emblem. At any rate, the mixed quality of the poem appears to affect its voice. To return briefly to those raindrops falling in the pond, I would suggest that when we have an overlapping of generic circles, we should not be surprised to find also an overlapping of voices. Furthermore, since it seems that if we really can discern meditative, allegorical, and emblematic elements here, perhaps we can take a drop or two more and recall the short prose form known as the resolve, or remind ourselves of the affinity presumed to exist between meditations and sermons. Or, perhaps better yet, we might recall North's self-assigned task of employing his own voice while leading the members of his household, family and servants, in morning and evening devotions.

The third poem under consideration here, an untitled work of fifty lines, provides a striking contrast to the first two. Not only does its voice speak in the first-person singular from the outset; the personal pressure behind it seems markedly greater, and the subject matter apparently is the speaker's own life. It begins,

> When after chyldhood Tyme had shew'd on mee
> The Comick entrance of lyfes Tragedye. . . .[55]

Of course the phrase "lyfes Tragedye" will convey only a limited threat if the speaker is to prove a Christian, but at the commencement of the poem it serves to introduce some of the briars that all flesh is heir to. The poet next observes that when he had through study and discourse discovered "The rule of Microcosme to bee my own" (l. 4),[56] his soul, "noe more in wardshipp" (l. 5), claimed her own sovereignty. The motivation of the soul was good. She resolved "To visitt all her coasts" and to "settle Vertue there" (ll. 7–8), a virtuous resolution, indeed, for a young man to make, and an appropriately colonistic metaphor for a poet whose uncle, Roger North, was a companion voyager with Sir Walter Raleigh and, in fact, was an explorer in his own right.[57] I would not press the matter so hard as to fall into any "biographical fallacy"; I would suggest simply that analysis of the text at such a point need not involve banishment of the poet from consideration.

For a while the soul proved successful in her colonizing efforts. She governed by the light of reason and made headway in clearing her coasts of vice. The use of the word "rooted" here in connection with vice (l. 13) may remind us in passing of those well-rooted weeds in North's garden poem. Inevitably, however, the progress of the free-sailing soul was impeded. The least clear passage in all of North's verse occurs here, but apparently the soul was led to falter by some "naturall defects of mynd" (l. 16) and by "much infirmity" of body (ll. 19–20). Caught up in external matters, the realm of accidentals, the soul became aware of problems with "Fortunes, Freedom, Freinds" (l. 23). In other words, though this poem, like the first two, works chiefly with a major, central metaphor—this time that of sailing—it differs by activating that metaphor more extensively, perhaps partly because the metaphor itself inherently involves action. Nevertheless, we are at the same time moving not farther from but closer to autobiographical verse. The strain on the North family's fortune, the circumscribing of North's personal freedom (which was one of his continuing concerns and, as we shall see, the central subject of his next meditative poem), and even the difficulties of friendship—all these are matters sprung from life.[58]

Continuing, the poem narrates how the soul, "Devoyd of counsell" (l. 29), began to grieve so excessively that "discontent had allmost form'd dispayre" (l. 31). Since verses which reflect the practice of religious meditation should end positively, the course of the poem must change. Consequently, as when we move from octave to sestet in a Petrarchan sonnet, we come to a shift. God, says the speaker, secured "my Soule [and note that this time it is not merely *the* soul] / From sharp dispayre, and purg'd my mynd from fowle / Terrene affections" (ll. 37–39). God teaches the old Christian lesson (indeed, it often had been classical, too) of the utter unimportance of worldly goods and goals. Furthermore— and here the autobiographical underpinning of the poem surfaces again—the restoring of the soul is accompanied, as certainly is not always the case, by "Some outward blessings" (l. 44). According to this poem, the external world, though incapable of making the soul happy, may nonetheless enhance whatever degree of content the soul otherwise happens to have attained.

Having brought the soul to a point of relative content in the narrative, the poem has only to end with the affirmation that the speaker (no longer merely the abstract "Soul") is saved, "restor'd by pow'r divine" (l. 47), particularly by that aspect of God which *is* the Savior, and that he himself may therefore look forward with "hopes" (the opposite of his earlier "despair") to "blest Eternitye" (l. 50). We have moved in this poem, it should be noted, from memory through understanding to a merger of a mortal will with God's.

Although the approach to the subject in this poem is quite figurative once again, the narrator is more insistently present than in either of the first two poems we have examined. It is now "My Soule," "my mynd," and "my hopes" that are set before us, and it is now the events of North's life, not merely of all men's lives, that surface—though discreetly and never specifically. The more extensive and effective use of the first-person singular voice is very likely one of the features of the poem that give it a greater immediacy and, not at all incidentally, make it sound more like North's meditation in prose.

Some of these points may be reiterated with regard to the next of North's meditative poems. An untitled work of forty-two lines, it has perhaps the strongest of all North's openings and proceeds at once to examine with energy a subject of continuing concern to him. Because this is the best of North's meditative poems as well as one of the better representatives of his verse as a whole, it may be well to present it here in its entirety:

> Noe Noe, I ever did and must denye
> Him to bee happy that wants Libertye,
> Discourse may make our ills afflict vs lesse,[59]
> But such defects admitt not happines;
> Whoe is not master of his how'rs, but still   5
> Must frame his actions to anothers will,
> Hee may enioy a forc't content of mynd,
> But force is nere with happines combyn'd.
> Lyfe is scarse lyfe, if not with freedom blest,
> Whoe craves not that with dullnes is possest.   10
> If some imprison'd birds desyre it not,
> T'is or vnknown to them, or quite forgott,
> It is the cheife perfection of the Soule
> That noe externall force can it controule,
> And till t'is from the bodyes prison free,   15
> It nere shall have a true felicitye.[60]
> But now I fynd my selfe deserve much blame
> In thus discoursing on an empty Name,
> For happy freedom evrywhere doth sound,
> But (Eccho lyke) is noe where to bee found,[61]   20
> The greatest Prince some servitude must beare,
> The happyst lyfe hath diverse crosses heere,
> Lawes, Rules, Observances the bridles are
> Which curbe our inclynations evry where,
> By these the better natures are inclyn'd.   25

Theyre own perverse affections others bynd,
Hee whoe to his affections giues full sway
In taking freedome, freedome casts away,
And none lesse truly happy is then hee
Whoe happy in this life exspects to bee.   30
Since then the nature of our earthly ioye
Requyres a bitter mixture of annoye,
Lett vs not fondly[62] anchor cast in these
These soe exsposed, soe tempestuous seas,
I the true Neptune dayly will implore,   35
To guyde mee till I find the blissefull shore,
To swell my sayles soe with his breath of grace
As I lifes western straights may safely passe,
And, ere my feeble tymber'd bark bee spent,
Find the Pacifick Sea of true Content,   40
Where wee, yett passengers, those ioyes may tast,
Which the blest hav'n shall fully yeeld at last.

Despite its free use of apothegm and aphorism (in fact, partly by *means* of them), this poem takes us still more obviously and directly into the mind of the speaker. That the mind is North's mind or a very accurate facsimile of it is the sort of point that raises problems for critics, but it is a point that should be made. A crucial factor in the background of this piece on liberty is that Dudley North took it upon himself to be so dutiful a son that people were moved to comment upon his obvious self-subjugation—socially proper and enjoined by the catechism, but still extreme.[63] We are told how he stood, hat removed, when in the presence of his father. And the dimension of time here is significant: North's father lived to be eighty-four, leaving his son holding his hat, as it were, until the age of about sixty-five.[64] Apparently North managed very well (too well, his wife thought) to honor his father's wishes,[65] but at the same time we find him returning in both poetry and prose to the simultaneous necessity and anguish of denying his own personal desire for liberty. One of the most outspoken of his statements occurs in the opening of his twelfth "occasional":

Of all my inward conflicts, none hath appeared more like an Earthquake in shaking the whole frame of my nature, than that which raised it self upon the consideration of (and sitting down under) some pressures carrying with them a constant deprivation of outward freedom; which freedom . . . hath been always too far considered by me as the ground of external happiness. (p. 96)

The "occasional" goes on to report a turning point in his life, however, at the time when he realized that his fetters had been wrought "by a Divine hand" (p. 97).

In the poem under consideration the turning point (indicated this time by the rhetorically emphatic "But" of l. 17) marks a turning from protest to acceptance. Even princes are not free, and the happiest man must bear "crosses" (l. 22)—a pun of obvious usefulness in a poem that is aimed, as usual, towards heaven.[66] Since none here below may know unmixed joy, the speaker comes to realize that he should not cast anchor in the "tempestuous seas" of everyday life (l. 34), but ask God—"the true Neptune"—"To guyde mee till I find the blissefull shore" (ll. 35–36).[67] The man / ship figure, which assumed a rather specialized, colonizing form in the preceding poem, assumes in this one a form that is very common in the literature of the period and may be traced back to various passages in the ancients.[68] Here it leads North to write of "lifes western straights" (l. 38) and "the Pacifick Sea of true Content" (l. 40), which phrases bring him about as close as he ever comes to the characteristically conceited thought and diction of John Donne.[69] Peaceful content here, the poem concludes, is a foretaste of joys that will be known fully only when our ship finally comes in to the "blest hav'n" (l. 42)—and to the extent that we can trust North's poetic skill, we may enjoy the similarity of sound here between "hav'n" and the literal word it displaces.

The voice of this poem is more obviously dual than that of any we have heard previously. The protesting voice that speaks out in the first part contrasts strikingly to the rationalizing voice that sounds in the second. According to traditional meditative strategy, we might recall, reasoned discourse is supposed to lead to an arousal of the affections. This poem gives us an initial extra step. It opens with the speaker's unworthy affections (note his phrase "perverse affections," l. 26) and uses these as a sort of dramatic backdrop or prelude against which he then presents the restoring of reason's power, leading at last to the appropriate affection of near-joy and a proper attitude of devotion.

Whether or not the dramatic shift of voice really is conveyed by a reminiscent reporter (as in the preceding poem), the shift ostensibly occurs during the course of the poem. One might observe that the metrical rules governing the lines constitute a kind of restraint that is operative from beginning to end, but the more important fact is that the speaker's thought appears to evolve by negating itself within the poem.

It is worth observing also that there is nothing specifically Christian in the thought. Plato and Epictetus say much the same things. This is not because Christian elements have been suppressed, however, but because the poet takes them so utterly for granted. In other words, we can grasp the quality of the voice in the poem better, as well as weigh the content more justly, if we know not merely other seventeenth-century meditative poems but other meditative poems by Dudley North, as well as other writing by him, and, for comfort's sake, as much as possible about his life.

It has taken me a while to lay my cards on the table, but at this point, with virtually all deployed, we are ready to approach the fifth of North's meditative poems. The work now at hand is almost certainly one of the last he wrote, for in it he tells what age has brought him, and he does so in terms that persuade us he is by no means dealing with imaginary problems. With thanks to Marianne Moore, I would suggest that there are real toads in Dudley North's poetic garden. Or at least there are toads as real as can be consigned to paper. This poem is also the longest of North's meditative verses, eighty-three lines (the odd number resulting from North's use of a triplet at ll. 31–33). Furthermore, North has given this poem a striking title: "An Essay in the Way of Gratitude."

The gratitude conveyed by the poem exceeds a Christian's everyday, garden-variety supply; the poem is an expression of gratitude to God for having allowed the writer to survive a serious illness. The more interesting term here is "Essay." Wherever North learned it first, I am inclined to recall at this point yet another generic drop in the literary pond. One might note that North knew his father held Montaigne's *Essais* to be a formative influence in his life,[70] and that he himself owned a copy of Bacon's *Essayes*. As a matter of fact, it turns out that in the foreword which the younger North composed for his poems he refers to them all as "imperfect essayes."[71] With such a phrase in such a context he probably means to suggest something of the unpolished, "extemporall" quality of his verse. Certainly some of his poems sprang from particular occasions. Even with regard to his love poems, he assures his wife, some "are not without a reall obiect, nor were it iniurious to any, if you should assume it to yourselfe to bee the person intended."[72] Furthermore, in the collection as a whole he clearly is "essaying" a wide variety of forms (satires, sonnets, and the like). On the other hand, it is only when we reach this final poem in the manuscript that he returns explicitly to the term "essay." Since the term is so capacious, perhaps we could justify placing this work in a line of poems which in another forty years would boast Pope's *Essay on Criticism*. It happens to share, however, the characteristics of North's other meditative verse.

This poem is also one of the most personal—meditative or otherwise—that has come down to us from North. Here is no intermediate, standard symbol (such as city or garden), presumably chosen as a medium of communication but managed somehow (like the glove in a handshake) so as to be a barrier between us and the speaker. The emotion of the speaker—and his word for it is "zeal"—shines clear in his opening lines:

> What better can poore I to God returne
> For many peereles mercyes, then to burn
> In Zeale, and from that holy fyre to rayse
> A lasting monument[73] vnto his prayse. . . .

Of course he goes on at once to confess his inability to thank God properly, since, like all men, he can thank God profusely but never adequately.

The momentum of the poem then slackens as he gives us— North gives us, not a Strephon, a Democritus, or some gray persona—North gives us in verse some autobiographical facts. They are succinct, frank, and straight from life:

> Some years in warr he [God] gave me sure protection
> And in sadd plagues he freed me from infection[74]
> Hee blest mee in relation coniugall. . . .[75] (ll. 13–15)

Then North tells how he was stricken by illness. His heart was humbled. He learned again—and the lesson was difficult for a man of position—that "externalls" (l. 29) are not to be trusted. He begged for ease, he says, from his pain, from his "nephritick tortures" (l. 39), a suffering old man learning more than ever now about what he once had termed "lyfes Tragedye."[76] Far from the writer working with the figure of man as city, farther still from the young man making witty love poems for a lady, he tells at last, virtually with joy, how he managed "to voyd" his "ragged stones" (ll. 40–41). The subject is startlingly personal, certainly unlovely, and perhaps grotesque. Humor would have been one way to gain distance from its grimness. In other contexts poets *did* whet their wits on kidney stones.[77] In the present poem, however, there is only earnestness, for no sooner had North found relief from his extreme suffering than he was again laid low. To shorten the story, we may turn to his son Roger, who later reported how "his father died a miserable martyr to the stone."[78]

The "Essay in the Way of Gratitude" continues at some length, then finally closes by directing our thoughts once again to heaven:

> Glory to God whoe doth vs mortalls blesse
> With Power t'attayne eternall happinesse. (ll. 82–83)

This time the price of arrival at a pacific port has been highest of all for the poet as a man, and I should think that it would be hard for any reader to miss the human quickening in his voice. It is not likely to be contrived. If ever in his verse North demonstrates Donne's idea of "white sincerity" (and I am quite aware that sincerity is a non-quality among some critics), it is in this poem.[79] The exultant yet chastened voice here is that of one who has just learned, perhaps learned all over again, that God's power is supreme.[80]

IV

The goals of this study have been complex, partly because I have tried to show how several topics, no one of them simple, impinge on one another. First, I have offered the suggestion that five poems by the fourth Lord North may be viewed in relation to the seventeenth-century tradition of religious meditation. Second, I have attempted to show that, while they are not so purely meditative as to wear with ease the generically restrictive term "meditation," all five can bear the modal adjective "meditative" with reasonable comfort. Third, I have made some suggestions about the quality and range of voice in North's meditative verse. And fourth, I have tried to indicate the relation of these poems to some of the extra-literary influences which contributed to the shaping of the mind and outlook of Dudley North.

Along the way, certain recurring characteristics in the poems have had to be recognized. We have seen that the poems are all written in rhyming iambic pentameter lines (four out of five in couplets) and that they are fairly extended; that whatever the originating subject may be, they eventually turn our attention towards heaven; and that while all are concerned with spiritual matters, none springs directly from a scriptural event. If we have been struck also by the repeated pattern in them of fall followed by renewal, that should not puzzle us, for it is psychologically convincing, artistically effective, theologically sound, and, in light of meditative practice, traditionally correct.

We also have seen considerable variety within these poems, and not least in the matter of voice. As I have arranged them here for discussion, the first and second poems, with their controlled, rather schoolmasterish quality, are eventually succeeded by the zealous thanksgiving of the fifth. In each and all, nonetheless, behind the various voices, is a mind that is basically one, a mind that is serious, committed, and conservative, a mind that is altogether in keeping with what we learn elsewhere about Dudley North. Having read them, we can understand better what North meant by saying, "I professe not to know any pleasure exceeding . . . Contemplation in matters Divine."[81] We can understand better what North's father meant when he spoke of his son as having "a minde bent to the more noble speculative and generous thoughts. . . ."[82] And even allowing for exaggeration, we can understand also what North's son Roger meant when he wrote that our poet "was a christian speculatively orthodox and good; regularly charitable and pious in his family, rigidly just in his dealing, and exquisitely virtuous and sober in his person."[83] The fact is that North is a fine illustration of the not-necessarily-smoothly-cobbled English *via media*, and that fact is in part conveyed, if not stated, in his verse.

Especially intriguing, moreover, is that if we arrange the poems in the sequence I have suggested, we may perceive an apparent movement towards confluence in the voices of persona and poet. What we really discern, of course, is a thought-provoking range of differences, not a progression; variety, not development. We know too little about dating to talk with any certainty about progression or development, but the variety of the poems, operating within the limits we have seen, is noteworthy, I think, and significant.

From a consideration of the range of voices in these verses I would move on to postulate that we can expect meditative verse to be expressed at least sometimes by a voice which is scarcely distinguishable from that of the poet.[84] It is true that meter and rhyme do a certain amount of formalizing, and that such conventional devices as the inversion of elements create distance between the poet and his work, and between his work and us. It is true that, though the writer be North or anyone else, he cannot really put his mind on paper. Nevertheless, the aim of meditative verse involves its sincerity. It is this very sincerity that sometimes made W. H. Auden uneasy when he tried to read religious verse.[85] Such verse can be too personal. If there is a sense in which it is in danger of becoming an intrusive artifact thrust between the writer and his God, as the seventeenth-century Puritans feared, there is also a sense in which it is in danger of seeming a rather strange offering to be viewed by any outside reader. On this last score, of course, North's slate is clean. Neither he nor his family published his verse.

Although it appears that North's religious or meditative voice (or variety of voices) sometimes takes us very close, indeed, to the man himself, this does not mean, of course, that his meditative verse is better or worse for the fact. The autobiographical element in a literary work is always neutral so far as evaluation is concerned. The importance of its presence in the work of North or of any other writer lies in its potential for putting us in closer touch with meaning.

Since the goal of every critic's pilgrimage is meaning, let us conclude by noting again that light on our way is provided not only by North's life and by his other works, but also by those of his contemporaries. When there has been time to consider the latter with care, conceivably Fulke Greville will prove to be the writer of importance closest to North in manner and matter. If we seek writers of meditative verse who are closer in both time and art, however, it may be necessary to turn to such men as John Hagthorpe and Robert Aylett.[86] That is to say, Dudley North's poetic charge was not great, and his mechanical skills were not always at the ready. Nevertheless, his poems now deserve a place in that body of works—the poetic pool, perhaps we may say—that finally determines our concept of what meditative verse really is. Modest though they are in achievement and intent, they should help us to see a bit better some of the works of even the finest seventeenth-century poets.

Notes

1. The manuscript volume on which this study is based was acquired by Perkins Library, Duke University, in 1969. A complete description is planned for an edition now in progress.

2. Louis L. Martz, *The Poetry of Meditation: A Study in English Religious Literature* (New Haven, 1954; rev. ed., 1962).

3. Richard Sibbes points the way back to still earlier times, noting that Paul urged Timothy to meditate, that David and Isaac meditated, and that God commanded Joshua to meditate (*Divine Meditations and Holy Contemplations* [London, 1638], A7^v-A8^r).

4. Martz, *Poetry of Meditation* (1962), pp. 43–53, 324.

5. Henry Montagu tried to sort the matter out: "Meditation or recognition, I saw was but a reiterated thought, proper to production either of good or euill. . . . But Diuines doe now dedicate Contemplation to diuine mysteries. Which affecting our soules, and exciting our wils, produceth some holy resolution. We meditate, saith one, to know God; we contemplate to loue God" (*Contemplatio mortis, et immortalitatis* [London, 1631], p. 4).

6. Martz, *Poetry of Meditation*, p. 14.

7. *Ibid.*, p. 15.

8. *A Treatise of Mentall Prayer* (an English version printed at St. Omer in 1627), p. 64; the passage is concerned particularly with degrees of meditative skill.

9. Reprinted by Martz in *The Meditative Poem: An Anthology of Seventeenth-Century Verse* (New York, 1963), pp. 1–23. In his *Scala meditatoria* (1483), John Wessel Gansfort presented a method with twenty-three steps.

10. *The Saints Everlasting Rest*, quoted by Martz, *Poetry of Meditation*, p. 154; Baxter discussed, pp. 153–175.

11. From a discussion in Barbara Kiefer Lewalski, *Donne's Anniversaries and the Poetry of Praise: The Creation of a Symbolic Mode* (Princeton, 1973), p. 81. See also U. Milo Kaufmann, *The Pilgrim's Progress and Traditions in Puritan Meditation* (New Haven, 1966); and Norman S. Grabo, "The Art of Puritan Devotion," *Seventeenth-Century News*, 26 (1968), 7–9. If the word "soliloquies" is puzzling, one may turn to Anthony Batt, who writes of "THE BOOKE OF S. AVGVSTIN, BISHOPP OF HYPPON, Commonlye called his Soliloquies, that is, the secret discourses and conferences of his soule with God" (*A Heavenly Treasure of Confortable Meditations and Prayers*, trans. Batt [St. Omer, 1624], p. 189). The attribution to Augustine is "suppositious."

12. Lewalski discusses the similarity, pp. 85–86.

13. Hall, p. 7. Perhaps it should be noted that Hall alludes to his dependence on Roman Catholic precursors in the field of meditation (A4$^{r&v}$).

14. *Ibid.*, p. 7.

15. Hall, *Meditations and Vowes Divine and Morall* (London, 1605), p. 61. One might add that while Roman Catholic meditations usually concerned some mystery of the faith, meditators sometimes were encouraged also to call to mind such things as the rising and setting of the sun, the multitude of stars, the fowl in the air, and the fish in the water. Richard Broughton, citing St. Cyprian, writes: "Let these and such other workes of God be spectacles for the beleuing Christians to meditate vpon" (*A New Manual of Old Christian Catholick Meditations, & Praiers* [n.p., 1617], p. 13).

16. Hall, *Arte of Divine Meditation*, pp. 84–85.

17. For an example of seventeenth-century awareness of the problem at hand one may turn to John Hagthorpe: "perchance thou thinkst it strange to see so sad matter, as Meditations drest in Verse; not considering how the same Musick that plaies your *Spanish* Pauin and Lauolto, is sometime fitted to a Lachrimae. That thou findst here so many kinds of Verse for one continued matter, maruell not: varietie is the best preuention for sacietie [*obs.*, satiety]" (*Divine Meditations, and Elegies* [London, 1622], p. 1 of "To the Reader").

18. At present the best readily available accounts of North are Augustus Jessopp, *DNB*, XIV (Oxford, rept. 1959–1960), 596–597; George Edward Cokayne, *The Complete Peerage*, IX, rev. ed. H. A. Doubleday and Lord Howard de Walden (London, 1936), 656–657; and Mary Frear Keeler, *The Long Parliament, 1640–1641: A Biographical Study of Its Members* (Philadelphia, 1954), p. 286. There are also a number of miscellaneous references of interest in Lawrence Stone, *The Crisis of the Aristocracy: 1558–1641* (Oxford, 1965). Usually harder to find but extremely valuable are the lives written by Roger North, particularly as presented in the edition of Augustus Jessopp, *The Lives of the Right Hon. Francis North . . . ; the Hon. Sir Dudley North; and the Hon. and Rev. Dr. John North*, 3 vols. (London, 1890).

19. Two epigraphs which appear on the title page of *A Narrative* provide brief but accurate glimpses of its contents: "*Curse not the King, no not in thy thought*" (Ecclesiastes, 10:20) and "*Rebellion is as the sin of Witchcraft*" (I Samuel 15:23).

20. *Observations and Advices Oeconomical*, pp. 41, 99.

21. *Ibid.*, p. 116.

22. *Ibid.*, p. 63.

23. *Light in the Way to Paradise*, p. 119.

24. Students of the period have overlooked almost entirely the third Lord North's *A Forest of Varieties* (London, 1645), which appeared subsequently, revised, as *A Forest Promiscuous of Several Seasons Productions* (London, 1659). The only significant exceptions that I know are L. A. Beaurline, "Dudley North's Criticism of Metaphysical Poetry," *HLQ*, 25 (1962), 299–313; Edward W. Tayler, who included some of North's critical writing in *Literary Criticism of Seventeenth-Century England* (New York, 1967); and a brief reference in Rosalie L. Colie, *The Resources of Kind: Genre-Theory in the Renaissance*, ed. Barbara Kiefer Lewalski (Berkeley, Calif., 1973). Since the submission of this essay, at least two other works have become available: Margaret Crum, "Poetical Manuscripts of Dudley, Third Baron North," *Bodleian Library Record*, 10 (1979), 98–108; and Robert J. Parsons, "Autobiographical and Archetypal Elements in the Verse of the Third Lord North," Ph.D. dissertation, Duke University (1980).

25. A poem he wrote at seventeen on the death of Queen Anne turns up in a Cambridge University memorial volume: *Lacrymae Cantabrigienses: In obitum serenissimae Reginae Annae* (Cambridge, 1619, p. 26); an epigram in *Light* brings the biography of Edward North to a close (p. 36); and an elegy on the death of his father was included in a privately printed, unpaginated collection assembled by William Carew Hazlitt, *Inedited Poetical Miscellanies 1584–1700* (London, 1870).

26. Perkins MS North, fol. 2ʳ.

27. Conversely, one "divine" poem by North which someone might prefer to include among his meditative works is "Who's This Appears in Crimson Dye," a poem on the Passion.

28. All but two of the "divine" poems are based on particular scriptural subjects (e.g., the Annunciation, the Ascension, and Pentecost), and there are four paraphrases of particular scriptural passages. Two others are a hymn and a dialogue. While all of these poems concern topics suitable for meditation, all, I believe, have a rather different "feel" from the poems selected here for discussion.

29. The lines of one poem rhyme *abab*.

30. Two passages from Cicero may be of interest: "But the entire discourse I have attributed, not to Tithonus, as Aristo of Ceos did, (for there would be too little authority in a myth), but, that I might give it greater weight, I have ascribed it to the venerable Marcus Cato . . . " (*De Senectute*, I); and (from *De Amicitia*, I): "in reading my own work on *Old Age* I am at times so affected that I imagine Cato is the speaker and not myself. But as in that book I wrote as one old man to another old man on the subject of old age, so now in this book I have written as a most affectionate friend to a friend on the subject of friendship." (Both quotations are from The Loeb Classical Library, *Cicero*, tr. William Armistead Falconer [London, 1946, rept. of 1923], pp. 11 and 113.)

31. "And though I fayle in art, yett this will bee exsprest, / That I our cursed Achans and theyr deeds detest" (Perkins MS North, fol. 28ʳ, ll. 9–10); for greedy Achan, see Joshua 7:1, 18–24.

32. *Transformations in the Renaissance English Lyric* (Ithaca, 1970), p. 81.

33. "To the Reader," Epigram 2, Bk. I, in *Small Poems of Divers Sorts* (London, 1658), the first p. 137.

34. Perkins MS North, fols. 33^r–34^r.

35. See Leonard Barkan, *Nature's Work of Art: The Human Body as Image of the World* (New Haven, 1975).

36. "Chap. VI. An Amplification . . . by Way of Comparison to a Cittadell Beseiged and Betrayed" (*Divine Meditations, and Elegies*, p. 15). Hagthorpe calls this poem a meditation, but I would not lean very hard on the fact.

37. E.g., The Folger Shakespeare Library has North's own copies of Samuel Marolois, *Fortification ou architecture militaire tant offensive que defensive* (The Hague, 1615), and Hendrik Hondius, *Description & breve declaration des regles generales de la fortification*, trans. by Albert Girard (The Hague, 1625).

38. See C. H. Firth and R. S. Rait, ed., *Acts and Ordinances of the Interregnum, 1642–1660*, vol. I of 3 vols. (London, 1911), pp. 106, 111; 145–146; 223, 227; 614, 621; 1072, 1078.

39. Perkins MS North, fol. 42^r.

40. See Stanley Stewart, *The Enclosed Garden: The Tradition and the Image in Seventeenth-Century Poetry* (Madison, 1966), and A. Bartlett Giamatti, *The Earthly Paradise and the Renaissance Epic* (Princeton, 1966). Cf. George H. Williams, *Wilderness and Paradise in Christian Thought* (New York, 1962).

41. *Two Sermons Preached at White-hall in Lent, March 3. 1625. and Februarie 20. 1626* (London, 1627), pt. I, p. 14.

42. *A New Herball* (London, 1551), Bvi^r. Like certain other plants, aloes had a dual tradition, but North's word "bitter" makes it clear that he intends nothing pleasant.

43. Ophelia says, "There's rue for you, and here's some for me. We may call it herb of grace o' Sundays . . . " (*Hamlet*, IV.v.180–181). Rue was the herb of repentance, and repentance a sign of grace (Henry N. Ellacombe, *The Plant-Lore and Garden-Craft of Shakespeare* [London, 3rd ed., 1896], p. 276).

In his *Light in the Way to Paradise* North uses herbgrace in another allegorical situation:

> . . . by an ascent . . . we come to the garden of Spiritual consolation, a place not only pleasing, but usefull, for there we may discern at a considerable distance, the rock of Faith, and the temple of Holiness, as also the way to them. And in that Garden may be gathered herb of Grace usefull for Nutrition and Sustentation, and *Salvia* (or the hope of Salvation) as an incentive to Perseverance. . . . (pp. 48–49)

In a prose prayer, dropping all indirection, he states the importance of grace:

> *We confess, that of our selves without thy especial grace we cannot step one step towards thee, by our actings in any Religious duty; yet by means of that grace we are enabled so far to act, as to obtain acceptance at thy hands in Jesus Christ, which is sufficient for us. (Observations, K3^v)*

44. *The Seconde Parte of William Turners Herball* (Cologne, 1562), p. 123^r. John Gerard cites Pliny as saying that rue is an antidote against poisons (*The Herball or Generall Historie of Plantes* [London, 1597], p. 1075).

45. The pun was still more obvious when the name of the plant was spelled as Gerard did: "there is not any which are ignorant what *Thymum durius* is, I meane our common Garden Time" (*The Herball*, p. 458).

46. Bacon, "Of Gardens," *The Essayes or Counsels* (London, 1629), p. 270; I cite from North's own copy, now in The Folger Shakespeare Library. See also Ellacombe, pp. 313–315.

47. See, e.g., Ricardo J. Quinones, *The Renaissance Discovery of Time* (Cambridge, Mass., 1972).

48. In his *Light in the Way to Paradise* North writes that the best light is the light eternal from the sun of righteousness: "*Our light in the way to Paradise (at the best) is but a reflexion of this righteous Sun's rays . . . *" (A2$^{r&v}$).

49. Alexander Nowell, *A Catechisme, or First Instruction . . .* , trans. Thomas Norton (London, 1570), 79^r.

50. Though obviously it is futile to try to identify North's weed, one may be tempted to ponder the following passage from his father's *Forest of Varieties*:

> There is an evill Herb they call Twitch [i.e., couch grass or dog's grass], which hath over-run it [a piece of my ground], of such nature, that having once possessed a ground, the soyle must be wholly altered and over-come, or no good thing will thrive committed unto it. . . . Some soyles are cured by much breaking, some by fire, some by inundation. . . . (p. 162)

Gerard describes the difficulties posed by the long, jointed roots of twitch (*Herball*, p. 22).

51. Cf. Hebrews 12:29: "our God is a consuming fire."

52. One such book is Gervase Markham's *Farwell to Husbandry* (London, 1625); see pp. 20, 32. Markham has in mind especially gorse, furze, and broom. Because of the importance of the fens to Cambridge in general and Dudley North in particular, it is of interest to find burning specifically recommended for improving fenland (Walter Blith, *The English Improver Improved* [London, 1652], p. 61). In light of the elder North's comments on twitch, perhaps it is worth noticing also that the generic term "twitch-fire" came to refer to "a fire for burning twitch or other weeds" (*Oxford English Dictionary*, XI [Oxford, rpt. 1961], 543).

53. *Georgics*, Bk. I, ll. 84–93 (Loeb Classical Library, *Virgil*, vol. I, trans. H. Rushton Fairclough [Cambridge, Mass., 1940; rpt. of rev. ed., 1935], pp. 86, 87).

54. Hall, p. 150.

55. Perkins MS North, fol. 39^r. The stage / life comparison, another commonplace of the time, was ancient in origin. See Thomas B. Stroup, *Microcosmos: The Shape of the Elizabethan Play* (Lexington, Ky., 1965), and Frances A. Yates, *Theatre of the World* (Chicago, 1969).

56. Cf. "to call our selves a Microcosme, or little world, I thought it onely a pleasant trope of Rhetorick, till my neare judgement and second thoughts told me there was a reall truth therein" (Sir Thomas Browne, *Religio Medici* [London, 1643], p. 77).

57. Roger (1585?–1652?) was with Raleigh on the latter's final and disastrous voyage to Guiana (1617). On returning he was deputed the difficult job of reporting to King James on the outcome of the voyage (23 May 1618). After much perseverance, Roger North eventually managed to establish a plantation in Guiana (1627), but legal problems kept him from developing the plantation as he would have liked. Back in England, he seems to have spent a good deal of time at Kirtling, his brother's home in Cambridgeshire.

58. *Re* "Fortunes": In North's youth his father apparently spent lavishly in an attempt to keep up with others at court; Lawrence Stone uses the Norths as an illustration of his statement that "As the tide of extravagance ebbed in the 1630's it left behind it on the beach a litter of debris" (*Crisis*, p. 584). The third Lord North explained himself in verse:

> I thought the bounty of a bounteous Prince
> Would never faile to recompence desert;
> But sad experience hath taught me since,
> Saints must be prayed, and Courting is an Art. (*The Forest*, p. 208)

Among other things, he had indulged himself in building. For a variety of reasons, then, his son had financial worries. In his *Observations*, our North writes that

> It was an Observation of my Fathers . . . That the *English* Gentleman can hardly be prosperous in government of his Estate; for whereas the Genius of some other Nations prompteth them to particular excesses; as the *Italian* to curiosity of House and Furniture; the *French* man to bravery in Habit of Clothes and other matters of Parade, as abundance of Pages and Laquays, &c. And the *German* to variety and excess in Drinking; but they are all frugal otherwise. Our *English* man affects all these together, as also that of our own, which is, a number of Menial Servants, and great plenty in Diet. Of this I shall make no application, but say concerning the Observation, *Valeat quantum valere potest*. (pp. 112–113)

Re "Friends": North corroborates this allusion to youthful problems with friends in the "Preface" to his *Observations*. There he admits (anonymously, since no author's name appears on the title page), "*I lived with my Parents at their* London *habitation, and having no employment I surfeited of Idlenesse, taking my pastime with some of the most corrupt young men of those dayes. By Gods grace I quickly found this unfit for continuance, and therefore I prevailed with My Father to send me beyond Sea to travel . . .* " (A3^v-A4^r).

59. Note that this is the second time we have seen North acknowledge the value of "discourse."

60. The metaphor of the soul caged or imprisoned in the body is, of course, traditional; cf. John Webster, *The Duchess of Malfi* (IV.ii.128–130): "Didst thou ever see a lark in a cage? such is the soul in the body . . ." (ed. John Russell Brown, Revels Plays [Cambridge, Mass., 1964], p. 123).

61. North alludes to the story of the nymph Echo, who, being spurned by Narcissus, hid in a wood until at last nothing remained of her but her voice. Ovid tells about her in his *Metamorphoses*, Bk. III.

62. I.e., foolishly.

63. Nowell, *Catechisme*, 13^v–14^r, 61^r. Henri Estienne, commenting on the device of the Prince of Wales and its motto *Ich dien* (I serve), says it alludes "to that of the Apostle, *The heire while he is a childe, differeth nothing from a servant*" (*The Art of Making Devises . . .*, trans. Thomas Blount [London, 1650], A3^v-A4^r). Stone, citing Lovejoy, discusses the belief "that peace and order could only be preserved by the maintenance of grades and distinctions and by relentless emphasis on the overriding need for subjection of the individual will to that of superior authority" (p. 21). Such subjection must have been costly to some individuals. Joel Hurstfield explores "The Paradox of Liberty in Shakespeare's England" in *Essays and Studies 1972*, ed. T. S. Dorsch (London, 1972), pp. 57–82.

North himself, in his *Observations*, tells of an apposite incident in the family of Robert Dudley, Earl of Leicester:

> As he was sitting at his Table with many other Noblemen, a Letter was delivered to him, whereby appeared that an Earl was dead whose Heir served him in his House, being somewhat remote in blood from the deceased, whereupon he called the Gentleman to him, and acquainting his Guests with the Letters substance, made him presently to sit at the Table above himself and many other of the Lords. (p. 96)

64. Roger North, son of our poet, writes:

> There never was an instance of filial duty to a parent more eminent than that of Sir Dudley North to his father. He lived to a good old age before the barony descended upon him, and had stood as an eldest son of a peer at the state in the House of Lords at sixty-three. He never would put on his hat or sit down before his father, unless enjoined to do it. So far was he from moving any thing to him that he knew would displease him, and so egregious was this dutiful demeanour that all people took notice of and admired it. (*Lives*, I, 35)

65. E.g., she "made it a grievance" that Sir Dudley had to contribute so much for household expenses during the years when he and his immediate family lived sometimes with Lord North at Kirtling (Lady Frances Bushby, "Memoirs of Some of the North Family During the Tudor and Stuart Dynasties" [typed in London, 1893], p. 163 [Bodleian MS Eng. Hist. c. 408]).

66. A "cross" is, of course, any impediment, but the seventeenth century frequently called on the religious overtones of the word. E.g., Henry King writes that "Any crosse by him [God] throwne vpon vs, awakes the slumbring faculties of our soules" (from *Two Sermons . . .*, pt. I, p. 8). Cf. Robert Fletcher, "The Times" (*The Poems and Translations*, ed. D. H. Woodward [Gainesville, Fla., 1970], p. 185); and Vaughan's "Day of Judgement" (*The Complete Poetry of Henry Vaughan*, ed. French Fogle [New York, 1965], p. 147).

67. Cf. the following passage from the elder North's *Forest*: "Thou, Oh God, art the Starre, the Loadstone, the *Neptune* of our voyage in this world, be thou my current, my guide, and to thee be all my Sacrifice" (p. 144).

68. Paul J. Korshin writes that "The ship in distress is a common symbol both for the

state in turmoil and for the soul troubled by sin; its deliverance suggests or foreshadows a greater deliverance by God of sinful man" (*From Concord to Dissent: Major Themes in English Poetic Theory 1640–1700* [Menston, Yorkshire, 1973], p. 56). See also Kathleen M. Grange, "The Ship Symbol as a Key to Former Theories of the Emotions," *Bulletin of the History of Medicine*, 36 (1962), 512–523; and Earle Hilgert, *The Ship and Related Symbols in the New Testament* (Assen, The Netherlands, 1962). North's father was fond of the image.

69. Cf. Donne's "Hymne to God My God, in My Sicknesse" (Martz, *Meditative Poem*, pp. 136–137).

70. *Forest*, p. 153.

71. Perkins MS North, fol. 1ʳ.

72. *Ibid.*, fol. 2ʳ.

73. One might read this as a rare hint that North thought his verse would survive; for the conventional quality of his figure see O. B. Hardison, Jr., *The Enduring Monument: A Study of the Idea of Praise in Renaissance Literary Theory and Practice* (Chapel Hill, N.C., 1962).

74. East Anglia suffered frequently from "sadd plagues"; see, e.g., L. J. Redstone, *Our East Anglian Heritage* (London, 1939), p. 121.

75. North's relationship with his wife appears to have been one of the happiest elements in his life. On 5 May 1668 Lady North wrote to a young lady and her fiancé wishing them "all the true Ioys, that can attend a married life. which none can be more truly sensible of then[,] Madam[, signature]" (British Library Add. MS 29,551, 413ʳ).

76. "*Nephriticall* patients . . . are troubled about their Kidneyes, especially with the ston . . . " (Helkiah Crooke, *Microcosmographia: A Description of the Body of Man* [London, 1631; 2nd ed.], p. 189).

77. Abraham Cowley compares an operation made by Dr. Scarborough for the stone to one of the feats of Moses:

> . . . like *Moses*, Thou
> S'trik'st but the *Rock*, and straight the *Waters*
> freely flow.

("To Dr. Scarborough," p. 35 of *Pindarique Odes*, in *Poems* [London, 1656].)

78. *Lives*, II, 317.

79. Donne uses the phrase in "La Corona," No. 1, l. 6 (Martz, *Meditative Poem*, p. 79).

80. It is interesting that *The Booke of Common Prayer* (1603 [i.e., 1604]) tells the minister to exhort a sick person thus:

> And for what cause so euer this sicknesse is sent vnto you, whether it be to try your patience for the example of other, and that your faith may bee found in the day of the Lord, laudable, glorious, & honourable, to the increase of glory and endlesse felicitie, or els it be sent vnto you to correct and amend in you whatsoeuer doeth offend the eyes of your heauenly Father: know you certainly, that if you truely repent you of your sinnes, and beare your sicknesse patiently, trusting in Gods mercy, for his deare Sonne Iesus Christes sake, and render vnto him humble thankes for his fatherly visitation, submitting your selfe wholly vnto his will, it shall turne to your profite, and helpe you forward in the right way that leadeth vnto life euerlasting. (P4ᵛ)

81. *Observations*, p. 121.

82. *Forest*, p. 158.

83. *Lives*, I, 6.

84. Common sense tells us, of course, that a particular meditative poem may be highly contrived, artificial in the modern sense. On the other hand, a "curious" setting forth, "artificial" in the older sense, may modify a poet's voice without obliterating it. As evidence one might cite Robert Southwell's "A Phansie Turned to a Sinners Complaint":

> And though I seeme to use
> The faining Poets stile,
> To figure forth my careful plight,
> My fall, and my exile:

Yet is my greefe not fain'd,
Wherein I starve and pine. . . .

(*The Poems of Robert Southwell, S.J.*, ed. James H. McDonald and Nancy Pollard Brown [Oxford, 1967], p. 40.)

Or we might turn again to Richard Baxter, another writer who did not believe in the impossibility of sincerity in verse: "Herbert," he says, "*speaks* to God *like one that* really believeth a God, *and whose business in this World is most* with God. Heart-work *and* Heaven-work *make up his Books*" (*Poetical Fragments* [2nd ed., London, 1689], A5ʳ). Herbert well knew the dangers of curling metaphors and perhaps seldom escaped them, but he held nonetheless that "The finenesse which a hymne or psalme affords, / Is, when the soul unto the lines accords" ("A True Hymne," *The Temple* [Cambridge, 1633], p. 163).

For some further reading see H. R. Swardson, *Poetry and the Fountain of Light* (Columbia, Mo., 1962); A. S. P. Woodhouse, *The Poet and His Faith: Religion and Poetry in England from Spenser to Eliot and Auden* (Chicago, 1965); Isabel G. MacCaffrey, "The Meditative Paradigm," *ELH*, 32 (1965), 388–407; William H. Halewood, *The Poetry of Grace: Reformation Themes and Structures in English Seventeenth-Century Poetry* (New Haven, 1972, 2nd printing; 1st printing, 1970); Lucien Carrive, *La poésie religieuse anglaise entre 1625 et 1640* (Caen, 1972); and Vernon Ruland, *Horizons of Criticism: An Assessment of Religious-Literary Options* (Chicago, 1975). Since the submission of this essay, a number of pertinent publications have appeared, including Anthony Low, *Love's Architecture: Devotional Modes in Seventeenth-Century English Poetry* (New York, 1978); and Barbara Kiefer Lewalski, *Protestant Poetics and the Seventeenth-Century Religious Lyric* (Princeton, 1979).

85. "Postscript: Christianity & Art," *The Dyer's Hand* (New York, 1962), p. 458.

86. We have met Hagthorpe earlier. For Aylett see *Divine, and Moral Speculations in Metrical Numbers, upon Various Subjects* (London, 1654).

IV

Humanism in the Music of the Renaissance

Edward E. Lowinsky
University of Chicago, Emeritus

Introduction

When we speak of humanism we have in mind the revival of Greek, classical Latin, and Hebrew, we think of the intensive study of Plato's philosophy, of Tacitus' history, Horace's poetry, Homer's and Virgil's epics, and the Old and New Testaments, all in their original languages, we think of the feverish search for manuscripts of Greek and Roman writers of antiquity, of the many newly discovered authors such as Sophocles, Herodotus, Plutarch, Epicurus, of Roman writers such as Lucretius, Tacitus, and some of Cicero's works, we think of the development of eloquence and rhetorics as well as of grammar, text criticism, and philological method.[1] All these activities were born of and kept alive by a burning enthusiasm for poetry and letters, by a new sense of the music and the power of language, and by a delight in the achievements of an ancient secular culture based on reason, ethics, and a vision of beauty.

The art historian has long known what a profound influence the humanistic movement exercised on the evolution of paintings, sculpture, and architecture. The study of iconography, developed by a whole generation of art historians under the leadership of

The present paper goes back to a lecture first given in 1956. Some of its ideas were expressed in a review of D. P. Walker's *Der musikalische Humanismus im 16. und im frühen 17. Jahrhundert (The Musical Quarterly*, XXXVII [1951], 285–289, esp. 286–287); others were presented at the Eighth Congress of the International Musicological Society in New York, September 1961. The occasion was the Round Table discussion of "Verse Meter and Melodic Rhythm in the Age of Humanism" (see *Report of the Eighth Congress, New York 1961*, ed. Jan LaRue, vol. II [Kassel, 1962], pp. 67–71, esp. 67–69). By far the greatest part of this paper is published here for the first time. The music examples offered at the lecture were illustrated with the aid of a tape recording which I owe to the kindness of Professor Miriam Terry, Director of the Vocal Ensemble at the School of Music at the University of Washington, where I read this paper in 1956 in abbreviated form. I am deeply indebted to Professor Terry and her musicians.

Warburg, Panofsky, Saxl, Wind, and many others, has made it abundantly clear how strongly the choice of pictorial themes and programs was guided by the fresh reading of ancient poets and philosophers and how the choice of new subject matter affected formal representation.[2]

In the history of music, on the other hand, it is still a widely held view that except for some pedagogical and antiquarian exercises in academic circles in Germany, France, and Italy, the humanistic movement hardly touched music and, at any rate, did not seriously affect its evolution.[3]

I shall try to suggest another view. Let me preface my remarks with two references, one to a Latin treatise on counterpoint written in 1477 by the Flemish composer and theorist Johannes Tinctoris, the other to a treatise of 1581 by the Italian composer and theorist Vincenzo Galilei, father of the famous physicist. Both speak of ancient Greek music and its possible relationship to the music of their time. Tinctoris, every inch a realistic Fleming, rejects the Pythagorean notion of the harmony of the spheres; he expresses in no uncertain terms his scepticism concerning the merits of ancient Greek music and declares that the counterpoint of the Flemish school is so marvelous that it should be considered suitable even for the immortal gods of the ancient Greeks.[4]

Vincenzo Galilei, on the other hand, rejects Flemish counterpoint as a mere tickling of the ears devoid of rhyme and reason. What made ancient Greek music great, what gave it its much praised miraculous effects, was that it had one concern only: to follow the poet's text, to adapt the quantity of its meter, to express the meaning of the words, their passions and conceits, all of which was rendered even more eloquent by gesture and accent of the performing musician.[5]

Both Tinctoris and Galilei speak of vocal music. Tinctoris is chiefly interested in consonance, dissonance, and counterpoint. Galilei, on the other hand, is the spokesman for the Florentine Camerata which was intent upon resurrecting the ancient Greek music drama; to him music is merely a means to intensify the expression of the spoken word. What happened in the interval between 1477 and 1581? Can it be shown that the humanistic movement had anything to do with this radical reorientation of musical aesthetics? Do we know what the humanists' ideas were regarding the proper relationship between word and tone? Is there such a thing as humanistic music of the Renaissance?

1. *The German Humanistic Ode and Its Italian Origins*

It may appear strange that the first documents of "humanistic music" are not to be found in the Netherlands, which was leading in music, or in Italy, which was leading in humanism, but in a country which was leading neither in music nor in humanism, in Germany. In 1507 Erhard Oeglin of Augsburg published the first collection of Horatian odes and epodes set to music for four parts[6] by Petrus Tritonius, pupil of the German humanist Conrad Celtis.[7] Here was a novel experiment in music. Nineteen poems of Horace were set in the rhythm dictated by the various classical meters in simultaneous four-part declamation.[8] Every syllable of the text had one note only; no repetition of a sentence or part of a sentence was tolerated; there were no more than two note values, a long and a short note, the long having twice the duration of the short note. They were painstakingly adapted to the long and short syllables of the Latin meter. No attention was paid to rhythmic variety beyond what the meter afforded, not the slightest concession made to counterpoint; all voices moved in one and the same metric step. No passing notes or dissonances gave relief; sharps or flats were used sparingly to preserve the purity of the modes. Solemn declamation of the Latin poem heightened by the sound of four-part harmony: this was the humanist's idea, for musicians had little to do with this fruit of humanistic endeavor. Petrus Tritonius, alias Treibenreif from Bozen, teacher at the Latin school in Brixen, student of Celtis first in Ingolstadt and later in Vienna, had never before published music of his own, nor did he do so after 1507.[9] He was an instrument of Conrad Celtis and set the Horatian odes *ductu Cunradi*, as he says in his preface, "under Conrad's guidance."[10]

It is understandable that music historians have tended to belittle the musical significance of the humanistic odes.[11] Yet, a few facts are well worth considering: these odes solved, if with a sword's blow, a problem that universally plagued composers of the period: how to adapt music to words. The ascendancy of contrapuntal writing had resulted in a one-sided emphasis on luxuriant melody, intricate polyphony, and polyrhythm, in which the text was all but drowned. The humanistic odes showed a new path that was to have unforeseen consequences. Besides, the four-part harmony offered a novel sound, the like of which German ears had not heard; it was to have a decisive influence on the Protestant chorale, which took over simple four-part harmony from the humanistic ode.[12] The success of the humanistic ode is demonstrated by several new editions of the Tritonius opus and by the growing literature of Latin odes to which now famous composers such as Ludwig Senfl, Benedictus Ducis, Paul Hofhaimer and many others made comprehensive contributions.[13] Neo-Latin school dramas featured musical numbers in the style of the humanistic ode, and they became very popular in sixteenth-century Germany.[14] Even before the Reformation, the humanists had forged a strong bond between ode composition and religion. Celtis himself added to Tritonius' *Melopoiae* of 1507 a list of hymns that could be sung to the four-part odes. Perhaps the most flattering compliment received by Tritonius consists of the three-part intabulations for solo lute of nineteen of his four-part ode compositions, that is, without the texts, in Hans Judenkünig's *Utilis et compendiaria introductio* (Vienna, 151?).[15]

It has been the general consensus of music historians that "humanistic ode composition received its initiative, its artistic goal, and its methods from learned German humanists."[16] Yet, I believe that the humanistic odes are another case in which German industry and methodic spirit have elaborated upon an Italian idea (a more famous one being Silbermann's development of the pianoforte invented by Cristofori of Padua). In Franchino Gafori's treatise *De harmonia instrumentorum musicorum*, published in 1518 but already completed in 1500, we find a musical setting of the Sapphic ode of an Italian humanist, Lancino Curzio, a poet at the Milanese court of Ludovico il Moro with which Gafori was connected. In four lines Curzio condensed the ancient philosophy of music, according to which the movements of the seven planets concord with the seven modes of music and the seven strings of the lyre played by Orpheus:

> Musices septemque modos planetae
> Corrigunt septem totidemque chordis
> Thracis antiqui lyra personabat
> Cognita silvis.[17]

The seven planets control the seven modes of music; and the lyre of the ancient Thracian, well known in the forests, resounded with that same number of strings.

As mentioned earlier, Gafori had Greek writings on music translated into Latin. He knew perfectly well that the Greeks cultivated music for one voice only. To satisfy both the historical truth and his inborn Italian love of consonance, he set Curzio's Latin ode twice, in the Dorian and in the Hypodorian mode, and observed, with tongue in cheek: "should two reciters wish to enunciate the poem together in these two modes, they would find the two melodies charming the ear with most agreeable harmony" (Ex. 1). For this break with classical tradition he did not escape the censure of Glareanus, who otherwise professed great admiration for him (save, of course, for his treatment of the modes).[18]

Conrad Celtis, Tritonius' teacher, had visited Italy in 1486; he had gone to Rome, Bologna, Florence, Ferrara, Padua, and Venice. Celtis' teacher, Rudolf Agricola, had spent ten years in Italy. Agricola's teacher, Johann Wessel, had received his training in Italy, just as did the later German humanists Mutianus Rufus and Ulrich von Hutten; Tritonius himself had gone to Italy to study at the University of Padua, where he acquired a *Magister artium* title in 1502, five years before the publication of his odes in Augsburg. Undoubtedly, it was in Italy that Tritonius came in contact not only with the new style of writing music in four-part harmony, but also with the *modo di cantar versi latini*, namely in long and short notes in simultaneous four-part declamation. Petrucci printed an example in his first book of frottole in 1504, which suggests that similar compositions may have been sung years earlier.

Evidence that the idea of the humanistic ode preceded Petrucci and even Gafori and that it was not so much the musicians who were interested in humanism as the humanists who were interested in music is provided by the *Grammatica brevis* of Franciscus Niger published in Venice in the year 1480.

In dealing with the metrical foundation of poetry, Niger concludes with these observations on music:

It is proper that the poet have an instrument fitting for poetry, playing on which he should conceive his poems in imitation of the ancient poets who composed no verse without melody, for they were called *carmina* from *canere*, to sing. For unless they were sung, their divine name was converted to the vilest and basest thing. Vocal harmony resides in the voice which executes the well-composed poems. It has five species, the grave heroic, the warlike heroic, the elegiac, the sapphic, and the lyric.[19]

To illustrate the five species, Niger, Francesco Negro by his Italian name, published Latin verses together with musical notation. Although his melodies have drawn the attention of the historian of music printing, they have been largely neglected by the historian of the humanistic ode, even though they are the earliest printed examples of that genre.[20] In 1480 they appeared without staves, the melody being suggested by up- and downward motion of the notes; in Niger's *Opuscula Vergiliana* of 1500 and in an edition of the *Grammatica* of 1501 they are placed on staves. A comparison with the book of 1480 demonstrates that the higher and lower position of the notes indeed signified the melodic movement and that the melodies of 1480 and 1500 are basically the same. In a new edition of Niger's *Grammatica brevis* published in 1514, the five melodies for the five meters can be found again.[21]

Niger adhered to the ancient tradition of monodic song. The melodies demonstrate the humanistic view of music as a mere servant of poetry. Indeed, some of these melodies of 1480 anticipate the dryness and the speech character of the early Italian monodies of the Florentine Camerata a century later—on a much more primitive level, of course. Niger and the musicians of the Camerata drew their inspiration from the same source, the ancient Greek concept of the unity of poetry and music. An example of Niger's melodies is his setting of distichs from Ovid's *Fasti* (VI: 771–772; I: 70–71):

> Tempora labuntur, tacitisque senescimus annis,
> et fugiunt freno non remorante dies.
> Prospera lux oritur: linguis animisque favete!
> nunc dicenda bona sunt bona verba die.
>
> > Time slips away, and we grow old with silent lapse of years:
> > There is no bridle that can curb the flying days.
> > A happy morning dawns. Fair speech, fair thoughts I crave!
> > Now must good words be spoken on a good day.
> >   (Loeb Classical Library)

Here we find a clear text setting without repeats of words or phrases and strictly syllabic declamation (Ex. 2). However, the division of long and short syllables is not regulated by the meter, but by a curious blend of metrical and word accent. Moreover, Niger uses two more note values than do the later German ode composers. His notation shows not only semibreves and breves but longs as well (to mark the end of the phrases) and, most remarkably, dotted semibreves. No doubt the note following was sung as a minim, not as a semibreve. But here Niger was not enough of a musician; the fault could not be the printer's, for it would have been just as easy to create a type for a minim by adding a stem to a semibreve as it was to produce a longa by adding a stem to the breve. A musician would of course have written it—and I use modern notation—as follows:

ta - ci - tis - que   se - ne - sci - mus   an - nis

This is the way the frottolists notated the scansion of ancient meters. Surely, in actual performance, singers reciting humanistic odes adapted the long and short syllables to their deeply ingrained sense of musical meter. Proof of this is the introduction of the dotted note by Niger—a refinement absent from the notation, but hardly the performance, of the German ode.

In all of this I posit Niger to be the author of the melodies. It would have been hard for an Italian musician to write such unmelodious tunes and notate them in contravention of the common tenets of contemporaneous music. Many humanists, as we shall see later, wrote their own tunes to ancient poetry. One of them, a friend of Niger's, was the Platonic philosopher Marsilio Ficino (1433–1499), who improvised music "for the Latin verses sent to him by his humanist friends," accompanying himself on the lyra.[22]

When Conrad Celtis came to Venice, Franciscus Niger's *Grammatica* had been out for six years; indeed, it is quite possible that Celtis met Niger in person.[23] To obtain full confirmation of Celtis' Italian inspiration, we need only turn to his own writings. Even as Albrecht Dürer wanted it to be known that he considered the Italians masters of perspective and of the design of the human body, so Conrad Celtis made it amply clear that he viewed Italy as the home of the liberal arts, of the study of literature and of music, poetry's sister.

A Sapphic ode expresses his fervent vision: "Ad Apollinem Repertorem poetices ut ab Italis ad Germanos veniat" ("To Apollo, the Inventor of Poetry, that he may leave Italy and come to Germany"):

Phoebe qui blandae citharae repertor,
Linque delectos Helicona, Pindum et,
Ac veni in nostras vocitatus oras
    Carmine grato.

Cernis ut laetae properent camaenae,
Et canunt dulces gelido sub axe.
Tu veni incultam fidibus canoris
    Visere terram.

Barbarus quem olim genuit, vel acer
Vel parens hirtus, Latii leporis
Nescius, nunc sic duce te docendus
    Dicere carmen

Orpheus qualis cecinit Pelasgis,
Quem ferae atroces, agilesque cervi,
Arboresque altae nemorum secutae
    Plectra moventem.

Tu celer vastum poteras per aequor
Laetus a Graecis Latium videre,
Invehens Musas, voluisti gratas
    Pandere et artes.

Sic velis nostras rogitamus oras
Italas ceu quondam aditare terras;
Barbarus sermo fugiatque, ut atrum
    Subruat omne.

    Phoebus, who invented the sweet lyre, answer our prayers; leave your beloved Helicon and Pindus and come to our land invoked by the poetry you love;

    you see how our country-bred muses hasten to meet you and with what charm they sing under our cold sky. Do you yourself come, visit this country as yet untutored by the lofty music of your lyre.

    So must the barbarian, born of warrior or rustic stock, ignorant of Latin culture, now learn beneath your guidance the speech of poetry,

    singing as Orpheus sang to the Pelasgians, when beasts of prey, nimble deer and tall forest trees followed him as he plucked the strings.

> You it was who deigned to leave Greece, passing swiftly and gladly over the wide sea to visit Latium with the Muse in your train; your pleasure it was to reveal the arts you love.
>
> So now we pray you: Come to us as you came to Italy. Let barbarian speech be driven out and the whole fabric of darkness collapse.[24]

And in his famous oration recited in 1492 at the University of Ingolstadt, in which he challenged German princes and German youth to follow up the political conquest of Italy of the past with an emulation of Italian love of letters of the present, he referred specifically to music and its part in the literary education of the young when he said:

It is therefore a wise practice on the part of the cities of ancient Greece and of modern Italy to instruct their children from the very beginning in the works of the poets. For in them they learn to recognize musical songs and sweet modulations of harmony (to which their age is peculiarly responsive), and their tender spirits, normally prone to laziness and indolence, are stimulated to industry, so that they are inspired to learn and to linger over their studies with joyful enthusiasm and eagerness. . . . This is the type of teaching which Aristotle prescribes, when he advises that young people should be trained in music. For harmony rouses the native talent of boys so that they bend their energies towards oratory and musical composition.[25]

Niger personified the uncompromising humanistic stand of precise imitation of ancient Greek musical practice; his melody is designed to give a lift to the declamation, no less—and certainly no more. Gafori, a humanistically inspired and educated musician, aimed to please both humanists and musicians by combining faithful observation of the Sapphic meter with elegant melody and agreeable consonance in two parts recited homorhythmically (see Ex. 1). Celtis-Tritonius, inspired by Italian models, made further concessions to the modern ear by allowing four-part harmony, although they knew that Greek music had neither harmony nor counterpoint. We choose as an example Tritonius' setting of the second ode of Horace's first book of *Carmina* (Ex. 3):

Jam satis terris nivis atque dirae
Grandinis misit Pater et rubente
Dextera sacras jaculatus arces
    Terruit urbem.

> Enough already of dire snow and hail has the Father sent upon the earth, and smiting with his red right hand the sacred hill-tops has filled with fear the City.
>
> (Bennett, Loeb Classical Library)

Music historians have paid little attention to the art with which Tritonius solved the problems set by the strict limits imposed by Celtis. The melodic fluency of the tenor distinguishes it as the clear point of departure. In a simplified form the melody might go like this:

The harmonic setting too shows unusual skill. The key signature of one flat in each of the four voices marks the piece as belonging to the transposed Ionian mode. The four phrases begin and end on F. Phrase one elaborates the relationship between tonic and subdominant; phrase two concentrates on the dominant, articulating it through reference to the supertonic and the sixth degree, sliding then into the first inversion of the subdominant; phrase three dwells on the relation between tonic and relative minor; the last phrase echoes in its clear-cut cadence (V-I-IV-V-I) the concise and energetic ending of the Sapphic meter, which follows three lines of eleven syllables with one line of five syllables.

One problem usually remains unnoticed. *Iam satis* has no fewer than thirteen stanzas. Skilful, indeed attractive, though Tritonius' setting is, it would strain the listener's endurance to hear the same setting repeated twelve times. Sebastian Forster, in the *Melodiae Prudentianae et in Virgilium* (Leipzig, 1533),[26] turning from Horace's odes to Virgil's epic, recognized the problem. He selected the first seven verses of the *Aeneid* and set them in continuous fashion (Ex. 4):

> Arma virumque cano, Troiae qui primus ab oris
> Italiam, fato profugus, Laviniaque venit

litora multum ille et terris iactatus et alto
vi superum saevae memorem Iunonis ob iram
multa quoque et bello passus, dum conderet urbem
interretque deos Latio; genus unde Latinum
Albanique patres atque altae moenia Romae.

> I sing of arms and of a man: his fate
> had made him fugitive; he was the first
> to journey from the coasts of Troy as far
> as Italy and the Lavinian shores.
> Across the lands and waters he was battered
> beneath the violence of High Ones, for
> the savage Juno's unforgetting anger;
> and many sufferings were his in war—
> until he brought a city into being
> and carried in his gods to Latium;
> from this have come the Latin race, the lords
> of Alba, and the ramparts of high Rome.[27]

(Allen Mandelbaum)

The through-composed technique results in a larger harmonic arch. Also writing in the transposed Ionian mode on F, Forster makes use of the subdominant of the relative minor. G minor occurs in the second, third, and the penultimate phrases with excellent effect, in the latter supported by E-flat major and C minor. The last three phrases are remarkable in their harmonic and melodic design. In phrase five the soprano melody surges up to its highest point, to descend in two slow curves to the low point, while the harmony veers to D and G minor, to return at the end to the tonic.

At the same time as the Italian madrigalist broke away from the strophic design of the frottola, the German ode composer, in a telling example, abandoned the stanzaic structure of the original ode as conceived by Celtis and executed by Tritonius. It is not without significance that Forster's new effort occurs in a work dedicated to strophic hymns of the fourth-century poet Prudentius,[28] dear to the humanists because he could serve as Christian apologist for the revival of the meters used in pagan poetry.[29]

II. *Metrical Declamation Versus Musical Expression*

To place the German ode into its historical context, we need to know how Italians and Netherlanders dealt with texts by Horace and Virgil. Michele Pesenti, frottolist from Verona, wrote a four-part setting of Horace's ode 22 (Book I):[30]

> Integer vitae scelerisque purus
> non eget Mauris iaculis neque arcu
> nec venenatis gravida sagittis,
>   Fusce, pharetra
>
>> He who is upright in his way of life and unstained by guilt, needs
>> not Moorish darts nor bow nor quiver loaded with poisoned arrows,
>> Fuscus
>>   (Bennett, Loeb Classical Library)

A humanist would have scanned the Sapphic meter of Horace's ode:

Integer vitae scelerisque purus.

Pesenti lightheartedly converted the classical meter into the regular four-four meter of the Italian eleven-syllable verse (Ex. 5):

Integer vitae scelerisque purus.

Yet, the often repeated assertion that a correct scanning of ancient verse in "modern" music awaited the arrival of the German humanistic ode leaves out of consideration Gafori, who represents a practice that must have been observed by other humanistically inclined musicians and musically inclined humanists in Italy.[31]

There were of course other differences between German and Italian practice. Tritonius started from a previously composed tenor. Pesenti wrote the four parts simultaneously; his harmonic setting is much simpler, and his rhythm has the bounce of the popular frottola. Tritonius' setting has dignity, harmonic variety, and, through its irregularity, a distinctly more interesting rhythm. Artistically superior, the German ode nevertheless owes its principal idea to the Italians.

This is even more evident from the four-part settings of odes and hymns with which Johannes Cochlaeus, humanist, historian, theologian, and musician, concluded his treatise on music, *Tetrachordum musices*, published in Nuremberg in 1511.[32] Clement Miller has shown Cochlaeus' indebtedness to Tritonius both in general and in revealing detail. He has also noted the differences between Cochlaeus and Tritonius with great precision.[33] One might add to his observations that Cochlaeus created a compromise between the classical German style of Tritonius and the Italian *modo de cantar versi latini*.[34] His hymn for St. John illustrates his ode style:

> Ut queant laxis resonare fibris
> Mira gestorum famuli tuorum,
> Solve polluti labii reatum
> Sancte Joannes.
>
> > Free from guilt your servants' unclean lips, holy John, that they may be able to sing with clear voices the wonders of your life.[35]

Here we have a setting (Ex. 6)[36] in which the rigid observation of the meter is loosened by the addition of two note values, the dotted minim and the semiminim, to the point where it agrees with a regular musical meter. Tritonius would of course have written (we abbreviate the note values as does Miller):

Although the humanists, then and today, may consider it blasphemy, the question must be raised whether the boys who were supposed to perform these verses were not in fact reciting them, following ingrained habit, as dotted rhythms whenever one short note followed a long one. Cochlaeus, encouraged by Italian example, may simply have codified what was actually sung. The German musicians who followed Tritonius were undoubtedly intimidated by the authority of the humanists. Cochlaeus was a formidable humanist himself. He felt equally confident of his Latin prosody and his musicianship. There were few like him.

But we are getting ahead of our story. In 1510 Cochlaeus had become rector at the School of St. Lorenz in Nuremberg. Willibald Pirckheimer, wealthy patrician and ardent humanist, one of Nuremberg's most renowned figures at the time of the Reformation, friend and patron of Cochlaeus, was school inspector. He lent his poetical talents to writing a eulogy of the author of the *Tetrachordum musices* that appears right on the title page. Pirckheimer may well have given Cochlaeus the idea to add the four-part settings in humanistic style to his book, previous versions of which did not contain them.[37] Indeed, Cochlaeus may have found Petrucci's frottola books with their *versi latini* in Pirckheimer's library, which he praised as "so rich in books that a similar library in Greek and Latin cannot be found anywhere in Germany."[38] But there may have been manuscript sources for Italian settings of Latin poetry. Pirckheimer had studied at the universities of Padua and Pavia (1489–1495); he might have brought samples of Italian settings with him upon return to his native city. If he later acquired all Greek works of the Aldine Press, why should he, the music lover, not also have bought Petrucci's frottole prints? And if half of Schedel's library is still today in the Staatsbibliothek of Munich, could the huge run of frottole prints there not have come from Pirckheimer's library?

While a rapprochement took place between the ode styles of Nuremberg's Cochlaeus and Venice's Petrucci collections—parallel to the flourishing trade between the two cities—the positions of German humanists and Netherlandish composers with regard to the setting of ancient poetry were poles apart. A polyphonic setting of Dido's last words, *Dulces exuviae*, from the fourth book of Virgil's *Aeneid* (651–654) by the Netherlandish composer Marbriano de Orto (probably a Latinization of Van der Hove), one of the many Northern musicians who migrated to Italy, will illustrate the point (Ex. 7):[39]

> Dulces exuviae, dum fata deusque sinebant,
> accipite hanc animam, meque his exsolvite curis.
> Vixi, et, quem dederat cursum fortuna, peregi;
> et nunc magna mei sub terras ibit imago.
>
>   . . . O relics, dear
>   while fate and god allowed, receive my spirit
>   and free me from these cares; for I have lived
>   and journeyed through the course assigned by fortune.
>   And now my Shade will pass, illustrious,
>   beneath the earth.
>
>   (Mandelbaum)

Throughout the first half of the sixteenth century and beyond, these verses that Virgil put into the mouth of Dido before she killed herself from love and grief were so popular in Italy that their musical settings amounted to a genre in itself.[40] Special attention should be focused on De Orto's application of the text, for the setting of the text is the great bone of contention between humanists and musicians. Whereas the humanists give one note to a syllable, De Orto gives one, two, three, four, at times up to a dozen, notes to one single syllable. Whereas the humanist pays strict attention to quantity and meter, De Orto leaves all matters of prosody aside, frequently neglecting even the correct accent of the word. Whereas the humanist projects the text simultaneously in all four voices, De Orto, in typically Netherlandish fashion, lets every voice proceed with its own portion of the text so that the four parts hardly ever synchronize their declamation of the text. It is this drowning of the text in music that was the object of vehement protests on the part of the humanists. Yet, the Netherlandish master, while indeed forgetful of the poetic body—verse, meter, word, accent—was mindful of its soul: he tried to express in his music some of the emotion that lay behind the words. In this he was, as were so many other composers of the time, under the influence of Josquin des Prez, whose colleague he was as singer of the Papal Chapel in Rome, and who had set the same verses to music.[41]

The examples of humanistic, Italian, and Netherlandish music that we have studied set the stage for the great war now opening between humanism and counterpoint, the war of supremacy between text and music that was going to fill the sixteenth century with a lot of noise and quarrels in Latin and in the vernacular, and at the same time with some of the greatest vocal music ever written. The battle lines were neatly drawn: the Netherlandish position was one of unquestioned supremacy of music; its aim was ever greater refinement of rhythm, melody, counterpoint; its problems were how to reconcile voice-leading with harmony, consonance with dissonance, demands of text expression with demands of counterpoint. The humanistic position was one of unquestioned supremacy of the poetic text, and at the point at which we see it now, it does not acknowledge the existence of a problem: it has solved the only real problem, that of the proper relation between poem and music, by adopting the old Greek idea of subordinating music to poetry, of equating musical rhythm with poetic meter. The humanist felt that he had paid his debt to modern music by clothing metrical declamation in four-part harmony. Yet, when listening to a work like De Orto's *Dulces exuviae*, he must have felt uneasy: to be sure, he could always deride the ignorance displayed with regard to a proper accentuation of Latin and the impossibility of following the text at all, but he could not laugh away the fact that this music was oddly expressive of Dido's state of mind in a way in which the humanistic ode was not. Humanistic thinking on this point can be followed in the long dedicatory address of the humanist Simon Minervius to the second series of humanistic odes published in 1534, in which the famous Swiss composer Ludwig Senfl used the tenor part of the Tritonius odes and gave them a fresh harmonic setting. Minervius, an intimate friend of the late Tritonius, wrote that the latter grew dissatisfied with his odes and wished that the great Senfl try his hand at them. He then reports how fate guided Senfl and himself to the court of Munich, and how carefully he cultivated Senfl's friendship until their relationship had matured to the point where neither would refuse a favor asked of the other. It was then that he told Senfl of Tritonius' greatest wish. Minervius makes it plain what in his opinion qualified Senfl for this task:

For even though Ludovicus be second to none in all that one may praise in a musician . . . he has nonetheless something indefinably his own, and that is that even as an illustrious poet lends expression to his words and moves the passions of his audience, so he too knows how to breathe life into his tones by setting the grandiose in a lofty, the moderate in a calm, the agreeable in a sweet, the sad in a somber manner and with all his art concentrates on the expression of the emotions. This can be found in all of his works, and it will not go unobserved in these compositions which he, in an elegant autograph, inscribed to my name and dedicated to me in such manner that he did not even keep a copy of it for himself.[42]

Several things are clear: it is not the composer who is interested in humanism, it is the humanist who courts, nay, virtually ensnares the musician to do his bidding, to create a music apt to do justice to poetry. Furthermore, Minervius' letter should shatter the general contention that the aims of the German humanists were merely of a pedagogical nature. If it was ever true in the beginning it was no longer true in 1530, when Josquin's music with its new range of expression was known everywhere, when the breezy Italian frottola began to give way to the serious settings of Petrarch's *canzone* and the early madrigal, and when the new French chanson, essentially light and graceful, showed the emergence of a lyrical vein. The humanists now realized that if they wanted to keep in step with the new musical style, they must strive for expression in the same sense in which a great poet strives for it. However, at this point, i.e., about 1530, they still thought that this goal would be reached if only they could persuade great composers to lend their talents to the cause.

Interestingly enough, while Minervius is full of praise for the expressive qualities of Senfl's music and finds them in "all of his works," when it comes to the Latin odes, he modulates to a minor key and says no more than that they, that is, these qualities, "will not go unobserved" in the compositions at hand. Study of Senfl's setting of *Jam satis terris*, for which he took Tritonius' tenor part (Ex. 3), will show that far from exceeding his model, he remains behind it (Ex. 8).

Tritonius invented his *cantus firmus* for the tenor in a manner carefully calculated to result in a logical harmonic organism (see the analysis above). By transposing it one fifth higher and placing it into the second soprano, Senfl deprived the melody of the contrapuntal possibilities it had as a tenor. For harmonic reasons he had to keep Tritonius' key signature of one flat while transposing the *cantus firmus* to C; he ended up with a most unsatisfactory hybrid. Of thirty-eight triads, no fewer than nineteen, fifty percent, are C major chords, seventeen of them in root position. Compare this with ten appearances of F major in Tritonius' setting. More essentially though, Senfl has the C-major chord at all strategic points: at beginning and end of every single one of the four phrases (save the beginning of phrase three), whereas Tritonius terminated the first phrase on the subdominant B-flat major, the second on the dominant, C major, the third phrase on the relative minor, D minor, reserving a return to the tonic, F major, for the end of the piece. Senfl does not succeed in constructing the harmonic arch and the tonal logic of Tritonius. How could this have happened? Had he kept Tritonius' *cantus firmus* in the tenor, it would have been difficult to avoid conspicuous similarities. There were two ways out of this dilemma: he could have written his own *cantus firmus* or he could have composed four-part settings without *cantus firmi*. But this is not what his humanist friend had asked of him. However, even then Senfl, tied to the restrictions of the German ode style, would not have been himself; he would have lacked the freedom to write the music that Minervius, knowing his other works, expected of him.

We have a charming small example of what a freely composed ode of Senfl's would have looked like. The *Liber selectarum cantionum* published by Grimm and Wyrsung of Augsburg in 1520 (RISM 1520[4]) contains an Asclepiadean verse written as a riddle canon in form of a labyrinth, notated as a magic square in breves. Hans Joachim Moser furnished an ingenious solution, clothing it in the meter of the verse, which, in view of its syllabic declamation, was undoubtedly the composer's intention.[43] In an economic format, Senfl uses six chords—one in two forms, as octave-fifth and as a full triad—with splendid harmonic logic and variety, even though he submitted to a severe restriction, but one of his own choosing (Ex. 9):

> Salve, sancta parens, dulcis amor meus
> Virgo pia, salus mundi, coeli porta.
>
>> Hail thee, holy mother, my sweet love,
>> Thou, pious virgin, salvation of Man, door to Paradise.

The humanists failed to see that the severe limitations imposed on every musical element of the Latin odes made it impossible for music to unfold its expressive power: melody cannot soar freely when it is tied to the text in a manner preventing even the slightest melismatic movement; rhythm cannot speak eloquently when it is reduced to two note values; harmony cannot be expressive when dissonance is banished altogether. The text setting cannot be flexible if repetitions of phrases or single words for emphasis or climactic effect are ruled out. The range of expression is limited if the modes are painstakingly observed. This the humanists demanded, since they erroneously assumed that the traditional Dorian, Phrygian, and other modes were identical with the Greek modes of the same name. And finally: did not the humanists give one and the same musical setting to different poetic texts, provided they were in the same meter? How can one and the same music serve two or ten diverse texts? The humanists, after having carefully clipped the wings of the musical Pegasus, were dismayed to find that he could not fly.

III. *Glareanus' Advance*

Humanistic interest in the question of how to wed music to poetry did not remain confined to Germany proper: the Swiss humanist, Henricus Glareanus, in his *Dodekachordon*, published in 1547 but completed some ten years earlier,[44] claims the authorship of Latin odes which, he says, are now sung anonymously throughout Germany. While he does not mind seeing his offspring deprived of his name, he takes exception to his melodies being sung, one to two or more different meters.[45] This passage has been construed as if Glareanus had meant to say that each text ought to receive its own individual setting.[46] A careful reading shows that the Swiss author did not yet espouse so advanced a view. Study of his own odes, nineteen in number, confirms this conclusion. Not only does he give one and the same melody to several odes,[47] he works and reworks certain phrases within one ode and, more remarkably, in a number of different odes.[48]

Nevertheless, Glareanus is fully aware of the need to deviate from the common metrical pattern, "whenever the poet cries out."[49] Indeed, his desire for special emphasis leads him to abandon the sacred principle of humanistic declamation, one note to one syllable. He uses a five-tone melisma rising one third above the octave of the *finalis* of the Dorian mode in setting Horace's ode on the ship which carries Virgil, his friend, to Greece (ode 3 from Book I).[50] The passage celebrates the courage of the man who first braved the terrors of the sea: "Oak and triple bronze must have girt the breast of him who first committed his frail bark to the angry sea."[51] Again, there is nothing individual about this, inasmuch as the same melisma is used (in a lover's lament over Lydia's faithlessness) to praise those couples who never diverge from the path of mutual love: "Thrice happy and more are they whom an unbroken bond unites and whom no sundering of love by wretched quarrels shall separate before life's final day."[52] No other melisma occurs in Glareanus' odes.

In many small ways Glareanus shows his sensitivity to the meaning of the text. He tries to enlarge the limited repertory of musical devices in the ode composition of his day, quoting an ode by Robert Gaugin (1433–1501), also spelled Gaguin, French historian, professor of law, and "enthusiastic Ciceronian . . . [who] was hailed by the younger generation as the father of French humanism."[53] Gaugin's elegiac poem is interesting not only as a sample of French ode composition before 1501, but also for its use of a meter sign (C) and of *proportio tripla*, neither to be found in German ode settings.[54] Glareanus emulates the Frenchman's example, indicating a "more animated" tempo (₵) and using *proportio tripla* no less than three times to enliven the common meter.[55] To give his settings more fluency, Glareanus follows Cochlaeus and Gaugin in replacing Gafori's and Tritonius' breves and semibreves with semibreves and minims, thus escaping, he says, the observance of tactus.[56] To lend life to the quarrel between the lover and Lydia in the famous ninth ode of Book III, *Donec gratus eram tibi*, Glareanus suggests that Lydia's verses be sung by a girl: "and a wonderful pleasure will result."[57] "But," observes our author wisely, "it brings greater pleasure if one changes the harmony [i.e., melody] gracefully according to the subject matter. . . ."

Here Glareanus comes to the heart of the matter, and it is incumbent upon us to see to what extent he, the humanist—but also the devotee of Josquin—succeeds in adapting his tunes to the subject matter. We select two melodies, one for the simplehearted girl "who cannot spin for thinking on the bright beauty of young Hebrus,"[58] the other one, the lament of a sophisticated young Roman of the upper classes over fickle Pyrrha, whose new lover has no notion of how treacherous she is.

The first tune of five tones in major (Ex. 10) is like a child's rhyme in its brevity, simplicity, and formulaic character—Glareanus himself likens it to a dance—unique in the collection of musical settings.[59] Only the first verse is given:

Wretched the maids who may not give play to love nor drown their cares in sweet wine, or who lose heart, fearing the lash of an uncle's tongue.[60]

The second melody Glareanus presents as sample of a through-composed ode.[61] Its text is:

What slender youth, bedewed with perfumes, embraces thee amid many a rose, O Pyrrha, in the pleasant grotto? For whom dost thou tie up thy golden hair in simple elegance? Alas! How often shall he lament changed faith and gods, and marvel in surprise at waters rough with darkening gales, who now enjoys thee, fondly thinking thee all golden, who hopes that thou wilt ever be free of passion for another, ever lovely,—ignorant he of the treacherous breeze. Ah, wretched they to whom thou, untried, dost now appear so dazzling! As for me, the temple wall with its votive tablet shows I have hung up my dripping garments to the god who is master of the sea.[62]

The four verses appear as a long elegant monody in the Phrygian mode ranging over ten tones with well-contrived phrases artfully fitted together (Ex. 11). The building blocks consist mostly of tetrachords and hexachords. The opening phrase rises over two tetrachordal terraces extending over a sixth; the three following phrases descend, either stepwise over a space of a sixth, or over two joined tetrachords covering a hexachord. The plaintive character of the text is fairly mirrored in the prevailing downward trend of the melody and the emphasis on the falling semitone peculiar to the Phrygian mode. Deviations from this pattern invariably echo the "outcry" of love betrayed. In the second stanza, the leap of a rising octave occurs in "heu" (of which "alas" is but a pale reflection); the much more dissonant leap of a major seventh, rarely found in the art music of the time, occurs on the words "Ah, wretched they to whom thou, untried, dost now appear so dazzling!" (line 6). Just as unusual is the leap of a fifth upward, piled, almost immediately, on top of the leap of a seventh. When the deserted lover, not unlike the grateful survivor from a shipwreck, hangs up a votive picture to the god of the sea,[63] the melody returns to the beginning: the last three phrases are borrowed from the first stanza. Such returns to the beginning are quite common in Glareanus' settings, but they reveal a feeling for form rather than for expression. Moreover, we note that the plaintive melody of our ode, its first stanza at any rate, is also set to an entirely different text, the happy praise of Latona, mother of Apollo and Diana (Horace's ode 21, Book I).[64] Yet, when comparing Glareanus' monody with the four-part setting of the same ode by Hofhaimer (Ex. 12),[65] we must acknowledge the former's superiority both in melodic mastery (to be expected in a monodic composition) and certainly in expressiveness: not merely because Hofhaimer, like Tritonius and Senfl, wrote music for the first

verse only, but also because he evidently was thinking chiefly of
the ancient meter, hardly at all of the content of the poem, which
latter task would have called for a fresh setting of each verse.

Like most humanists, Glareanus sought to give added legiti-
macy to his enterprise by inserting metrical settings of religious
poetry; in his case we deal with a double "votive-ode," as it were:
the text presents "the Child Jesus addressing the human race." Its
author is the patron saint of humanists, Erasmus of Rotterdam,
"our teacher."[66] The text of the ode, *Cum mihi sint uni bona, quae
vel frondea tellus / Vel olympus ingens continet*, of which Glareanus
gives only the first four verses, must be a version unknown to
Erasmian scholarship; it seems to precede even the "first draft of
a later and much enlarged poem entitled *Expostulatio Iesu cum ho-
mine suapte culpa pereunte*."[67] The poem played a role in the history
of the Reformation. "In 1523 Zwingli dated the beginning of his
conversion to the reading of this poem eight or nine years earlier."[68] In its later form the poem was printed in 1514.

Glareanus stands midway between the world of the humanist
and the musician. His humanistic position is that of Celtis, for
whom expression lay in the poet's words alone, while music functioned as a soundboard, designed to enhance, but not to color or
express the text.[69] As a musician, on the other hand, he strove to
make music an increasingly faithful mirror of the text, a poem in
tones, as it were. The source of his inspiration, as we shall observe
later, was the newly flourishing literature of treatises on poetics.
Glareanus worshipped at both shrines, not always with an easy
mind.

iv. *Tyard and the* vers mesuré

The next step was taken in France. In 1552 the poet and humanist Pontus de Tyard, a canon and later a bishop, enters the
arena with a glowing defense of ancient poetry and music, issuing
a veritable call to arms addressed to French poets and musicians.
I refer to Tyard's *Solitaire Second*.[70] Like all of Tyard's writings, the
Solitaire Second appears in the form of a dialogue between Solitaire
and Pasithée, the lady whom Solitaire loves and courts.[71] Tinctoris
dedicated his dictionary of musical terms to his royal pupil, Bea-
trice of Aragon, but it took a Frenchman to introduce the genre
of a music treatise in form of a dialogue in which learning and

courtship were fused with an elegance the like of which was not known before in writings on music. It is for Pasithée, Solitaire confesses, that he studied Greek writings on music. It is the wide range of her interests and of her questions that guides all of his studies.

Tyard revived in typically humanistic fashion the ancient ideas about music as the art reflecting the harmony and symmetry of the human body. He quotes exact figures of proportions and says that this is a matter which Albrecht Dürer has reported "très curieusement" in his writings on the symmetry of the human body.[72]

Now if Tyard, who was no expert on art, could know of Dürer's work on the proportions of the human body, there is little reason to doubt that he, who was greatly interested in music, might very well have been acquainted with the musical experiments of the German humanists under the leadership of Conrad Celtis, who, incidentally, was an intimate friend of Dürer's.[73] At any rate, not only do Tyard's ideas on poetry and music agree with those of the Germans—which might be explicable by their common derivation from Greek sources—but Tyard shares with the German humanists the notion of how to set poetry to music, to wit, one note to a syllable and dividing all notes into long and short ones, the two basic note values for the long and short syllables of language.

But there are surprises in Tyard's stand: if he knew the German four-part odes—and I presume he did—he rejected two of the original positions taken by his German confreres: he did not care for the four-part settings,[74] and he made it plain that each text must have its own melody and that this melody must be expressive of the text. In this he went beyond Glareanus, drawing the logical conclusions from the latter's aesthetic premises. He was outspoken in his opposition to counterpoint. Here is what he says:

If it appears to be the aim of music to give to the text such a melody that everyone listening feels impassioned and drawn to the emotion intended by the poet, then the one who knows how properly to compose one single voice appears to me to attain better his professed goal, in view of the fact that the contrapuntal music brings to our ears nothing but a big noise from which one can derive no lively effect. But the simple and unaccompanied voice flowing sweetly and continuously according to the dictates of the meter chosen with regard to the verse is irresistibly ravishing. In this only means then did that overpowering effect of the ancient lyric poets reside who, wedding music to poetry (since they were born for each other), sang their verses, and often achieved the desired effect: for the simplicity observed in the singing of the metric verses is endowed with a secret and marvelous power.[75]

However, now Tyard takes a step so bold that it did not even enter into Celtis' considerations. He transfers the whole problem of the wedding of music and poetry from ancient Greek and Latin to modern French poetry. Even the manner in which he does it is remarkable. One generation before Vincenzo Galilei, Tyard published samples of the Greek letter notation of music—but in giving an example of how the Greek letter notation would look if added to words, he offers not a Greek, but a French, text and tune, and then transcribes both into modern musical notation (Ex. 13):[76]

> Plus, d'une paix rebelle,
> Votre douceur cruelle
> Au travail me dispose,
> Plus je repose.
>
>> The more your cruel sweetness
>> With rebellious peace
>> Disposes me to work
>> The more I rest.
>
> (Elliot Forsyth)

Pontus de Tyard envisaged practically the whole later development of French musical humanism. For in spite of its utter simplicity, the little air for one voice with which he illustrated his ideas is a *vers mesuré en miniature*—and *vers mesuré* is what later Jean de Baïf called the musical settings of French verse in which the meter was faithfully observed. Tyard complains—and he was neither the first nor the last Frenchman to do so—that the French poet is confronted with tremendous difficulties when trying to determine what syllables are short or long. While it is easy in Greek or Latin, it is well-nigh impossible in French and, indeed, this problem occupied the poets of the Académie de Poésie et Musique constantly, and Baïf, of whom more presently, devised his own orthographic system in which he tried to approximate the Greek language so as to facilitate the determination of the proper length of the syllables in a French verse.[77]

Tyard's substitution of French for classical languages corresponds, in beautiful symmetry, to Ronsard's development from a Neo-Latin to a French poet.[78] The two friends, both members of the Pléiade, shared the ideal of a union of poetry and music. In the preface to his odes, Ronsard wrote: "I shall revive, if I can, the use of the lyre resuscitated today in Italy, for the lyre alone should and can animate the verse and give it the right weight."[79] Ronsard called on the greatest French composers of his generation, Janequin, Certon, Goudimel, to set his verses to music—and they did. But two points might be made in this connection: it was a humanist, the amateur composer Marc-Antoine de Muret, who created the most sensitive and faithful musical declamation;[80] and—while Tyard broke radically with the polyphonic practice and used only two note values, long and short, according to the length of the syllables—Ronsard's composers adhered to the customary four-part setting and the rhythmic variety of traditional music within a prevailingly homophonic texture.

This homophonic texture was no novelty in the French chanson. One finds its beginnings in Petrucci's *Odhecaton* (no. 94, *La tura tu* by Bruhier)[81] and his *Canti B* (no. 29, *Et dunt revenis vous* by Compère, or no. 33, *Amours me trocte par la pance* by Lourdoys).[82] A generation later, when Attaingnant initiates his great series of chansons, syllabic declamation goes hand in hand with homophony in a limited number of works such as Claudin de Sermisy's *En entrant en ung jardin* and Janequin's famous *Ce moys de may* in Attaingnant's *Trente et une chansons musicales* (Paris, 1529),[83] while playing a smaller part in many others. It is almost twenty years later that one encounters isolated examples of radical homophony with syllabic declamation and superior accentuation. A splendid example is Arcadelt's *Si sa vertu et grâce* (from Attaingnant's *Vingtcinquiesme livre contenant XXVIII chansons nouvelles*, Paris, 1547).[84] But even here homophony yields at the final cadence to melismatic movement in the two middle voices. Kenneth Levy, in a brilliant paper, has sketched the background of this work.[85] Compositions like this may have served as models for the composers of Ronsard's verses and eventually for the *air de cour*, as Levy demonstrates.[86]

One wonders whether Tyard might not have approved of Arcadelt's *Si sa vertu et grâce*. For while he objected to the contrapuntal music of his time, he had the vision to foresee a polyphonic

music of the future that could do justice to his demands as a poet
and humanist:

Nevertheless, I do not think it impossible to adapt contrapuntal music
properly to the text, nor do I despair of our time: but the difficulty of
our language, not yet measured in certain length or shortness of syllables, and the little attention paid to this matter by our musicians who
all, or for the most part, are not men of letters and lack knowledge of
poetry, combined with the contempt, indeed, the ignorance of music on
the part of our poets, make me fear that it will take a long time until we
shall see good and natural examples of it.[87]

It took just about twenty years.

In 1570 Jean-Antoine de Baïf, French poet and humanist,
spurred on by Jean Dorat, Greek scholar of distinction, founded
the Académie de Poésie et Musique, supported by royal privilege,
in order to create a modern revival of ancient poetry and music
in the French tongue by bringing together poets and musicians.
The *vers mesuré* was the musical form that sprang from these efforts. The French solved the problem which had baffled the German humanists. The latter had blocked a solution by their inability to moderate the extreme position they had taken. The
French saw that the solution lay not only in mustering the best
musical talent available, but also in relaxing the strict conditions
attached to the musical setting of verse. While maintaining an essentially syllabic setting, they allowed enough melismatic orna-
mentation in the soprano to give flexibility and grace to the leading part. They took an entirely fresh approach to the problem of
a harmonic setting by releasing the accompanying voices from the
yoke of strict homorhythmic declamation; the lower voices were
allowed to roam freely and to enliven the soprano melody where
appropriate. With one stroke they rid themselves of rhythmic
poverty and harmonic dryness; the movement in the accompanying voices allowed eighth notes to animate the prevailing quar-
ter- and half-note steps of the soprano and it brought in passing
notes and dissonance. The field was now open for an exploration
of entirely new artistic possibilities by a combination of a metric
declamation of vernacular verse in the soprano with the expressive potentialities of an enriched rhythmic and harmonic palette
in the other voices. The French did away with the uniformity of
four-part settings as well. They used, within one and the same

composition, two, three, four, and five parts, and thus added a variable texture to variable rhythm and harmony. No wonder then that excellent composers such as Claude le Jeune (ca. 1530–1600) and Jacques Mauduit (1557–1627) developed a whole literature of the *vers mesuré* which has an artistic quality and spontaneity far superior to anything achieved by "humanistic" music before. Claude le Jeune's *D'une coline* (Ex. 14) goes with a text curiously similar to Goethe's *Heidenröslein* set to music by Schubert:

D'une coline m'y proumenant
Par la plu vert' et plu gaye saizon,
Quand toute choze rid au chams,
Je voy une Rôze vermeilléte
Qui toute fleuréte de fleur de beauté
Passe de bien loin.

Rechant à 3
    Je la voy de loin,
    Et je l'aime fort,
    Je la veu cuillir,
    Et la main j'y tens,
    Mais las c'est en vain.

Rechant à 5
    Je la voy de loin . . .

        Wand'ring on a greening hill
        In the freshest and gaiest season
        When all things in the fields do smile
        I saw a red rose blooming
        Which in beauty among flowers
        Surpassed ev'ry thing in sight.

        Seeing it from afar,
        Driven by desire,
        How I wish to pick it,
        Now I lift my hand.
        But, alas, in vain.

        Seeing it from afar . . .

Quite aside from a remarkable melodic gift and the crisp and vivacious Gallic rhythm, Le Jeune demonstrates his ability, already praised by his contemporaries, to endow the music with soul. The refrain, in a carefully built harmonic sequence, follows, step by step, the dramatic situation of the youth trying in vain to pick a rose, beautiful but remote. Yet, even the *vers mesuré*, notwithstanding its incomparably higher artistic level and the collaboration of splendid musicians, did not become popular beyond the walls of the Académie and the court, or consequential as a musical art form. With all its charm, it remained a genre outside the mainstream of music.

v. *Italy: Humanism Conquers Polyphony (Freminot, Willaert, Rore, Vicentino, Lasso)*

For the climax of the humanistic influence on music we must turn our attention to Italy. We studied Dido's lament set by De Orto at the end of the fifteenth century. Three settings of Virgil texts from the second third of the sixteenth century will demonstrate how far the musicians had gone to meet the humanistic challenge.

The first one, so far overlooked, is by the obscure Freminot, probably identical with Ferminot, mentioned by Eitner as composer of a four-part setting of an Italian text in a frottola print of 1531.[88] It occurs in MS 1209 D of the Biblioteca Civica of Bergamo, fol. 54ᵛ–55 (see Ex. 15). The manuscript has been dated as of ca. 1545.[89] Freminot's setting of *Dulces exuviae* might go back to the early 1530's. While written in the free polyphonic style of the period, it distinguishes itself by several features that clearly reveal humanistic influence. Foremost among them is the unusual configuration of the soprano. It is the only voice part that gives the words one note per syllable (save for the deceptive five-measure introduction). And not only is the text recited syllabically in the leading voice, but also with an accentuation uncommonly good, though not yet perfect. Why then did Freminot not go all the way and set the text in simultaneous syllabic declamation in all four voices? In that case measures six to eleven, for example, would sound like this:

instead of

Not only are rhythm and texture infinitely richer, the lengthened rhythms, the syncopations and resulting dissonances, the semi-tone appoggiatura with B-flat (m. 9) and the clash of a major seventh (bass and alto) with a minor seventh (tenor and soprano) in measure 10 resolving in the hollow sound of three parallel fourths add a poignancy that lend Dido's last words the bitterness without which her state of mind cannot be communicated. And at this stage music wishes nothing more urgently than to become portrayal in tones of the human psyche. To this end Freminot chose the low tessitura, the prevailing minor, the Phrygian mode which, with its downward pull and descending semitones, conveys the despair of Dido over Aeneas' betrayal. Artistic trends are never more obvious than when they appear in the work of a minor, indeed, a very minor, composer.

Writing probably a full generation later than De Orto, Freminot stands no less under Josquin's spell than his predecessor, but now the text comes out with great clarity in the soprano part, while the melismatic motion in the other voices is carefully confined to enhancing the meaning of the text: "free me from these cares" (mm. 20–23), "I have lived" (mm. 25–28), "I have journeyed through" (mm. 32–38), etc. Nor can Fortuna's uncertain step be depicted without rhythmic freedom of the voices and syncopation. Whereas De Orto's voices had basically the same character and outline, Freminot, to achieve his effects, had to give his voice parts contrasting roles—with mixed success. Assigning to the soprano the task of reciting the words syllable by syllable does bring out the text, but it weakens the leading part's ability to express it. It also creates a discrepancy between the voices.

This is the problem to which Adrian Willaert addressed himself in his setting of *Dulces exuviae*, published in 1545[90] (Ex. 16). His object is the same, but his means differ. For Willaert as for Freminot, the text stands in the foreground. But now all voices share in the task of making the words heard and felt. Willaert is aware of the dominating role of the soprano in projecting *and* expressing the text. The declamation is prevailingly syllabic, but in all voices alike. In contradistinction to the slow pace of Freminot's recitation in even breves and semibreves, which makes Dido appear as a tired old woman, Willaert's Dido, speaking in semibreves, minims, pointed dotted rhythms, and energetic upbeats, comes forth as a woman of strength and emotion. This impression is intensified by well-planned acceleration and the deft use of minim rests and melismatic motion in seminimims. The soprano melody, too, breathes sentiment and affection. It suffices to compare the two settings of the words "and free me from my cares" (*meque his exolvite curis*): one crawling, as it were, at snail pace in a small ambit, the other, with quickening step, rising from a low, semitone-centered range to a minor sixth, as in a pained outcry. The texture keeps a miraculous balance between counterpoint and homophony, giving melodic and rhythmic life without obstructing comprehension of Virgil's verses. A new clarity and quiet energy emerge, unifying music and text beyond anything that Freminot would have been aiming at or been able to achieve. Freminot already had the four voices meet in triads based on the root. In place of the older composer's strict modal observance, Willaert offers a harmonic texture of shimmering colors. In a nominally Phrygian mode and a harmonic ambit from E major through B-flat major (mm. 35–43) Willaert uses all major chords between these two poles. Careful notation of accidentals insures the frequent appearance of D major, A major, and E major chords mixed with G, C, and F major and the minor chords on E, A, D in a constantly changing blend that follows the sense of the words. Dido's offering of her life to the gods (*accipite hanc animam*) is expressed in a melodic ascent in major; the plea for release from her suffering (*[meque his] exolvite curis*) is set in minor chords; *Vixi*, whose two slow chords should be sung *decrescendo*, sounds like a choral sigh, whereas the "varied course" that Fortune imposed on Dido's life appears rhythmically accelerated in a modulatory movement gliding from E major through A, D, G, C, and F major into a cadence tending toward A minor but resolving in the single note A.

Willaert—"Adriano" as the Italians fondly call him—is the only composer in the context of our study whose humanistic mentors (whom he certainly had) are unknown. But humanism was so pervading an intellectual force in the Venice of his time (he held the post of chapelmaster at San Marco from 1527 to his death in 1562) that it did not take a single figure of overshadowing authority[91] to explain Willaert's turn to a style that held the equilibrium between the demands of humanism and of the art of music with a precision and finesse that aroused the admiration of all: musicians, humanists, connoisseurs, music lovers—and theorists. It is from his works that Zarlino deduced the famous ten rules of text underlay[92] and Kaspar Stocker, the German student, friend, and assistant of Francisco Salinas of Salamanca, drew the extensive treatment of the same problem in his tract *De musica verbali.*[93]

Even more important than the theorists were the composers who studied with Willaert, none of them more so than Cipriano de Rore. A Fleming, like his teacher, he had come to Italy to stay; he acquired such fame that after long years of brilliant activity at the court of Ferrara, and later at Parma, he became successor to his master at San Marco in Venice. Having absorbed everything there was to learn from the indubitably greatest teacher of the century, he added something entirely his own to the style and technique taken over from his model: a fiery, passionate temperament that endows his music with a sense of emotional power and urgency. Instead of the *ultima verba Didonis*, he chose the scene that shows the Queen in the first vehement reaction to Aeneas' betrayal, *Dissimulare etiam sperasti* (Ex. 17):[94]

Dissimulare etiam sperasti, perfide, tantum
posse nefas tacitusque mea decedere terra?
nec te noster amor nec te data dextera quondam
nec moritura tenet crudeli funere Dido?

> "Deceiver, did you even hope to hide
> so harsh a crime, to leave this land of mine
> without a word? Can nothing hold you back—
> neither your love, the hand you pledged, nor even
> the cruel death that lies in wait for Dido?"
>
> (Mandelbaum)

Instead of casting the scene in one continuous whole for a quartet of voices, as does Willaert, he divides it into three parts for five, six, and seven voices, building a steady crescendo. Like his master he faithfully observes long and short syllables, but he adopts more radically the humanistic demand to make the text clearly understood by giving Dido's words a strictly syllabic setting and an exceptionally articulate declamation. On the other hand, he rejects the humanistic principle to tie music to meter (word accent supersedes metric accent); he refuses to shun text repetition (indeed, right in the first line he reiterates Dido's *perfide* with marvelous effect) and he repeats whole phrases to increase or decrease tension; he declines tying all voices in lockstep to strictly synchronized declamation when excitement calls for a rhythmic crescendo to be reached only by staggering the rhythmic entries of the voices (mm. 32–36). Responding to the emotional state of a woman, a queen, deceived in love, he fashions the soprano melody of the strident initial lines of accusation prevailingly in large ascending intervals accompanied by harmonies chiefly in major. He uses small melodic steps and mainly minor harmonies in the third line where Dido reminds Aeneas of their love and the vows exchanged; he goes beyond the confines of the mode and sets the last line, in which Dido announces her determination to die, to an effective modulation, uniting in one phrase the (rarely used) B minor and B-flat major. Throughout the *prima pars* he shuns cadences altogether, achieving thereby an austerity novel in its dramatic conciseness.[95]

Rore also employed this style occasionally in his madrigals. Einstein shows how he "applies the free declamatory style of certain compositions from the second book of four-voiced madrigals to his five-part pieces, and this affords him an even greater freedom in alternating half-choirs of four and three voices."[96] The lengthy quotation from *Se ben il duol che per voi, donna, sento* (Book IV of five-part madrigals, 1557—"the last to appear during Rore's lifetime") is particularly interesting for us. It is written in a homophonic texture entirely devoid of full cadences, in the idiom of modulatory harmony, syllabic declamation, and a recitative-like melody: its rhythm is so free that Einstein dispenses with barlines—a condition that prevailed also in the German odes.

It is this wedding of humanistic principles in the broadest sense of the word with the principle of musical expression that gives Rore's music its special quality and explains why Monteverdi, forty years after the master's death, still referred to him as *il Divino Cipriano Rore*,[97] and why the first historians of melodrama speak of him as opera's spiritual father. Indeed, if the lower voices were executed by instruments and only the soprano sung, we would have an early model of dramatic monody (Ex. 18).[98]

We might ask what proof, direct or indirect, exists that Rore knew anything at all about the humanistic ode that we implicitly consider to be at the root of his setting of Virgil's verses. An answer is provided by the piece following *Dissimulare* in the Rore codex of Munich. It is the music to Horace's ode 9 of Book III, *Donec eram gratus tibi* (Ex. 19).[99] The dialogue between Horace and Lydia, already composed for one voice by Glareanus, who, as we saw earlier, proposed that it be sung alternately by a man and a woman, is here set for two choirs of four parts each, one for low and one for high voices, the two choirs uniting at the end when the quarreling lovers decide to make up. Here the syllabic declamation paired with homophonic texture is observed even more strictly; rests, syncopations, and dotted note values as well as rhythmic liberties of individual voices and small melismatic movements give occasional relief. Again, word accent replaces measured recitation. But there can be no doubt that only the humanistic ode could have provided the stimulus for a texture so far removed from the polyphonic style of Rore's general output. Being surrounded, wherever he worked, by men of letters, by humanists and poets, he might very well have been asked by one of his friends or patrons to write music corresponding to the humanistic ideals that were in the air quite generally.

Soon these musical tendencies assumed a bolder, more radical character. In their quest for an enriched scale of musical expression, the Italians grew fascinated by one aspect of Greek music which the German humanists had completely ignored and to which the French paid but scant attention: all Greek modes could be rendered in three different *genera*, the diatonic, the chromatic, and the enharmonic. The chromatic gender called for a series of half-tone steps, the enharmonic for a series of quarter-tone steps in succession. The use of such intervals lay entirely outside the medieval system of church modes; it presented difficulties of a practical, theoretical, and philosophical nature destined to arouse heated controversy.[100] The progressive wing of Italian and Italianate composers invoked the authority of ancient Greece to introduce chromaticism and even quarter tones into their new and highly experimental music.

The spokesman for the Italian avant-garde was Nicola Vicentino, whose patron was Cardinal Ippolito d'Este of Ferrara. As early as 1549 Vicentino instructed some gentlemen in Rome in the mysteries of ancient Greek music and in the art of how to apply the chromatic and enharmonic scales to modern music.[101] These gentlemen were sworn to secrecy, and Vicentino might have continued such secrecy, had it not been for the fact that, in 1551, he lost a wager in a public disputation with a singer of the Papal Chapel in a manner so decisive and accompanied by such publicity that he wrote his famous treatise *L'antica musica ridotta alla moderna prattica* ("Ancient music applied to modern practice"), publishing it four years later in the same Rome in which the event had taken place.[102]

Vicentino's objective was not so much a revival of Greek music as the creation of a modern music capable of the most intense and most varied expression. For this he needed a new aesthetics and new musical means; both were furnished by Greek theory.[103] The use of chromaticism was only one of many means to achieve such flexibility of the musical language. Other means were modulation from one key to another, use of dissonance in ways frowned upon thus far, prohibited intervals, a rhythm capable of great contrasts, *ritardando* and *accelerando* as well as dynamic shading in performance. To illustrate to what degree the humanistic ideas of text declamation had affected the music of the Italian madrigal, I take the opportunity to present a work not published in Vicentino's *Opera omnia*,[104] since it came to light only recently in the Tarasconi Codex, whose disappearance Einstein had deplored[105] and which has now surfaced in the Library of the Conservatorio Giuseppe Verdi of Milan.[106] Doubly significant because it is another large sixteenth-century manuscript in score,[107] and because it contains no fewer than eighty-nine madrigals of Cipriano de Rore—in both of these respects comparable to the huge Bourdeney manuscript acquired some twenty-five years ago by the Bibliothèque Nationale of Paris,[108]—it has a number of *unica*, among which is Vicentino's *Era sereno il ciel* (Ex. 20):[109]

Era sereno il ciel, chiara la luce
Del sol più che l'usato
Quel giorno che l'amato
Mio ben, mia speme e mia fidata duce
Mi dimostrò col suo leggiadro viso
Quanto di bel può darne il paradiso.

Ond'io ringratio amore
Che mi scorges[s]'all'hora
A mirar il splendor di quella luce
Ch'il suo regn'honora
E in cui si vede bellezza rara
Come stella nel ciel lucente e chiara.

> Serene the sky, more luminous the sun than ever
> That day, on which my love, my hope,
> My trusted guide revealed to me
> Her beauteous face, and with it
> How much delight the paradise can offer.

> Whence I give thanks to Amor,
> Who saw me then behold the splendor
> Of that light which exalts his reign
> In which one sees so rare a beauty
> As of the brightest star shining on heaven's vault.

Not a great poem nor, probably, a quite correct text. Eleven- and seven-syllable lines alternate irregularly. The rhyme scheme of the *prima pars* is *abbacc* and should perhaps be *dedeff* in the *secunda pars* instead of the *deaeff*. Should not the line in question read: "A mirar di quella luce il splendore" (in which case we would have the expected rhyme sequence)?

Vicentino's four-part madrigal is as interesting for what it does as for what it avoids. To begin with the latter: it steers clear of the traditional techniques of counterpoint of the period: there is no independent melismatic melody, no motivic work, no thematic imitation, no artful weaving of contrapuntal voices; even poly-rhythmic animation of harmony is carefully restrained. Instead, we find a recitative-like melody full of tone repetitions, moving mostly in note values of quarters and eighths, which, in *alla breve*, result in speech-like rhythm, overwhelmingly syllabic declamation reinforced by strong emphasis on homophony and pseudo-homophony, and a very restricted melodic ambitus. Vicentino moved from the solemn metric recitation of the Latin ode to a lively human speech melody rendered sophisticated through a tricky rhythm abounding in syncopation, upbeats, and unexpected accelerations, retards, and sudden stops, and made spicy through a harmony bristling with false relations, unusual dissonances, strange modulatory movements, and even direct chromaticism—none of which, oddly enough, seems justified by the text. We observe a change from the uniform four-part writing of the humanistic ode to a constantly varying texture turning from four to three and two voices, and even sudden compressions of four voices into one single note. All these are qualities that mark the work as a representative of humanistic principles in Italian secular music and of the maneristic style.[110] The musician copying the piece must have thought well of the composer, or else he had tongue in cheek when he wrote at the end of the *prima parte*: "Di Don Nicola Vicentino de i Vicentini arcimusico."

To distinguish between the traditional style and the so-called *nuova maniera*, Vicentino opposed *musica comuna* and *musica riserbata*, which latter he defined not only as music reserved for the aristocratic elite and the sophisticated ear but also as music reserved for the use of the chromatic and enharmonic *genera*.[111] The term *musica reservata* became a symbol and a slogan for the new trend of expressive realism in music. It emerges again in connection with the music of the foremost representative of the new aesthetics, Orlando di Lasso, in whose immense oeuvre we encounter proofs of familiarity with humanistic ideas on the musical settings of classical poetry. We quote the initial verse of his six-part setting of Virgil's famous first eclogue, *Tityre, tu patulae* (Ex. 21), a poem that has been considered to hold a "key to the literary tradition of Europe."[112]

> Tityre, tu patulae recubans sub tegmine fagi
> Silvestrem tenui musam meditaris avena;
> Nos patriae fines et dulcia linquimus arva:
> Nos patriam fugimus: tu, Tityre, lentus in umbra
> Formosam resonare doces Amaryllida silvas.

>> Thou, where this beech doth spread her close-leafed tiers,
>> Liest outstretched, O Tityrus, and wooest
>> The sylvan muse with that slim reed of thine;
>> We from our country's bounds, her dear, dear fields,

> We from our country's self must fly; while thou
> Dost idle here in shade, teaching the woods
> To echo "Amaryllis beautiful."

To demonstrate that he knew well how to scan the hexameters, the composer observed the meter strictly[113] in the first lines of the *prima* and *secunda pars*, while straying from it in the remainder of the poem, indicating thereby that he belonged to the tradition of Willaert and Rore who assigned priority to meaning over meter. On both counts the work merited to be rated as *musica reservata*— and, indeed, it was.[114] Compared with Tritonius or Forster, Lasso, like Willaert, Rore, and Vicentino, expands the harmonic space. In this setting it embraces seven major and four minor chords between E major and B-flat major, a number of sixth chords and syncopated dissonances, allowing thereby greater liberty in the choice of unusual harmonic combinations.

Another motet clearly written under humanistic inspiration is his wedding poem *Pronuba Juno*.[115] But it is in the five-part setting of a capricious Neo-Latin poem which—in studied opposition to the ancients' praise of gods and heroes—curses the plague of beasts and humans, the flea, that Lasso honors the principles of the humanistic ode writers almost to a T.[116] Boetticher, who usually prints poems written in classical meters true to the metric alignment, failed to recognize that this poem consists of four distichs and that Lasso carefully distinguished between hexameters and pentameters:[117]

> Bestia curvafia pulices proch posoniensis
>   Progenies pungunt. Bestia curvafia.
> Persimilis peditum passum[118] proterva pediclis
>   Praefocanda pigra. Bestia curvafia.
> Perlustrat pectus poplites pellesque politas
>   Propugnat passim. Bestia curvafia.
> Pellantur pulices pelagus perdatque pediclos
>   Profundum pastos. Bestia curvafia.

> The crooked beast, the flea, woe, the poisonous
> Race stings. The crooked beast!
> Just so stings the louse the wanderer's foot.
> The lazy, wanton breed that should be crushed,
> It crawls through breast and hollow knee,
> Attacks at random the clean skin, the crooked beast!
> May all the fleas be routed! May the deep sea
> Swallow up the lice sucked full [of blood]! The crooked beast!

We quote the first distich (Ex. 22, mm. 1–11). Throughout, Lasso maintains the meter in strict homophony. Only at the pronunciation of the curse, at the fourth distich, where the poisonous insects are sent to their death in the depths of the sea, does the composer set four voices in syncopation against the immovable tenor; still every voice part observes the meter meticulously. Even here where Lasso sets out to write in the simplest harmonic idiom of the century—in the 1570's the ode style had lost the novelty it had in 1507—he cannot suppress his individuality; it lights up in the modulatory harmony, in the isolated break with the homorhythmic pattern, in the variable texture, and in the institution of a full-voiced refrain *Bestia curvafia* which begins and ends the piece, and articulates the close of each of the four distichs, introducing thereby a form element quite unknown in the traditional ode composition. Also, while adhering to the humanistic position not to violate the integrity and continuity of the poetic text by repetitions, at the end, for final affirmation, he repeats the refrain.

Boetticher considers the text as belonging to the spheres of student poetry; this might explain Lasso's choice of a pattern at home in the humanistic ode created originally for the young students of Latin—a connection overlooked by Boetticher, who apologizes for the "questionable joke," which—he emphasizes—"the master permitted to be published only in French prints."[119] He feels sure that the work cannot "tarnish the image of Lasso's venerable Muse." Do we really need to apologize for the master's robust sense of humor, manifest in his German Lieder as well as in his French chansons or his Italian *villanelle* and *moresche*—a humor that does not shrink back from satirizing all classes of people, including monks and nuns?[120] Why should what we find acceptable in literature, in Shakespeare or Rabelais, become unacceptable in music? Why should we deny the great figures in music the full-blooded humanity that we admire in the writers and painters of the age?

And the musicians of the Renaissance, Lasso above all, share to a much greater degree in the literature and painting of their time than did those of preceding centuries. The Italian madrigal is unthinkable without Italian poetry; its evolution, as Alfred Einstein has so convincingly demonstrated in his *magnum opus, The Italian*

Madrigal, cannot be explained without constant reference to the changing tone and style of the texts. This goes for the various national song literatures as well. Lasso sets Italian, French, German, and Neo-Latin poems to music; nor does he shun the lowly poetry in Neapolitan dialect: and each literature calls forth a specific musical vein in him. If, in its beginnings, humanism in music manifested itself in the drastic curtailment of all musical elements, now, in the compositions of Lasso and his contemporaries, it had conquered music from the inside: rhythm, melody, harmony, consonance and dissonance, texture and structure, every single musical element now obeys the impulse of the poetic text. Not without good reason did Samuel Quickelberg, physician and humanist at the court of Munich, in the commentary on Lasso's *Penitential Psalms*, composed as a companion volume to the illuminated codex of the music, write: "He expressed [the content] so aptly with lamenting and plaintive melody, where necessary adapting [the music] to the subject and the words, expressing the power of the individual emotions, presenting the subject as if acted before our very eyes. . . . This kind of music they call *musica reservata*."[121]

For illustration of Lasso's *musica reservata* I choose a posthumous, undoubtedly late work in which the composer, at the height of his creative powers, paints a pastoral idyl in tones. As the painter's eye moves continuously back and forth from the object of his observation to his canvas, so Lasso follows in every tone of a rich five-part texture the various phases of an idyllic scene, indeed, every single concept of the text (Ex. 23):

> Dulci sub umbra sirium vitans
> piger dum fistulam inflo rusticam,
> cantans meos felix amores,
> candidam puellulam, hoedi et caprae
> attendunt ovesque me meae.
>
>> Under the sweet shade, shunning the midday heat, I rest, blowing upon the rustic flute. Happily, I sing of my loves, of the fair maiden. My goats, my kids and sheep listen to me.

My search for the identity of the poet remained fruitless. Certain it is that it is not a classical author. But my learned friend, Ernst Manasse, Professor Emeritus of Philosophy and Classics at North Carolina Central University, showed me that the Neo-Latin poet followed closely the pastoral models of Virgil: "Almost all of the motifs of *Dulci sub umbra* also occur in the *Eclogues*: the shepherd's rest in the shade, the rustic flute, the chant about his love and the beloved, the company of goats, sheep, and kids." He also assured me that my translation of "Sirius" as "midday" rather than "summer (heat)" was correct: "Sirius, in this context, may, as it does in the *Georgics*, not only mean the summer heat, but also, more specifically, the midday climax of a hot summer day" (letter of July 12, 1978).

The Virgilian poem inspired Lasso to an extraordinary effort. The beginning on an E-flat major chord, unusual for its time, and the softly gliding modulation from E-flat to B-flat major, F major, C minor, and G major are designed to paint the dark, sweet shade in which the shepherd rests. The recitation on the D-major chord evokes the brightness of the midday sun; the word *piger* ("lazy") is set on long-held C-major chords, the soprano limping behind the other voices and ending in the symbol of perfect laziness, a rest. On the words *dum fistulam inflo rusticam* ("while I play on the rustic reed") the soprano starts a sweet melody of undeniably pastoral inspiration, accompanied in parallel sixths by the tenor, and inverted in parallel thirds on its repetition an octave lower by the two tenors, while all the time the bass holds on to the low humming note of F as in a bagpipe concert. These are only a fleeting three measures, but they hold the key to the whole genre of the later instrumental pastorale which favors F major, a bagpipe pedal tone, parallel thirds and sixths, and simple and pleasant tunefulness. The first expansion into richly melismatic melody occurs on the word *cantans*. On the words *candidam puellulam*, the image of a fair maiden is invoked by a tercet of the high voices and by the graceful lines of the only passage in the motet employing extensively the fast-moving eighth notes. The concluding sentence, *hoedi et caprae attendunt ovesque me meae* ("the kids and the goats and my sheep listen to me"), offers the composer a chance for a unique ballet of sheep and goats. Even the text of the unknown poet participates through the intentional juxtaposition of the words *me meae* in a realistic sheep concert. An upbeat motif evoking the picture of a rearing goat is capriciously exploited in a confused jumble of stretti; one voice interrupts the other, the motif being sung alternately with the long notes on the strong beat and in syncopated fashion with the long notes on the weak beat. The motet concludes with yodel-like calls echoing from the mountains.

Lasso is the foremost tone painter of his time. The touchstone of his work is the originality of the music, its richness of imagination, its vivaciousness and variety stimulated by the images conjured up in the text of the poem. Lasso was indeed motivated by the professed aim of *musica reservata*, "to place the subject before our very eyes." His work is representative of the direction in which the music of the Cinquecento moved. The struggle between counterpoint and text was decided in favor of the text. Counterpoint was not abolished; it was transformed into a tonal language of the most subtle and flexible expressiveness. The transformation of counterpoint from an autonomous force obeying its own set of rules into a servant of poetry, following in rhythm, melody, harmonic color, and dissonance every nuance of the text, marks the reconciliation of Italian humanism with Netherlandish counterpoint.

vi. *Andrea Gabrieli's* Edipo tiranno

If in the last quarter of the sixteenth century a composer had taken it upon himself to set to music not just a few verses of a classical poet, but, say, the choruses for a whole Greek tragedy (not in Greek, but in Italian translation), if he had decided to adapt the humanistic principles in the way shown by Cipriano de Rore and Orlando di Lasso, what might his score have looked like? In the first place, we would expect to find fairly strict syllabic declamation of the text in a prevailingly homophonic texture. In compensation for the lack of melismatic melody and counterpoint, we would anticipate modulatory harmony, dissonance, variable texture, a rhythm dictated not by a poetic meter, but by the accent of the word—accent being understood as originating in the emotion as well as in the grammatical form of the word, and therefore of great diversity. If we found all that, should we then still have qualms about ranging these works among the fruits of humanistic inspiration?

We do in fact find all that, and more, in Andrea Gabrieli's choruses written for the performance of Sophocles' *Edipo tiranno* in the translation of Orsatto Giustiniani staged for the opening of Andrea Palladio's theater in Vicenza in the year 1585.[122] Both construction of the theater and the performance of the Greek tragedy were undertaken by the Accademia Olympica of Vicenza—which accounts for the whole idea and for the humanistic cast of the music. But Gabrieli goes beyond our expectations: unlike Rore and Lasso, he allows no repetitions of text save the occasional final line of a chorus; his harmonic spectrum includes the boldest chromatic colors,[123] intense rhythmic contrasts with a particularly intriguing use of rests; the variable texture has everything possible within a six-part framework, including solo passages. What emerges is a music of exceptional power, a blend of firmest melodic restraint, harmonic diversity, and rhythmic vitality, in which the text shines forth in austere beauty. Two examples may suffice:

> Doubled are the hymns;
> And the voice, often broken,
> Resounds with sobs and crying (Ex. 24).

Andrea Gabrieli, madrigalist turned humanist extraordinary, succeeds in uniting the opposites, strictest discipline of syllabic declamation with intense, if controlled, expression: "raddoppiano" doubles the rhythm, "inni" receives an air of solemnity in the slowing down and the chromatic progression from D to B major, the "voice" speaks in the recitation on a single chord, "interrotta" literally interrupts the word with a rest, "singulti" likewise imitates a sob by breaking the word into two parts, changing the harmony to the flat region and pausing for half a measure, "crying" is suggested in the harmonic movement from F to D major over a held note in the soprano.

> He who wickedness, sinful, does not abhor, nor flee (Ex. 25).

The rash steps of the wicked are depicted in the fast rhythm, the "sinful" is expressed in the prohibited leap of a diminished fifth in the soprano, the unusual skip of a seventh in the bass, and the jump from a G-major chord to a D-minor sixth chord, continuing with F major, G major and stopping cold in a repeated slow D major followed by a pause; this sequence of chords leading nowhere symbolizes the rejection implicit in "aborisce," while the succeeding three quick chords on C and G major, starting with an upbeat and stopping on a quarter note on the weak beat followed by a rest, picture "flight"—an ending in mid-air, as it were, never coming down to earth. (To achieve a conclusion, the G major would have to be anchored in an authentic cadence and end on the strong beat in a long note, as in Example 26.)

Gabrieli, even more radically than Rore in his Dido motet, steers clear of any and all cadential formulas. Music of this kind enables us to solve the riddle of a passage on *musica reservata* that has long puzzled musical scholars. The Besançon treatise on counterpoint from the acts of the Synod of Besançon (1571) was published by W. Bäumker a full century ago.[124] In 1938 Helmuth Osthoff noted for the first time the passage dealing with *musica reservata*.[125] The sentence in question says: "In rhythmo autem continuo clausulam fugies, ut fiat, quam vocant musicam reservatam" ("But in continuous rhythm you shall flee the clausula so as to bring forth what they call *musica reservata*"). The obstacle to a clear understanding lies in the concept "rhythmus continuus," which refers to a rhythm not interrupted by the syncopations of the traditional clausula. The ordinary cadential formulas with their syncopated rhythm and melismatic flourishes prevent syllabic declamation, which is an essential part of *musica reservata*, whose core resides in the close relationship between word and tone. As shown earlier, Zarlino's *fuggire la cadenza* has nothing to do with the radical avoidance of cadence as practiced by Rore, Lasso, Gabrieli, and other composers. Now we find it theoretically attached to the concept of *musica reservata* by the unknown author of the Besançon treatise.[126]

Leo Schrade, to whom we owe the first edition and study of *Edipo tiranno*, raises the question of Gabrieli's models. He rejects, in succession, the music for dramas performed in Venice and other North Italian cities (of which of course very little remains), the *canzona villanesca* or the *giustiniane* with their homophony, the settings of Horatian odes in Petrucci's *frottola* collections, declaring instead that "one sole category can have served as model: psalmody. The simplicity of composing in note-against-note technique brings to mind the fauxbourdon which one associates with psalmody and analogous genres"—an astonishing conclusion, considering that the fauxbourdon had been thoroughly dead for over one century and was held in low esteem by sixteenth-century theorists and composers alike,[127] astonishing also in view of the irreconcilable conflict between the two settings, the one in three-part fauxbourdon, the other in five-part triadic harmony; the former using one single chord form, the sixth chord (apart from the octave-fifth of beginning and end), the latter a whole gamut of diverse chords, consonant and dissonant; the former tied to the diatonic mode, the latter employing not only all possibilities afforded by *musica ficta*, but also by direct chromaticism; the former presenting a succession of constantly repeated psalmodic formulas adapted to the changing prose text, the latter freed of any formulas whatever, even those of the cadence, each line of the poetic text set afresh.[128]

The real model for Gabrieli's enterprise is the humanistic ode at the point of development to which great composers like Rore and Lasso[129] had brought it. Even madrigals such as Vicentino's *Era sereno il ciel* (Ex. 20) belong to the prototypes of Gabrieli's style, the slight contrapuntal freedom and the sparing use of traditional cadence formulas notwithstanding. But out of these elements the aged Venetian master shaped a unique ensemble of soloistic and choral combinations, presenting in his choruses the people of Thebes as they participate, with intense empathy, in the tragedy of Oedipus and Iocasta, which was also the tragedy of Thebes. Gabrieli preceded the opera of the Florentine Camerata composers by fifteen years. The choruses of Peri's and Caccini's operas were not imitations of those in *Edipo tiranno*. Unquestionably, however, they originated in the same humanistic tradition. While their music was conceived in a harmonic language closer to modern major and minor, the texture of their choruses was for the most part homophonic and their declamation answered the chief demands of the humanists. The Orphean myth that inspired medieval poets and musicians and became a humanistic symbol for music's power was seized upon by Peri and Caccini for their first operas in the *stile rappresentativo* of the Florentine Camerata.[130] Both use the chorus in the great humanistic tradition outlined here. I choose as example Caccini's chorus, *Se de boschi* (Ex. 26):

> Se de boschi i verdi onori
> raggirar su' nudi campi
> fa stridor d'orrido verno,
> sorgono anco e frond'e fiori

appressando i dolci lampi
della luce il carro eterno.

> Even if the green glory of the woods
> is stripped on the barren fields
> by the jarring noise of horrid winter,
> still the plants and flowers will grow again
> as the sweet light
> from the celestial chariot approaches.
>
> (Howard Mayer Brown)

Set for five voices in syllabic homophony, only two well-placed melismas quicken the step of the eight-syllable lines, six in all, twice repeated to new stanzas. If tone and style are close to the *vers mesuré*, the destination of the work for the wedding of Marie de' Medici and Henri IV of France may have acted as a supplementary reason.

In the case of Peri and Caccini we are well informed about the carriers of the humanistic tradition behind them; it is the Florentine Camerata in the homes of Count Bardi and Jacopo Corsi, meeting points of poets, scholars, and musicians.[131]

VII. *Andrea Gabrieli's Humanistic Mentor*

But who was the humanist responsible for the education of Andrea Gabrieli? The answer to this question is given in a treatise on poetics by Bernardino Daniello of Lucca printed in Venice in 1546,[132] overlooked so far by Andrea's biographers.[133] Daniello offers his "Poetics" in form of a dialogue between Trifone Gabrieli, his two nephews, Andrea and Jacopo Gabrieli, and himself. He puts the conversation in the month of May 1533[134] and places it at Trifone's small villa in Bassano, on the left bank of the river Brenta in the midst of the green valleys and pleasant hills of the Veneto.

Trifone Gabriele (also Gabrieli or Gabrielli), 1471–1549, was a patrician and one of the intellectual luminaries of Venice. Having entered the priesthood, he found that the passion for his studies caused him to neglect his ecclesiastic duties. In 1515, at Trifone's request, Pietro Bembo secured for him from Leo X an absolution from his priestly duties and the vow "not to read books of pagan authors" (*de libris gentilium non legendis*).[135] When he was proposed for the patriarchate of Venice in 1524, but not elected, Trifone wrote to his brother Francesco: "I thank the illustrious Senators [of the Republic of Venice], those who proposed, and those who opposed me; the former for the confidence they placed in me, the latter for the good they have done me. For others the mitres and the crowns! *Rura mihi et rigui placeant in vallibus amnes* ("For me the countryside, the gardens, and the rivers in the valleys"; Virgil, *Georgica* 2, 485).[136] Fleeing offices and honors, he gave himself entirely to the study of Greek, Latin, and Italian letters—surrounded by a circle of devoted students whom he instructed, free of charge, teaching above all Horace's *Ars poetica*, Cicero's *De oratore*, Virgil's verses, reading with them Dante and Petrarch, and discussing the beauties and the defects of each. He was known as the "Venetian Socrates" and he was immortalized in the works of his students, friends, and admirers. Donato Giannotti, the Florentine historian of Venice, in his *Libro dela Republica de' Vinitiani* (Rome, 1540, but concluded in 1527[137]) introduces Trifone Gabrieli in a dialogue as his chief authority for the constitution and history of Venice.[138] The dialogue is held in the villa of Trifone's lifelong friend and admirer, Pietro Bembo, who "held his mind in greater esteem than all human riches."[139] In 1553 Jason de Nores published a book on Horace's *Ars poetica* "in the interpretation taken over from Trifone Gabrieli's daily lectures."[140] In a dedication to his brother, de Nores reports how he received the news of Gabrieli's death, and gripped by unspeakable pain, broke out in tears, "for what more sorrowful, more bitter event could reach me in this life than the death of the man to whom I owe more than I can ever put into words." He then proceeds to eulogize his master in terms of infinite affection and esteem. Trifone, praised by innumerable other writers, even by the most mordant tongue of Christendom, his compatriot Pietro Aretino,[141] was to Andrea Gabrieli what the latter was to his nephew Giovanni, a father-like figure and a forming influence.[142] Alfred Einstein said of him: "Andrea aims to symbolize every concept that occurs in his text."[143] It was Trifone who taught Andrea how to read poetical texts, above all Dante and Petrarch. Judging from the constant flow of lines from Petrarch's *canzone* with which Daniello has him illustrate his arguments, one must deduce that Trifone knew the *Canzoniere* by heart.

That Andrea must have been a close second to his uncle we may infer also from Daniello's dialogue. At one point Trifone, in obvious reference to Horace's *Ars poetica*, distinguishes between the three styles (or "figures"); the "high" is grave and sublime, the "low" is humble and simple, and between these two stands the "middle."[144] Trifone cites examples for all three from Petrarch, "I' vo piangendo i miei passati tempi" for the sublime, and "Vago augelletto che cantando vai" for the low style.[145]

Thereupon Messer Andrea remarked, "if this *canzone* belongs to the low style, Sir, where would you place 'S'el pensier che mi strugge'[146] and its companion, 'Chiare, fresche, e dolci acque'?"[147]

And Trifone, seeing very well the point that Andrea was trying to make, replied without hesitation:

"In the same one. Granted, they are so charming, beautiful, and so sweet that their very charm, beauty and sweetness stand in the way of appearing lowly,"

by which he intended to show that these qualities, however attractive, had no bearing on the determination of the style to which they belong.

May 1533, in which the conversation took place, lies right in the middle of the years during which the madrigal grew to maturity. One generation later, we find in Andrea's first book of madrigals for five voices[148] an echo of Trifone's tutorship, a setting of *Vago augelletto che cantando vai*, and in the already mentioned *Concerti* of 1587, Petrarch's *I' vo piangendo i miei passati tempi*.

We should now be prepared for the discovery that Daniello's *Poetics*—and the poetics of the Cinquecento quite generally—created the prototype of the aesthetics of *musica reservata* both in the sense of music set aside for private use and music as painting in tones and expression of emotion. Quickelberg's *rem quasi actam ante oculos ponendo* is foreshadowed in Daniello's definition of the rhetorical figure "demonstration, which is used when one puts the subject matter as it were before the eyes of the audience in such manner that it seems to them as if they saw it acted just as the poet described it or as it really was and happened."[149] Nor should it surprise us that Giovanni Gabrieli, in the above-mentioned dedication to his uncle's and his own *Concerti* of 1587, one year after Andrea's death, praised him, among other things, for his ability to express the "energy" (from the term *enargía* in Aristotle's *Rhetoric*) "of words and concepts."[150]

Regarding the private use of *musica reservata*, this idea also is foreshadowed in Daniello's book; indeed, it is the point of departure for the dialogue.[151] Daniello, while a house guest of Trifone, enters his study one morning together with Jacopo and finds there Andrea, in his hand a book that he tries to hide. His curiosity aroused, he asks what book he was holding, and finds that Andrea was reading Horace's *Ars poetica*. Upon opening it he reads the following passage: "There once was the wisdom that knew how to divide the public from the private things,"[152] lines to which Daniello returns later: "Who was it who first divided the public things from the private? The poet."[153] Already in his dedication he distinguished the rhymers from the poets, "who spend long years and intense thought in the study of the classics, and, pale from effort, seek out the most inaccessible and secret places of that beautiful mount where the sacred muses stay."[154] The distinction between the public and the private sphere reminds us of the one made by Vicentino between *musica comuna* and *musica riserbata*.[155]

In one respect we are disappointed: Daniello's treatise offers no hint that the young Andrea, nephew of Trifone, is musically inclined. This may reflect the author's lack of interest in music; it may also tell us something about Andrea's personality. Alfred Einstein complained rightly that "the life of Andrea Gabrieli is veiled in an obscurity difficult to understand. We do not know exactly when he was born or when he died; no monument marks his last resting place. What we do know is that he was born in the quarter known as Canareggio, supposedly about 1510, though more probably about 1520—for it would otherwise be difficult to understand his late appearance in 1550, and he can in no case be older than Rore."[156] But as his tombstone testifies, Rore was born in 1516.[157] Einstein was understandably perplexed by the fact that Andrea waited until the 1560's to begin publication of his compositions, although occasionally a madrigal slipped into anthologies of the 1550's. Daniello offers a key to the solution of this riddle. Andrea must have shaped his life and person in emulation of the "Venetian Socrates," the man who fled honors and publicity, leaving publication of his ideas to his students. Trifone died in 1549. It seems that it took Andrea a long time to shake off the hold that his beloved uncle's image had on him—to judge by the fact that he did not begin to publish the rich treasure of his musical oeuvre that must have been accumulating over the decades before he had reached his mid-fifties. And in answer to our immediate question: if he was so shy that he did not even wish it to be known what he was reading, he was certainly not going to show off his musical talents during one of the discourses in his revered uncle's home.

Nevertheless, one precious notice reaches us at the very end of the book. Trifone calls the rhyme

a harmony of which the verse in the vernacular is richer than the Latin verse ("essendo la rima un'armonia che il verso volgare ha di più che il latino"), which you can see for yourself each time you ask a first-rate musician to sing to his own accompaniment a poem by Horace and then one by Petrarch. For there can be no doubt that the latter will fill the ear of a connoisseur with sweeter harmony than the former. And this will be due solely to the rhyme, which will accord more with the music and render greater sweetness to the degree that it is less remote from its companion rhyme.[158]

This observation is valuable for a number of reasons. It demonstrates Trifone's interest in music, it confirms that he was well aware of the settings of Horace's verses (probably the Italian ones in Petrucci's frottole prints, but possibly also those from northern sources that German humanists traveling in Italy might have brought with them), and it shows his familiarity with the current efforts to set Italian verse to music—again, he probably was well acquainted not only with the old frottole compositions by Cara, Tromboncino, and their companions, but also with the new vogue of madrigal writing in Venice and Rome. While the frottolists occasionally set verses by Petrarch, the canzone of the great trecento poet became popular among composers only with the madrigalists of the 1530's, except perhaps for a work standing between frottola and madrigal, the *Musica de meser Bernardo pisano sopra le Canzone del petrarcha* of 1520, a late publication by Petrucci.[159] Unlike the traditional humanists, Trifone preferred madrigal to ode, for the former gave more delight to the listener than did the latter—a preference that does honor to his musical judgment. Of course, in 1533 the distance between humanist and madrigalist was not so great as was the case between the humanist and the composer of polyphonic motets at about 1500. The madrigalist took the text as point of departure and used freely all musical elements to suit the words. Trifone gives an interesting reason: the vernacular verse is richer in rhyme than Latin verse—indeed, rhyme is virtually unknown in ancient Greek and Roman poetry. The writers of frottole, and of madrigals in particular, coordinated rhyme with cadential articulation; the harmonic, melodic, and rhythmic structure moves from line to line and rhyme to rhyme, creating a musical organism of far greater complexity, coherence, and purposeful direction than was possible within the plain settings of Latin odes.

With this brief observation, Trifone has revealed himself as a musical connoisseur of distinction, a man well equipped to provide the humanistic and literary education of one of Italy's great composers. Indeed, Trifone may well have pointed the way that Andrea chose for his course as a madrigalist. If "there is no master whose work so completely and faithfully reflects the Venetian life of the third quarter of the Cinquecento as does Andrea Gabrieli's,"[160] and if he was equally eminent as a madrigalist, a composer of state cantatas, of church and organ music, as he was of *canzoni alla villanesca* or *giustiniane* and *greghesche*, settings of popular poetry in dialect, in which he created together with the poet Antonio Molino, known under the name of Burchiella, the figure of Pantalone, then Trifone's aesthetics based on Horace's three styles served him marvelously well. For it gave him the philosophical underpinning for composing in the *stilus humilis*, in which he portrayed the lowly populace and the comic characters of Venice.[161]

Trifone does in fact speak about the music proper for comedy as against that suitable for tragedy, if only in passing. "The tragedies should contain choruses (since they are not used in comedies, where, between acts and lest the stage remain empty, one employs in their stead music for instruments and for voices and introduces a mixture of *moresche* and buffoons). . . ."[162]

It is not impossible that Trifone also exercised some influence on Adrian Willaert, Andrea's reputed teacher, whom he must have met during the latter's long years of residence in Venice in one of its patrician houses and "academies." If so, the two men surely felt immediate sympathy for each other, for they were remarkably similar in character. In a study of portraits of Willaert, I described him as "a man singularly lacking in vanity, indeed, in any attention to externals of any kind. . . . The simplicity of Willaert, his modesty and gentleness, are praised in contemporary accounts and shine through in the immense popularity that he enjoyed in an age and in a country torn by furious jealousies in politics and in art."[163] To this one should add that like Trifone, Willaert was idolized by his students. He was characterized earlier as "the indubitably greatest teacher of the sixteenth century."

VIII. *Conclusion*

Looking back from the Florentine music drama to the French *vers mesuré* and the German humanistic ode, we find in each case the humanist and poet taking the initiative and directing the musician—whether it is Celtis and Tritonius, Minervius and Senfl, Baïf and Claude le Jeune, Pietro Bembo and the Italian madrigalists, Trifone and Andrea Gabrieli, Count Bardi and Vincenzo Galilei, Caccini, and Peri, Ronsard and the later French chanson composers. Each time we encounter the same constellation: the humanist in search of ancient Greek music and music drama, or the humanistically inspired poet anxious to resurrect in the vernacular the old ideal union between poetry and music, and the musician who is encouraged, indeed charmed, bribed, and virtually ensnared by the humanist to serve his ends until, ultimately, he makes these ends his own. In the beginning of the sixteenth century, the humanist's attention was confined to the problem of a musical rendering of ancient Roman poetry that would produce a clear and strictly metrical declamation of the text in four-part music. It is the indisputable merit of German humanism to have defined the issue, clearly and sharply.

At the end of the century, the humanist and the humanist-musician had enlarged their vision; not content with serving the poetic body alone, they fixed their attention now on the soul of poetry, its imagery and emotion, with the result that painting in tones and musical expression became the chief focus of vocal composition, while precise and sensitive declamation were more and more taken for granted. It is this movement that led to the great stylistic reforms of the baroque age. In the Florentine music drama of the outgoing Cinquecento, counterpoint is replaced by monodic song with instrumental accompaniment; most choruses are set in the humanistic tradition of simultaneous harmonic declamation. Italy was the last country in which humanism helped to create a new form of music, but it was the only one that gave the world a musical form that proved viable: opera.

Yet, the influence of humanism on music, north and south, goes far beyond the creation of specific musical forms. The humanistic movement had a fundamental part in shaping modern music in the broadest sense of the word; it produced a new relationship between word and tone, a new concept of music as expressive of human emotion. The humanistic movement, in the final analysis, gave the decisive impulse to that humanization of music to which we owe Bach's *St. Matthew Passion* as well as Mozart's *Marriage of Figaro*, Beethoven's Ninth Symphony as much as Schubert's Lieder, and which conquered its old antagonist: counterpoint—that is, music as autonomous structure—not by suppression, but by transformation.

IX. *Epilogue*

This paper would be historically incomplete without a word on one of the seminal works of twentieth-century music, Schönberg's *Pierrot lunaire*, written in 1912. Stravinsky called it "the solar plexus as well as the mind of early twentieth-century music," and admitted, fifty years later, that its "real wealth . . . sound and substance . . . were beyond me as they were beyond all of us at that time. . . ."[164] It is generally praised as one of the great avant-garde works of our time.

It is that; but it is also a *summa* of the European tradition, and in particular the one sketched out in the foregoing. In this work for *Sprechstimme* and eight instruments (played by five performers), the old problem of how to make the words in a polyphonic texture understood while at the same time bringing them alive in tones has been solved in a manner both novel and radical. The text of the "three times seven poems" is given to one single person, a soprano; it is neither spoken nor sung. In a unique experiment that turned out to be a masterwork, the pitches of the *Sprechstimme* are indicated and the singer is expected to intone and quickly leave them, rising or falling to the next note in a sort of vocal glissando. Eschewing the spoken word—a solution tried in the melodrama of the eighteenth, nineteenth, and twentieth centuries—Schönberg evades the unbridgeable gap between music and speech. Shunning recitative-like melody, he steers clear of tedious formula. Returning to the principles of Conrad Celtis, whom he probably never heard of, he used one tone—or shall we say one tone spectrum—for one syllable, he observed strictly the natural stress of the spoken word, and he did away with all repetitions of words or phrases not found in the original poem. Thus the text comes out with incisive clarity and in its full integrity. What the Camerata critics of the madrigal denounced as the *laceramento della poesia* is thus avoided. Unlike Celtis-Tritonius, Schönberg gives the spoken word the most flexible rhythmic form, embedding it besides in a contrapuntal texture of the most varied instrumental colors that spring clearly, color as well as design, from the multiple and often contradictory images and impulses of the poetic text. What had been a problem with which generations of composers since the Renaissance had wrestled, how to make the word in music understood as well as "seen" and felt, Schönberg solved in *Pierrot lunaire* in a singular manner. The atonal freedom of the musical language has long obscured the undeniable truth that in this work two traditional problems of Western vocal music, intelligibility of the sung word and expressivity of the text, have been solved by the free use of some of the earliest humanistic principles in the vocal music of the West. Schönberg's falling back on old forms and techniques, canon and fugue, passacaglia and waltz, does not really affect the nature of the music. The return to the central problem of Western aesthetics together with the revival of some of the earliest means of solving it touches the vital nerve of one of the commanding works of European music.

1. Franchino Gafori, *Musices septemque modos*

De harmonia musicorum instrumentorum (1518), fol. 89ᵛ

Mu - si - ces sep - tem - que mo - dos pla - ne - tae

Cor - ri - gunt sep - tem to - ti - dem - que chor - dis

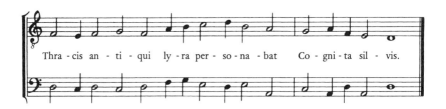

Thra - cis an - ti - qui ly - ra per - so - na - bat Co - gni - ta sil - vis.

2. Franciscus Niger, *Tempora labuntur*

Grammatica brevis (1514), fol. 88

Tem-po-ra la-bun-tur   ta-ci-tis-que se-ne-sci-mus an-nis

Et fu-gi-unt fre-no   non re-mo-ran-te di-es.

Pros-pe-ra lux o-ri-tur: lin-guis a-ni-mis-que fa-ve-te

Nunc di-cen-da bo-na   sunt bo-na ver-ba di-e.

3. Petrus Tritonius, *Jam satis terris*

after Vecchi, *Dalle Melopoiae*, Table II

Jam sa - tis ter - ris ni - vis at - que di - rae

gran - di - nis mi - sit pa - ter et ru - ben - te

dex - te - ra sa - cras ja - cu - la - tus ar - ces ter - ru - it ur - bem.

4. Sebastian Forster, *Arma virumque cano*

after Vecchi, *Melodiae Prudentianae*, p. 29

Ar - ma vi - rum - que ca - no, Tro - iae qui pri - mus ab o - ris

I - ta - li - am, fa - to pro - fu - gus, La - vi - nia - que ve - nit

Li - to - ra mul - tum il - le et ter - ris ia - cta - tus et al - to

Vi su - pe - rum sae - vae me - mo - rem Iu - no - nis ob i - ram

Mul - ta quo-que et bel - lo pas - sus, dum con - de - ret ur - bem

In - ter - ret - que De - os La - ti - o; ge - nus un - de La - ti - num

Al - ba - ni - que pa - tres at - que al - tae moe - ni - a Ro - mae.

5. Michele Pesenti, *Integer vitae*

after Cesari, *Le frottole*, p. 35

Edward E. Lowinsky

6. Johannes Cochlaeus, *Ut queant laxis*

after Miller, *Cochlaeus*, p. 85

Ut que-ant la - xis re - so - na - re fi - bris,

Mi - ra ge - sto - rum fa - mu-li tu - o - rum, Sol - ve pol -

- lu - ti la - bi - i re - a - tum, San - cte Io - an - nes.

7. Marbriano de Orto, *Dulces exuviae*

Picker, *Chanson Albums*, pp. 292–95

8. Ludwig Senfl, *Jam satis terris*

after Liliencron, "Die Horazischen Metren," p. 53

Jam   sa - tis   ter - ris   ni - vis   at - que   di - rae

gran - di - nis   mi - sit   pa - ter   et   ru - ben - te

dex - te - ra   sa - cras   ja - cu - la - tus   ar - ces   ter - ru - it   ur - bem.

9. Ludwig Senfl, *Salve sancta parens*

after Moser, *Hofhaimer*, p. 163

Sal - ve san - cta pa - rens dul - cis a - mor me - us

vir - go pi - a sa - lus mun - di coe - li por - ta.

10. Henricus Glareanus, *Miserarum est*

Dodekachordon, p. 193

Mi - se - ra - rum est   ne - que a - mo - ri   da - re   lu - dum

Ne - que dul - ci   ma - la   vi - - no   la - ve - re aut   ex -

A - ni - ma - ri   me - tu - en - tes   pa - tru - ae   ver - be - ra lin - guae.

11. Henricus Glareanus, *Quis multa gracilis*

Dodekachordon, p. 189

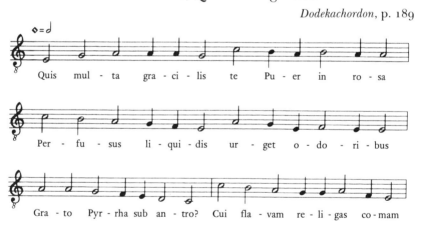

Quis   mul - ta   gra - ci - lis   te   Pu - er   in   ro - sa

Per - fu - sus   li - qui - dis   ur - get   o - do - ri - bus

Gra - to   Pyr - rha sub an - tro?   Cui   fla - vam   re - li - gas   co - mam

Sim - plex mun - di - ci - is? heu quo - ti - ens fi - dem

Mu - ta - tos - que De - os fle - bit, et a - spe - ra

Ni - gris ae - quo - ra ven - tis E - mi - ra - bi - tur in - so - lens.

Qui nunc te fru - i - tur cre - du - lus au - re - a,

Qui sem - per va - cu - am, sem - per a - ma - bi - lem

Spe - rat ne - sci - us au - rae Fal - la - cis, mi - se - ri qui - bus

In - ten - ta - ta ni - tes. Me ta - bu - la sa - cer

Vo - ti - va pa - ri - es in - di - cat hu - mi - da

Su - spen - dis - se po - ten - ti Ve - sti - men - ta Ma - ris De - o.

12. Paul Hofhaimer, *Quis multa gracilis*

Moser, *Hofhaimer*, p. 114

Quis mul - ta gra - ci - lis te pu - er in ro - sa
per - fu - sus li - qui - dis ur - get o - do - ri - bus
gra - to, Pyr - rha, sub an - tro? Cui fla - vam re - li - gas co - mam?

13. Pontus de Tyard, *Plus d'une paix rebelle*

Solitaire second, pp. 26–27

Plus, d'u - ne paix re - bel - le,
Vo - tre dou - ceur cru - el - le
au tra - vail me dis - po - se, Plus je re - po - se.

14. Claude le Jeune, *D'une coline m'y proumenant*

Expert, *Les Maîtres Musiciens*, XIV, 91

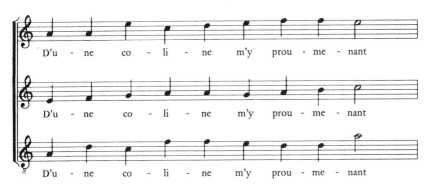

D'u - ne co - li - ne m'y prou - me - nant

D'u - ne co - li - ne m'y prou - me - nant

D'u - ne co - li - ne m'y prou - me - nant

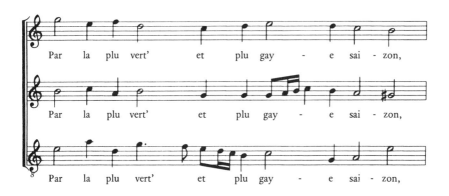

Par la plu vert' et plu gay - e sai - zon,

Par la plu vert' et plu gay - e sai - zon,

Par la plu vert' et plu gay - e sai - zon,

Quand tou - te cho - ze rid au chams,

Quand tou - te cho - ze rid au chams,

Quand tou - te cho - ze rid au chams,

Je voy u - ne Rô - ze ver - meil - lé - te

Je voy u - ne Rô - ze ver - meil - lé - te

Je voy u - ne Rô - ze ver - meil - lé - te

Qui tou - te fleu - ré - te de fleur de beau - té

Qui tou - te fleu - ré - te de fleur de beau - té

Qui tou - te fleu - ré - te de fleur de beau - té

Pas - se de bien loin.

Pas - se de bien loin.

Pas - se de bien loin.

Rechant à 3

Je la voy de loin, Et je l'ai - me fort,

Je la voy de loin, Et je l'ai - me fort,

Je la voy de loin, Et je l'ai - me fort,

Je la veu cuil - lir, Et la main j'y tens,

Je la veu cuil - lir, Et la main j'y tens,

Je la veu cuil - lir, Et la main j'y tens,

Mais las c'est en vain.

Mais las c'est en vain.

Mais las c'est en vain.

15. Freminot, *Dulces exuviae*

MS Bergamo 1209 D, fol. 54ᵛ–55

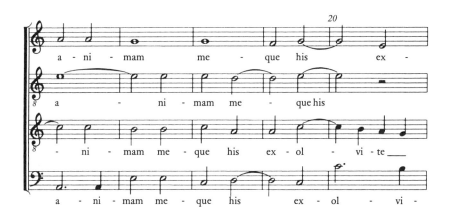

1) orig.: dum

1) orig.: dum

2) orig.: terris, in all voices

16. Adrian Willaert, *Dulces exuviae*, mm. 1–29

Opera omnia, II, ed. Zenck, 59

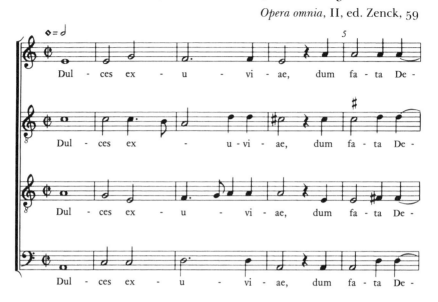

17. Cipriano de Rore, *Dissimulare etiam sperasti (1.p.)*

Opera omnia, ed. Meier, XIV, 6–8

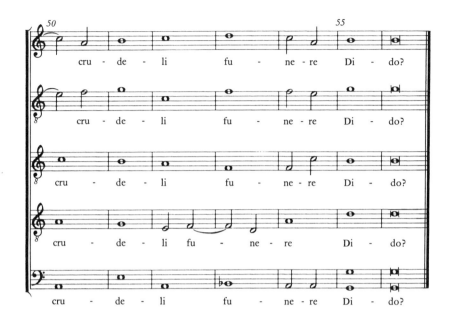

18. Cipriano de Rore, *Dissimulare etiam sperasti (1.p.)*

Dis - si - mu - la - re e - ti - am spe - ra -

- sti, per - fi - de, per - fi - de, tan - tum Pos - se

ne - fas,   ta - ci - tus - que me a

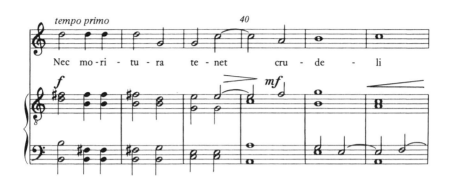

19. Cipriano de Rore, *Donec gratus eram tibi*, mm. 1–41

Opera omnia, ed. Meier, VI, 16–17

20. Nicola Vicentino, *Era sereno il ciel*

Tarasconi Codex, f. 33

*) The sharp is placed before the preceding F, which I consider a mistake in this context.

21. Orlando di Lasso, *Tityre, tu patulae*, mm. 1–14

Werke, ed. Haberl, XIX, 68

22. Orlando di Lasso, *Bestia curvafia*, mm. 1–11

Sämtliche Werke, Neue Reihe, I, ed. Boetticher, no. 13

23. Orlando di Lasso, *Dulci sub umbra*

Werke, ed. Haberl, XI, 49

24. Andrea Gabrieli, "Si raddoppiano gl'Inni"

Edipo tiranno, ed. Schrade, p. 174

25. Andrea Gabrieli, "Ne le sceleratezze"

Edipo tiranno, ed. Schrade, p. 221

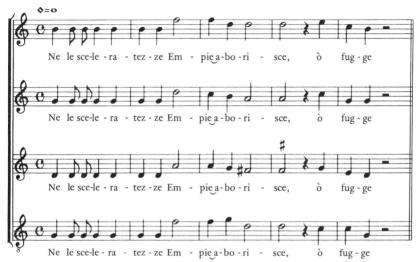

26. Giulio Caccini, *Se de boschi i verdi onori*

L'Euridice (1600), p. 25

Notes

1. Indispensable are the studies of Paul Oskar Kristeller, especially "Humanist Learning in the Italian Renaissance," *Renaissance Thought*, II, *Papers on Humanism and the Arts* (New York, 1965), pp. 1–19; "The Moral Thought of Renaissance Humanism," *ibid.*, pp. 20–68; "European Diffusion of Italian Humanism," *ibid.*, pp. 69–88; "Humanism and Scholasticism in the Italian Renaissance," *Studies in Renaissance Thought and Letters* (Rome, 1956), pp. 553–583. For a penetrating and lively account of the German scene, see Lewis W. Spitz, *The Religious Renaissance of the German Humanists* (Cambridge, Mass., 1963); for an imaginative, intelligent, and beautifully illustrated discussion of the international scene, see André Chastel, *The Age of Humanism, Europe 1480–1530* (London, 1963).

2. I shall confine myself to citing the fundamental works of two scholars, Aby Warburg, *Gesammelte Schriften*, ed. G. Bing, 2 vols. (Leipzig, 1932), and Erwin Panofsky, *Hercules am Scheidewege und andere antike Bildstoffe in der neueren Kunst, Studien der Bibliothek Warburg*, vol. XVIII, ed. Fritz Saxl (Leipzig/Berlin, 1930); *idem, Studies in Iconology, Humanistic Themes in the Art of the Renaissance* (New York and Evanston: Harper Torchbooks, 1962).

3. Different is of course the situation in the field of musical theory. Franchino Gafori was the first theorist of music to have Greek music treatises translated into Latin for his own use. He also is one of the first theorists to write not in the monks' Latin of the medieval musicians but in the classical Latin cultivated by contemporary humanists. In this he was preceded by Johannes Gallicus, student of the great humanist Vittorino da Feltre of Mantua. But whereas there is an unbridgeable gulf between Gallicus' humanistic Latin and his reactionary views on music—he opposed not only secular music, but all polyphony, advocating instead strict confinement to Gregorian chant in church music—Gafori strove, in his first great treatise, *Theorica musica* of 1480, to bring style and content of his work into close harmony: he wrote the first truly humanistic treatise on music, basing himself on the musical mythology, aesthetics, and theory of the ancient Greeks as transmitted chiefly by Boethius; see P. O. Kristeller, "Music and Learning in the Early Italian Renaissance," *Journal of Renaissance and Baroque Music*, I (1947), 255–274, esp. 266–268, reprinted in *Renaissance Thought*, II, pp. 142–162, esp. 153–156, and Lowinsky, "Music of the Renaissance as Viewed by Renaissance Musicians," in *The Renaissance Image of Man and the World*, ed. B. O'Kelly (Columbus: Ohio State University Press, 1966), pp. 129–177, esp. 132–141 and 150–151.

The first Renaissance writer on music who knew Greek—and was justly proud of it, mentioning frequently his close relationship with Erasmus, the sixteenth-century humanists' oracle—was the Swiss humanist Henricus Glareanus. His *Dodekachordon*, published in Basel in 1547, was a pioneering work in the recognition of the Ionian and Aeolian modes, the forerunners of major and minor, in a principled aesthetic attitude based on humanistic ideas, and a deep understanding of the music of Josquin des Prez, the first great composer to make the text the source of his inspiration. What contribution humanistic writings made to music and how they influenced and eventually transformed musical theory still awaits detailed investigation (Lowinsky, "Music of the Renaissance," pp. 154–161). For Glareanus, see Clement A. Miller's monumental translation and introduction, *Heinrich Glarean, Dodecachordon*, 2 vols., Musicological Studies and Documents, 6 (American Institute of Musicology, 1965); see also Bernhard Meier, "Heinrich Loriti Glareanus als Musiktheoretiker," *Beiträge zur Freiburger Wissenschafts- und Universitätsgeschichte* (Freiburg im Breisgau, 1960), pp. 65–112.

4. "Concords of sounds and melodies, from whose sweetness, as Lactantius says, the pleasure of the ear is derived, are produced, then, not by heavenly bodies, but by earthly instruments with the co-operation of nature. To these concords the ancient musicians—Plato, Pythagoras, Nicomachus, Aristoxenus, Philolaus, Archytas, Ptolemy, and many others, including even Boethius—most assiduously applied themselves, yet how they were accustomed to arrange and to form them is almost unknown to our generation. And if I may refer to my own experience, I have had in my hands certain old songs, called apoc-

rypha, of unknown origin, so ineptly, so stupidly composed that they rather offended than pleased the ear.

Further, although it seems beyond belief, there does not exist a single piece of music, not composed within the last forty years, that is regarded by the learned as worth hearing. Yet at this present time, not to mention innumerable singers of the most beautiful diction, there flourish, whether by the effect of some celestial influence or by the force of assiduous practice, countless composers, among them Jean Ockeghem, Jean Regis, Antoine Busnoys, Firmin Caron, and Guillaume Faugues, who glory in having studied this divine art under John Dunstable, Gilles Binchoys, and Guillaume Dufay, recently deceased. Nearly all the works of these men exhale such sweetness that in my opinion they are to be considered most suitable, not only for men and heroes, but even for the immortal gods. Indeed, I never hear them, I never examine them, without coming away happier and more enlightened. As Virgil took Homer for his model in that divine work the *Aeneid*, so I, by Hercules, have used these composers as models for my modest works, and especially in the arrangements of the concords I have plainly imitated their admirable style of composing." Johannes Tinctoris, *Liber de arte contrapuncti* (1477), dedication; translated in Oliver Strunk, *Source Readings in Music History* (New York, 1950), pp. 198–199. For the Latin text, see *Johannis Tinctoris opera theoretica*, II, ed. Albert Seay (American Institute of Musicology, 1975), pp. 12–13.

5. "Consider each rule of the modern contrapuntists by itself, or, if you wish, consider them all together. They aim at nothing but the delight of the ear, if it can truly be called delight. They have not a book among them for their use and convenience that speaks of how to express the conceptions of the mind and of how to impress them with the greatest possible effectiveness on the minds of the listeners; of this they do not think and never have thought since the invention of this kind of music, but only of how to disfigure it still more, if such a thing be possible. And that in truth the last thing the moderns think of is the expression of the words with the passion that these require, excepting in the ridiculous way that I shall shortly relate, let it be a manifest sign that their observances and rules amount to nothing more than a manner of modulating about among the musical intervals with the aim of making the music a contest of varied harmonies according to the rules stated above and without further thought of the conception and sense of the words. And if it were permitted me, I should like to show you, with several examples of authority, that among the most famous contrapuntists of this century there are some who do not even know how to read, let alone understand. Their ignorance and lack of consideration is one of the most potent reasons why the music of today does not cause in the listeners any of those virtuous and wonderful effects that ancient music caused." Vincenzo Galilei, *Dialogo della musica antica e della moderna* (1581), translated in Strunk, *Source Readings*, pp. 312–313.

"When the ancient musician sang any poem whatever, he first considered very diligently the character of the person speaking: his age, his sex, with whom he was speaking, and the effect he sought to produce by this means; and these conceptions, previously clothed by the poet in chosen words suited to such a need, the musician then expressed in the tone and with the accents and gestures, the quantity and quality of sound, and the rhythm appropriate to that action and to such a person. For this reason we read of Timotheus, who in the opinion of Suidas was a player of the aulos and not of the cithara, that when he roused the great Alexander with the difficult mode of Minerva to combat with the armies of his foes, not only did the circumstances mentioned reveal themselves in the rhythms, the words, and the conceptions of the entire song in conformity with his desire, but in my opinion at least, his habit, the aspect of his countenance, and each particular gesture and member must have shown on this occasion that he was burning with desire to fight, to overcome, and to conquer the enemy. For this reason Alexander was forced to cry out for his arms and to say that this should be the song of kings. And rightly, for provided the impediments have been removed, if the musician has not the power to direct the minds of his listeners to their benefit, his science and knowledge are to be reputed null and vain, since the art of music was instituted and numbered among the liberal arts for no other purpose." *Ibid.*, p. 319.

6. Musicologists have long wondered why Celtis and Tritonius should have preferred four-part to monodic settings, since they well knew that the ancient Greeks and Romans had neither polyphony nor harmony. There was undoubtedly a double motivation: to bring these settings close to the ear and preference of the contemporaneous musician and music lover, and to legitimize the whole enterprise by approximating it as much as possible to the church music of the period. This is the reason why so many publications of humanistic odes contain sacred songs to texts written in ancient meters. Celtis, in a little-observed passage of his poem "To the Music Lovers" (*Ad musiphilos*) inserted in Tritonius' opus, speaks of the

> carmina, quatuor
> Vocibus, ut vates et sacra templa canunt.

See Édith Weber, *Musique et Théâtre dans les Pays Rhénans*, vol. I, 1: *La musique mesurée à l'antique en Allemagne* (n.p., 1974), 180, and Giuseppe Vecchi, *Dalle "Melopoiae sive harmoniae tetracenti[c]ae" oraziane di Tritonio (1507) alle "Geminae undeviginti odarum Horatii melodiae" (1552)* (Bologna, 1960), p. 9. The passage alludes to "four-part music as sung by priests and in places of worship." Glareanus, too, followed these tactics, as we shall see below (section III).

7. *MELOPOIAE SIVE HARMONIAE TETRACENTICAE super XXII genera carminum Heroïcorum Elegiacorum Lyricorum & ecclesiasticorum hymnorum per Petrum Tritonium et alios doctos sodalitatis Litterariae nostrae musicos secundum naturas et tempora syllabarum et pedum compositae et regulatae ductu Chunradi Celtis foeliciter impressae. . . . Impressum Augusta vindelicorum ingenio & industria Erhardi Oglin . . . Qui primus nitidas pressit in aeris notas Primus et hic lyricas expressit carmine Musas, Quatuor et docuit vocibus aere cani.* The title has been printed artfully so as to result in the image of a wine cup; this is hinted at by the marginal inscription, *Crater Bachi* (see Weber, *La musique mesurée*, I, 179, and Vecchi, *Dalle Melopoiae*, p. 19). For illustrations of the two woodcuts at the beginning and the end of the book showing Apollo playing the *lira da braccio* on Mount Parnassus and the nine Muses in a heavenly concert with Apollo, see *Die Musik in Geschichte und Gegenwart* (hereafter *MGG*), IX, pl. 119; a much superior illustration of the former appears in Chastel, *Age of Humanism*, p. 15. This work also contains a number of other illustrations bearing on the life, work, and death of Celtis. For a specimen page of the music, see *Musik in der Reichsstadt Augsburg*, ed. Ludwig Wegele (Augsburg, 1965), p. 55, and Georg Kinsky, *A History of Music in Pictures* (New York, 1951), p. 73, pl. 2.

Tritonius' odes were brought out in old clefs and original note values by R. von Liliencron in the appendix to his study on "Die Horazischen Metren in deutschen Kompositionen des 16. Jahrhunderts," *Vierteljahrsschrift für Musikwissenschaft*, III (1887), 26–91; 49–91. They are now available in modern clefs and reduced to one-fourth of the original note values in Giuseppe Vecchi's edition, *Dalle Melopoiae*. This work adds the metrical analysis of each ode, given in the original print but omitted by Liliencron, and takes the 1552 edition of Tritonius' odes by Petrus Nigidius into account, correcting a number of errors in the *editio princeps*. In an informative introduction, Vecchi lists (p. 16, n. 34) the contents of the second series ("geminae") of the non-Horatian *carmina* and their metric forms covered in Tritonius' opus; he quotes in full (pp. 14–15) Nigidius' dedication, from which we learn that he reprinted not only Tritonius' *Melopoiae*, but also Aldus Manutius' *De Metris Horatianis Tractatus* of 1526 (see Weber, *La musique mesurée*, p. 239) and a number of odes on sacred texts and hymns. Liliencron, in his edition, had also provided Senfl's and Hofhaimer's settings of the verses selected by Celtis-Tritonius. On the latter's *Harmoniae poeticae* (Nuremberg, 1539), see H. J. Moser, *Paul Hofhaimer, ein Lied- und Orgelmeister des deutschen Humanismus* (Stuttgart, 1929), p. 67. Moser gives a complete edition of Hofhaimer's 35 settings of Latin meters (Appendix, pp. 112–128), of which Liliencron offered only the 19 that Tritonius had set. On Hofhaimer's relations to Celtis and the Nuremberg humanist Willibald Pirckheimer, see pp. 25 and 162.

8. The three settings omitted by Liliencron are on texts by poets other than Horace; they are probably the ones that were set to music by "other learned musicians of our literary sodality," as the title says (see note 7).

9. This is true, strictly speaking, even if he were indeed identical with the anonymous editor of the *Hymnarius: durch das gantz Jar verteutscht . . . Getrukht zu Sygmundslust . . . 1524,* as F. Waldner has argued in his "Petrus Tritonius und das älteste gedruckte katholische Gesangbuch," *Monatshefte für Musik-Geschichte,* XXVII (1895), 13–27, esp. 18–19.

10. Simon Minervius, a close friend of Tritonius, about whom we shall hear later, echoed these words when he, in the preface to Senfl's odes, said of Tritonius' work that it had been done *ductu et auspiciis Cunradi . . . hortatu preceptoris* ("under the guidance and auspices of Conrad . . . with the encouragement of his teacher"). To translate these words as "at the command and direction of Conrad, according to the instruction of his teacher" ("auf Befehl und Vorschrift des Konrad Celtis, nach Anweisung seines Lehrers"; see Renatus Pirker's valuable study, "Beiträge zur Entwicklungsgeschichte der vierstimmigen Humanistenode," *Musicologica Austriaca,* I [1977], 136–153; 141), seems exaggerated. The author believes that Treibenreif had become a victim of Celtis' "malicious sense of humor"—a speculation based on untenable premises: (1) that Treibenreif's humanistic name Tritonius was Celtis' invention; (2) that it might be derived not only from "Tritonia," that is, Pallas Athene, and mean "disciple of Pallas Athene"—a clever explanation—but also from *tritonus,* the *diabolus in musica,* and stand for "Misstöner," the "maker of discords." Surely a student of Celtis and *magister artium* from the University of Padua could make up his own Latin nickname. Nor is it reasonable to suspect Celtis of trying to mock the man whose cooperation he sought not alone in his musical enterprise but also in a great unfinished work, *Germania illustrata,* for which he asked Tritonius to prepare a description of the Adige Valley, the region in which he was born; see two letters from Tritonius to Celtis, nos. 242 and 282, in Hans Rupprich, *Der Briefwechsel des Konrad Celtis* (Munich, 1934). To derive the name Tritonius from *tritonus* would scarcely have occurred to humanists thoroughly trained in Latin grammar. The tone of genuine admiration and affection of Tritonius' letters to Celtis rules out the possibility of any animosity between the two, even though the relationship between Celtis and some of his students in Ingolstadt, as Pirker notes, was demonstrably bad (see their letter, no. 174). However, there were also students in Ingolstadt who were deeply grateful to Celtis, as may be seen from the letter of Bernhard, Count of Waldkirch the Younger (no. 50) and especially from the testimony of famous humanists who had been his students in Ingolstadt, men such as his successor at the University of Ingolstadt, Jacob Locher (see no. 208) and Johann Aventinus, who followed Celtis from Ingolstadt to Vienna (see no. 253). Rupprich calls him "founder of scientific German historiography, disciple, favorite, and successor of Celtis" (p. 428, n. 4).

I should add that Pirker's very recent article came late to my attention. I have tried to work his main ideas, as far as pertinent, into the present study (see note 23).

11. For a different appraisal, see the writer's review of D. P. Walker, *Der musikalische Humanismus,* in *The Musical Quarterly,* XXXVII (1951), 286–287.

12. This is also the opinion of Friedrich Blume; see his *Die evangelische Kirchenmusik* (Potsdam, 1931), pp. 43ff, 80; see also Friedrich Blume, *Das Zeitalter der Reformation,* separate print from *Geschichte der evangelischen Kirchenmusik,* ed. Ludwig Finscher (Kassel, 1965), pp. 47–48.

13. The most thorough and detailed bibliography of humanistic odes in Germany is to be found in Édith Weber's work cited in note 6, vol. I, 1, pp. 25–78. For analysis and bibliography of the new Latin renderings of the psalms in metric form and the ancient and contemporaneous hymns in classical meters, see *ibid.,* ch. VIII, IX, X. For brief surveys, see the article of Karl-Günther Hartmann on "Die humanistische Ode" in *MGG,* IX (1961), cols. 1841–1846, and the entry on "Odenkomposition" in *Riemann Musik-Lexikon,* 12th ed., III, ed. H. H. Eggebrecht, 647–648.

14. R. von Liliencron, "Die Chorgesänge des lateinisch-deutschen Schuldramas im XVI. Jahrhundert," *Vierteljahrsschrift für Musikwissenschaft,* VI (1890), 309–352, with 21 music examples (pp. 353–387); Weber, *Musique et Théâtre,* vol. II: *Le théâtre humaniste et scolaire dans les Pays Rhénans.* See also E. Refardt, "Die Musik der Basler Volksschauspiele des 16. Jahrhunderts," *Archiv für Musikwissenschaft,* III (1921), 199–219 (including three pages of music).

15. See Howard M. Brown, *Instrumental Music Printed Before 1600: A Bibliography* (Cambridge, Mass., 1965), pp. 23–24, which also lists where some of them are available in modern reprints.

Oddly enough, the most comprehensive publication of humanistic odes, including Judenkünig's three-part intabulations of Tritonius' odes, although in print for some seventy-five years, seems to have bypassed musicological attention. I refer to the work of Eduard Stemplinger, *Das Fortleben der Horazischen Lyrik seit der Renaissance* (Leipzig, 1906). Not only does the author offer a survey of Horace imitations, emulations, parodies, and influences in post-Renaissance Western literature of surprising richness, he presents us also with the musical settings of the various Horatian odes, including compositions of lesser known authors such as the Swiss Joannes Frisius or Michael from Augsburg alongside those of Tritonius, Cochlaeus, Senfl, Hofhaimer, and Glareanus. Finally, this is the only book that contains all nineteen intabulations of Judenkünig. Stemplinger had succeeded in persuading Oswald Körte, author of *Laute und Lautenmusik bis zur Mitte des 16. Jahrhunderts* (Leipzig, 1901), to transcribe these works. One may forgive the historian of literature if he failed to recognize that Judenkünig, rather than composing the pieces, had merely given a condensed version (three instead of four voices) of the Tritonius settings.

16. See Helmuth Osthoff, "Vergils Aeneis in der Musik von Josquin des Prez bis Orlando di Lasso," *Archiv für Musikwissenschaft*, XI (1954), 85–102; esp. 85. This was the situation in 1956, when I sketched the Italian background of the German humanistic ode in the first version of the present paper. In the meantime, the article of K.-G. Hartmann mentioned in note 13 has demonstrated the Italian contribution to the origin of the German humanistic ode. Hartmann showed that even the earliest German ode settings for three voices in Jacob Locher's drama *Historia de rege francie* (1495) were clearly indebted to Italian models. On Locher, see note 10. For new evidence, see note 23.

17. This is, not by accident, the seventh stanza of the fifteen that the poet composed in the tenth of the twenty chapters on modes of Book IV of *De harmonia*. Gafori gave the chapter the following title: *De Septem modorum et Planetarum convenientia sapphico carmine et Dorica atque hypodorica modulatione descripta Caput decimum* (Chapter 10 on the concord of the seven modes and planets depicted in a Sapphic ode set in a Dorian and Hypodorian mode). The poem opens with this verse:

> Gaphuri tandem modulis levata
> Musa: non longum dea carmen adde
> Musicae: alterna vice nomen unum
> Nectit utrasque.

> At length, o Muse, refreshed by Gafori's modes,
> Add now, Goddess, a less long poem to [the treatise on] Music
> For one name binds Muse
> And Music in turns.

The poem is printed on folio 89 of the work; see the facsimile edition in *Bibliotheca Musica Bononiensis*, Sez. II, N. 7 (Bologna, 1972).

18. *Dodekachordon*, p. 180; Miller, *Dodecachordon*, I, 210.

19. "Decet enim vatem habile poeticae instrumentum habere: quo modulante carmina condat: ad priscorum imitationem poetarum qui sine melo nullum versum componebant: Carmina enim a canendo ideo dicta sunt: quia nisi decantata fuerint: divinum nomen in turpissimum foedissimumque convertunt. Vocalis harmonia in voce consistit: qua composita carmina decantantur. Huius species sunt quinque, scilicet heroica gravis: heroica bellica: elegiaca: sapphica: et lyrica" (fol. 87 of the Milan, 1514 edition). See my presentation at the Round Table on "Verse Meter and Melodic Rhythm in the Age of Humanism," in *Report of the Eighth Congress*, II, 67–68.

20. An exception, in addition to Hartmann's article, is Édith Weber's work on *Musique et Théâtre dans les Pays Rhénans*. In her chronological list (I, 26), Niger's book is dated as of 1420 and lined up between sources of 1404 and 1437—a mistake corrected in the discus-

sion on pp. 132–133. There a staffless example is given as illustration, but no mention is made of later editions with staves, nor is Niger's individual mode of notation observed.

There exist of course earlier written examples of Latin verses in classical meters set to music. One occasionally finds a statement such as that "Hugo von Reutlingen had already composed odes in correct scansion in 1332"; see Hans Engel in the Round Table discussion on "Verse Meter and Melodic Rhythm," p. 68, to which the present writer made the following response: "Hugo von Reutlingen, however, did not actually compose Latin odes; in a theoretical work (*Flores Musicae*, ed. C. Beck, Stuttgart 1868, 2. Abt. p. 66) he gave an example of how to scan hexameter and pentameter in a Latin mnemonic verse devoid of poetic significance and in a setting for one voice. There is no connection between this *Merkvers* on scanning and the humanistic ode, neither in intent, nor in poetic or musical form, nor in historical influence" (*ibid.*). For medieval settings of classical poetry, see Friedrich Ludwig's valuable synopsis in *Handbuch der Musikgeschichte*, ed. Guido Adler, 2 vols. (2d ed., Berlin, 1930), I, 160. (The neumatic notation is too imprecise to allow unambiguous transcription.)

21. For a partial facsimile of the melodies in the editions of 1480 and 1485 (without staves), and 1501 with staves, see Frederick R. Goff, "Early Music Books in the Rare Books Division of the Library of Congress," *Music Library Association Notes*, 2d ser., VI (1948), 58–74, esp. 67 (the irregular staves in 1480 have been entered by a contemporaneous hand). This article contains further bibliographic references. Confining himself to incunabula, Goff does not mention later editions such as *Francisci Nigri . . . de Grammatica libri decem . . . Impressum Mediolani per Gotardum de Ponte . . . 1514*, which is part of my library. It must be based on an earlier edition of 1507, for it contains a dedication of the Milanese printer of that year.

The various editions of Niger's *Grammatica* contain divergent readings of the five melodies that would warrant comparison. The kindness of my former student, Jeffrey Kallberg of the University of Chicago, who used a working period at the Library of Congress in Washington to collate, at my request, the three editions before 1500 preserved there, enables me to make a beginning. He studied two copies of the *editio princeps* (Venice, 1480), one in the Rare Book Division, the other in the Music Division, and one copy of Basel, Michael Wennsler, ca. 1485, and another one of Basel, Jacobus Wolff, 1499. From his meticulous descriptions it is fair to draw the following conclusions: The two copies of Venice, 1480, agree precisely; they may be held to come from the same printing, if the musical notation may be taken as a criterion. The copy from the Rare Books Division has some staves inked in by hand. The edition of Basel, ca. 1485, also lacking printed staves, follows the music examples of Venice, 1480, but not with the precision desirable. For one thing, the dots are omitted, and at times a note is missing or erroneously added. Not infrequently the interval spaces between the notes deviate from those of 1480. Obviously, Venice, 1480, has the better readings. I must presume, nevertheless, that it is not free of error. *O decus Phoebi*, the fourth melody illustrating the Sapphic meter, is set to the fourth and last verse of Horace's thirty-second ode of Book I. It ends on the words *Rite vocanti*. These words, against humanistic principles, are repeated (no less than three times)—and not as one might expect to the same number and rhythm of notes. While I should like to think that Niger supervised the printing of his melodies, I cannot believe that he would have approved of the strange repeats. If the 1485 Basel print is lacking in precision, in part because the printer failed to understand details of the notation such as the dots, it can be confidently asserted that the printer of Basel, 1499, although he places the notes on staves, was entirely untouched by any familiarity with music and musical theory. He confuses the verses, setting the second line of *O regina novam* to the melody of the first line of *Bella per hermatios* and vice versa, although number and stress of syllables differ. Similar confusion occurs elsewhere. In many instances rhythm and intervals are plainly wrong. For illustration of the *species lyrica* 1499 uses a different text and melody. It is hard to escape the conclusion that the musical competence of the printers varied widely, but that none of the printers employed a musical proofreader—a situation parallel to the lack of literary proofreader in frottola prints of the second decade of the sixteenth century (see *Eustachio Romano, Musica duorum*, ed. from the literary estate of Hans T. David by Howard

Mayer Brown and Edward E. Lowinsky [*Monuments of Renaissance Music*, VI; Chicago, 1975], preface, p. xvi).

22. P. O. Kristeller, "Music and Learning," p. 272.

23. Persuasive evidence for this hypothesis is now available in Renatus Pirker's extraordinary discovery that the second of the two choral numbers of Celtis' *Ludus Dianae* (performed in Linz on March 1, 1501, before Maximilian I, Queen Bianca Maria, and two members of the Sforza family) borrowed one of the five melodies from Niger's *Grammatica brevis* (*O decus Phoebi*) for the soprano of the Sapphic strophe set for three parts ("Beiträge zur Entwicklungsgeschichte," p. 137). The song is not only "metrically slightly changed" but also melodically. But there is no doubt that Niger is the source of the soprano melody of *Regis eternas resonemus omnes* (see R. von Liliencron, "Die Chorgesänge des lateinisch-deutschen Schuldramas," p. 359). For the original melody, see Niger, *Grammatica* (fol. 88ʳ of the 1514 edition). The differences in the pitches of the melody may have their origin in the fact that early editions of Niger do not provide staves; hence the notes could not be placed with precision (see note 21).

24. *Selections from Conrad Celtis, 1459–1508, edited with Translation and Commentary by Leonard Forster* (Cambridge, 1948), pp. 20–21. An earlier version in the *Ars versificandi et carminum* (1486) had added to the title two words, interesting in our context, "cum lira": "ut ab Italis cum lira ad Germanos veniat"; see Adalbert Schroeter, *Beiträge zur Geschichte der neulateinischen Poesie Deutschlands und Hollands* (Berlin, 1909), pp. 1–2. That Celtis indeed had a musical instrument rather than a mere metaphor in mind may be deduced from the text of the poem. For a comprehensive critical biography, see Lewis W. Spitz, *Conrad Celtis, The German Arch-Humanist* (Cambridge, Mass., 1957). The same author drew an incisive intellectual portrait of Celtis in *The Religious Renaissance of the German Humanists* (see note 1), chap. V. A summary of the life and works of the German humanist is given in Heinrich Hüschen's article on Celtis in *MGG*, II, cols. 950–954. For a miniature portrait in the words of Erwin Panofsky, see below, note 73.

We know next to nothing about Celtis' musicianship. Hüschen, who wrote the best article on him, reports that in his *Vita* he is praised as devoted music lover, *musicae pertinax amator* (Rupprich, *Briefwechsel des Konrad Celtis*, p. 611). The *Vita* actually says *utriusque musicae pertinax amator*. This one word makes out of music, pure and simple, the two great divisions of music of the time, *cantus planus*, Gregorian chant, and *cantus figuratus*, polyphonic music. It transforms Celtis from a mere lover of music to a student of both monodic chant and polyphonic music (*studiosus* can be used as synonym for *amator*; see Lewis and Short, *A Latin Dictionary* [Oxford, 1966], p. 101). That Celtis also sang, and played the lute and the viol, we know from an unimpeachable source. In Cracow, at whose University he studied between 1487 and 1489, Celtis had a Polish mistress of noble family, Hasilina von Rzytonic. We have a letter of hers written in Czech, the language used at the Polish court at the time, and dated simply "1500" (Rupprich, pp. 432–433; German translation, pp. 434–435), in which she, who was married, protests vehemently Celtis' using her name in his love poems (primarily the first book of his *Amores*) and exposing her and her family to universal shame. At the end of this letter she accuses him in these words: "But, as I hear, you do not only write about me, you also sing and play the lute and the viol." The meaning of these words is, I believe, the following: "Bad enough to be the subject of a Latin poem—worse yet to figure in a song, performed in public and to the accompaniment of the lute or viol," that is, to be serenaded—*in absentia*, to be sure—in the manner of the famous courtesans of the time.

In his *Tractatus de condendis epistolis* (1492), Celtis wrote, as a sample of a love letter, a missive to Hasilina asking for her love in the most candid terms (Rupprich, p. 644).

25. Forster, *Selections*, p. 63.

26. A modern edition was published by Giuseppe Vecchi (see note 6), tables 1–20.

27. *The Aeneid of Virgil, a Verse Translation* (Berkeley, Los Angeles, London, 1971), p. 1.

28. Already in 1515, in Vienna, Wolfgang Grefinger had published the first collection of Prudentius' hymns set according to humanistic principles: *Aurelii Prudentii Cathemerinon . . . Cujus singulis Odis singulas harmonias quatuor vocum. . . . Hieronymus Vietor calcographus . . . in studiosorum communem utilitatem adjecit: componente aliquando eas Domino Wolfgango Graefin-*

ger . . . Cum Rudolfi Agricolae . . . Praefatione (see Othmar Wessely, art. "Wolfgang Grefinger," *MGG*, V, cols. 764–769).

29. Glareanus, in the last chapter of Book II of his *Dodekachordon* (1547), in which he treats of the setting of Horatian odes to music, writes with reference to the Roman poet: "May those who assert that the lightness of this author is perhaps too little suited to church songs pardon me in this matter, although they can certainly see that the early church fathers were in no wise fearful of arranging hymns for general use according to the form of this same poet's verses, and to prescribe them for the choir after merely changing the text"—and he concludes with the assurance that it is his purpose to "bring the profane into the service of the sacred" (see Miller, *Dodecachordon*, I, 210–211). While Glareanus must have thought primarily of Prudentius, who had used the various ancient meters more systematically than anyone else, he may have deliberately referred to "the early church fathers" to evoke the figure of the venerable St. Ambrose, Bishop of Milan, creator of the Roman Catholic hymn, who likewise used classical meter for his verses.

30. *Le Frottole nell'Edizione Principe di Petrucci*, transcribed by Gaetano Cesari, ed. by Raffaello Monterosso with an introduction by Benvenuto Disertori (Cremona, 1954), vol. I (books I, II, III); book I, fol. 44, p. 35.

31. In my report on "Verse Meter and Melodic Rhythm," p. 67, the German humanistic ode was shown to consist of five elements: "(1) a Latin ode of ancient origin, preferably by Horace, (2) strictly syllabic declamation, (3) elimination of all text repetition, (4) exclusive use of short and long notes to fit the short and long syllables of Latin meters, and (5) four-part harmony, to the exclusion of counterpoint in any voice. Already in 1504, Petrucci printed an ode by Horace, *Integer vitae*, with music by Michele Pesenti. . . . The humanistic scanning of the Sapphic meter . . . is discarded for a more musical one, similar to the Italian eleven-syllable verse. . . . Otherwise, the ode fits the German definition." One might add that the Italian musicians found it hard to follow the orthodox line taken by German humanists. In Pesenti's ode a syncopation slips into the final cadence and one extra note occurs in the alto (m. 3): to avoid the leap of a seventh the voice skips down via the more vocal interval of an octave and goes up one step. Nor do the Italians mind setting Horatian odes in a much freer form (see Pesenti's *In hospitas per alpes*, the previous piece in the same book). The point to remember is that Italian composers furnished the models on which German humanists were able to develop their theory of the right way of matching word to tone.

32. See the translation of Clement A. Miller, with introduction and transcription, in *Musicological Studies and Documents*, 23 (American Institute of Musicology, 1970). The edition of 1512 has been published in facsimile by Georg Olms (Hildesheim and New York, 1971).

33. Miller, *Cochlaeus*, pp. 11–12.

34. Part of the title of Petrucci's *Libro quarto* of *Strambotti, ode, frottole, sonetti . . .* (RISM 1507²).

35. *The Hours of the Divine Office in English and Latin*, 3 vols. (Collegeville, Minn., 1964), II, 1881–1882.

36. I am giving Miller's transcription, adding only bar lines to demonstrate his thesis that the hymns and odes fit readily into a normal metrical scheme.

37. See Miller's introduction, p. 8. Franz Krautwurst, in his article on "Nürnberg" (*MGG*, IX, cols. 1745–1762, esp. 1751), notes the leading roles that poetry, rhetoric, and music played in the humanistic sodalities whose guiding spirits were Celtis, Hartmann Schedel, and Willibald Pirckheimer. Hartmann Schedel (1440–1514) is well known for the great *Liederbuch* which he himself largely copied in the 1460's (see Heinrich Besseler's article on Schedel in *MGG*, XI, cols. 1609–1612). Interestingly enough, the only music print in his great library was Tritonius' odes (*ibid.*, col. 1610). Pirckheimer, in his autobiography, describes what admiration the Italians had for his skill as an organ player and lutenist; see *Willibald Pirckheimer's Briefwechsel*, ed. Arnold Reimann and Emil Reicke, 2 vols. (Munich, 1940), I, 371, n. 2. This note is added to a letter from Dr. Lorenz Beheim, who sends Pirckheimer, upon his request, some Italian basse dances (letter of 8 June 1506).

38. "Tam dives librorum, ut similis bibliotheca utriusque linguae nusquam per Germaniam reperiri queat" (Lewis Spitz, *Religious Renaissance*, p. 325, n. 4). See also Emile Offen-

bacher, "La bibliothèque de Wilibald Pirckheimer," *La Bibliofilia*, XL (1938), 241–263. The selective list of books from Pirckheimer's library contains one work that holds a key position in our investigation: Franciscus Niger's *Grammatica*, Venice, 1480. We also know that Pirckheimer was personally acquainted and corresponded (at least since 1503) with Conrad Celtis (see the *Briefwechsel* cited in the preceding note, I, nos. 58, 59, 60, 63). It is quite possible that Willibald Pirckheimer belongs to the circle of German humanists who influenced Celtis and, through him, Tritonius in bringing out the 1507 edition of Latin odes. Pirckheimer's interest in music and ancient poetry makes it also likely that he heard some of the settings like Michele Pesenti's *Integer vitae* (Ex. 5) in Italy.

39. From MS 228 of the Bibliothèque Royale de Belgique, Brussels, no. 28; see Martin Picker, *The Chanson Albums of Marguerite of Austria* (Berkeley and Los Angeles, 1965), pp. 292–295. I have followed Picker's excellent reading to the letter except for some changes in the text underlay, introduced to meet a humanist's objections where feasible.

40. See Helmuth Osthoff's article cited in note 16; see also Oliver Strunk's admirable essay, "Vergil in Music," *The Musical Quarterly*, XVI (1930), 482–497. Allen B. Skei, in his "'Dulces exuviae': Renaissance Settings of Dido's Last Words," *The Music Review*, XXXVII (1976), 77–91, retraces Strunk's and Osthoff's steps, adding settings by Gregorius Peschin, Jacobus Vaet, and Jacob Handl.

Since Skei has been "unable to obtain a copy of Peschin's setting," a word on his composition might be in order. Apparently an *unicum*, it is to be found in the partbooks MS B 220–222 of the Proske Musikbibliothek in Regensburg, fol. 53 (soprano part). Set for three men's voices (alto, tenor, bass) in transposed Ionian on F, it is a nice, thoroughly unremarkable piece in imitative counterpoint that could be set to any text. The declamation is no worse nor much better than dozens of compositions of the period. I would estimate its origin as no later than 1530. It has no special expressive qualities; it proves that even when it came to the most emotional text it was still possible in the third decade of the century to write music hardly touched by humanistic ideas. Of course, we are dealing with the work of a small figure. Yet, we shall see later that even a minor composer can create a significant work fully in harmony with the humanistic trends of the time.

41. See *Werken van Josquin des Prés*, Wereldlijke Werken, Bundel V, ed. M. Antonowycz and W. Elders (Amsterdam, 1968), 4–7. The work has also been published by Helmuth Osthoff in *Fünf Vergil-Motetten* (*Das Chorwerk*, 54; Wolfenbüttel, [1956], pp. 5–8). On this setting, see Helmuth Osthoff, "Der Durchbruch zum musikalischen Humanismus," third public address, *Report of the Eighth Congress, New York, 1961*, II, 31–39, and Lowinsky, "Josquin des Prez and Ascanio Sforza," *Congresso internazionale sul Duomo di Milano, Atti*, ed. Maria Luisa Gatti Perer, 2 vols. (Milan, 1969), II, 17–22.

Although Josquin's setting "still shows the fine play of contrapuntal lines of the golden age of Josquin-Netherlandish music, but hardly a trace of attention to the meter" (Osthoff, *Das Chorwerk*, p. iii), its declamation surpasses that of De Orto in clarity through its good accentuation and its economic use of melismatic melody reserved for pictorial purposes. Strunk, in "Vergil in Music," compares Josquin's with Mouton's setting, which borrows the former's soprano part (pp. 485–487).

42. R. von Liliencron, "Die Horazischen Metren," pp. 30–31, n. 1; also É. Weber, *La musique mesurée*, I, 1, 182–184.

43. See Moser, *Paul Hofhaimer*, p. 163. We give Moser's version in a 1:4 reduction. The signs in parentheses are added.

44. See Clement A. Miller, "The *Dodecachordon*: Its Origins and Influence on Renaissance Musical Thought," *Musica Disciplina*, XV (1961), 155–166, esp. 159–162.

45. See Miller, *Dodecachordon*, I, 210: "Many years have elapsed since I, as a youth, composed certain songs to the Horatian odes, which some men later published throughout Germany without using my name; this has not distressed me, but it has pained me that certain songs which I had composed as belonging to certain odes they have attempted to apply in general to all, although this would be in no way possible, except to the great derision of learned men; yet especially it cannot occur in different genera, and not even in a single genus, if the sentences are not contained within the same periods."

46. See, for example, the article on "Odenkomposition," *Riemann Musik-Lexikon*, III,

Sachteil, 648: "Ihm zufolge (i.e., Glarean's *Dodekachordon*) sollten die musikalischen Sätze stets einstimmig und nur für eine Ode bestimmt sein."

47. His sixth melody (Miller, *Dodecachordon*, I, 214, second example) carries the beginnings of two texts: ode 19 from Book II and ode 27 from Book I. The seventh melody (pp. 214–215) also receives two texts: ode 15 from Book II, and ode 2 from Book III. He provides one and the same melody for verses by Martial and a hymn of Prudentius, *Pastis visceribus* (p. 216).

48. Compare, for instance, the melody on p. 212 with the second example on p. 213 or the one on p. 215 (ll. 3 and 4) with the first one of p. 216 (ll. 3 and 1). Renatus Pirker shows the technique of the "Mosaikbau" in Tritonius' ode settings ("Beiträge zur Entwicklungsgeschichte," pp. 142ff.) and in the Hebrew accents that Reuchlin published in his *De accentibus et orthographia linguae Hebraicae* (1518). Having received the 33 "accents" assembled in one continuous melodic line from the lector of Hebrew at the University of Ingolstadt, Reuchlin had them set for four voices by Christoph Schilling of Lucerne (p. 139).

49. *Dodecachordon*, I, 214.

50. *Ibid.*, p. 212.

51. *Horace, The Odes and Epodes*, Latin text with translation by C. E. Bennett (London, 1918: The Loeb Classical Library), p. 13.

52. *Ibid.*, p. 41; the melody appears in *Dodecachordon*, I, 213.

53. Wallace K. Ferguson, *Europe in Transition, 1300–1520* (Boston, 1962), p. 535.

54. *Dodecachordon*, I, 217. The one exception is Cochlaeus' *Veni creator spiritus* with the time signature ₵ (see facsimile edition, fol. F III). Here it should be remembered that Glareanus studied with Cochlaeus at the University of Cologne. His eulogy on music dedicated to "Johannes Cochlaeus of Bavaria" appears in the latter's treatise (see Miller, *Cochlaeus*, pp. 89–90).

55. *Dodecachordon*, I, 217.

56. *Ibid.*, p. 211.

57. *Ibid.*, p. 213. In the magnificent presentation manuscript of Cipriano de Rore's music made for Duke Albrecht V of Bavaria, Munich, Bayerische Staatsbibliothek, Mus. MS B, fol. 15, *Donec gratus eram tibi* is set for two choirs of four parts, one of low and one of high voices (see Ex. 19 below). As the dialogue changes between the lover and Lydia, so do the two choirs; see *Cipriani Rore Opera Omnia*, ed. Bernhard Meier, VI, *Corpus Mensurabilis Musicae*, 14 (American Institute of Musicology, 1975), 16–22.

58. *Horace, Odes and Epodes*, ed. Paul Shorey (Boston, 1901), p. 346.

59. *Dodecachordon*, I, 223.

60. *Horace*, Book III, ode 12, trans. Bennett, p. 223.

61. *Dodecachordon*, I, 219.

62. *Horace*, trans. Bennett, p. 19.

63. *Horace*, ed. Shorey, p. 161.

64. *Dodecachordon*, I, 219.

65. Moser, *Paul Hofhaimer*, appendix, p. 114, no. 5 (editorial accidentals added by the present writer).

66. *Dodecachordon*, I, 220.

67. See Wallace K. Ferguson, ed., *Erasmi Opuscula. A Supplement to the Opera Omnia* (The Hague, 1933), p. 28. The draft is printed on pp. 30–31.

68. *Ibid.*

69. Conrad Celtis, in his poem *ad musiphilos* accompanying Tritonius' *Melopoiae* (see note 6 above), speaks of the affects of the soul and the gestures of the body produced by the lutenist as he accompanies the [vocal] sounds:

> Affectusque animi gestuque in corpore pulsant
> Plectra simul mixto constrepitantque sono.

(Tritonius himself makes similar remarks in his long title.) Celtis also alludes to Orpheus, who is never missing when a Renaissance poet praises music. Yet, these are conventional ideas without real significance for the music of the odes. They are, however, proof that the humanists had absorbed the classical idea of the relationship between music and emotion before they were able to help the composers create such a music themselves. It had not yet dawned upon them that they were in fact obstructing the very possibility of such a relationship to emerge.

70. *Solitaire second, ou prose de la musique* (Lyons, 1555) (first ed., 1552).

71. Later on a third person enters the dialogue, "Le Curieus."

72. *Solitaire second*, p. 148.

73. See Erwin Panofsky, "Conrad Celtes and Kunz von der Rosen: Two Problems in Portrait Identification," *The Art Bulletin*, XXIV (1942), 39–54. Panofsky showed that the figure of the elderly man in Dürer's *Martyrdom of the Ten Thousand* leaning against the artist himself, who had included his self-portrait, was not, as thought before, that of Willibald Pirckheimer, but of Conrad Celtis, whom Panofsky describes as "a skilful Latin poet, a somewhat amateurish philosopher, epigrapher, archaeologist, geographer, and historian, the founder of several learned societies and, after all, the discoverer of Hroswitha of Gandersheim's Comedies and the *Tabulae Peutingerianae*, this stout, smallish man was one of the founders of German humanism and genuinely famous in his day" (p. 40).

74. He shared the distaste for the four-part settings of classical poetry with Glareanus, whom he quotes at length on the matter of modes and praises as "amateur et connoisseur de toutes disciplines" (*Solitaire second*, p. 119). Glareanus himself had referred to "those who in this time have set four-voice songs to the Horatian odes, in which one finds absolutely no trace of distinguished talent, aside from the harmony" (*Dodecachordon*, I, 210).

75. ". . .car si l'intencion de Musique semble estre, de donner tel air à la parole, que tout escoutant se sente passioné, et se laisse tirer à l'afeccion du Poëte: celui qui scet proprement acommoder une voix seule, me semble mieus ateindre à sa fin aspirée: vù que la Musique figurée le plus souvent ne raporte aus oreilles autre chose qu'un grand bruit, duquel vous ne sentez aucune vive eficace: Mais la simple et unique voix, coulée doucement, et continuée selon le devoir de sa Mode choisie pour le merite des vers, vous ravit la part qu'elle veut. Aussi consistoit en ce seul moyen la plus ravissante énergie des anciens Poëtes lyriques, qui, mariant la Musique à la Poësie (comme ils estoient nez à l'une et à l'autre) chantoient leurs vers, et rencontroient souvent l'efet de leur désir: tant la simplicité bien observée aus Modes de chanter est douée d'une secrette et admirable puissance" (*Solitaire second*, pp. 132–133).

76. *Ibid.*, pp. 26–27.

77. Frances A. Yates, *The French Academies of the Sixteenth Century* (London, 1947), p. 52. On Baïf's ideas see also D. P. Walker, "The Aims of Baïf's *Académie de Poésie et Musique*," *Journal of Renaissance and Baroque Music*, I (1946), 91–100, and the same author's article on "Jean-Antoine de Baïf" in *MGG*, I, cols. 1084–1086.

78. In a whimsical poem he confides that once upon a time he had hoped to earn his laurels writing in Latin. Upon discovering that he was not born for it, he decided to be rather second or third, or perhaps first, in his own language than the last, without honor, in Rome:

> Je fu premierement curieux du Latin:
> Mais cognoissant, helas! que mon cruel destin
> Ne m'avoit dextrement pour le Latin fait naistre,
> Je me fey tout François, aimant certe mieux estre
> En ma langue ou second, ou le tiers, ou premier
> Que d'estre sans honneur à Rome le dernier.

See Pierre de Nolhac, *Ronsard et l'Humanisme* (Paris, 1921), p. 22. Nolhac offers a well-documented account of the poet's life and his intellectual and artistic development with special reference to the world of humanism.

Ronsard's career can be viewed as a French echo of Pietro Bembo's change from staunch Ciceronian to the defender and protagonist of the *volgar lingua*; see Giuseppe Toffanin, *Storia Letteraria d'Italia, Il Cinquecento*, 3rd ed. (Milan, 1945), pp. 87ff. Inasmuch as he prepared the way from frottola to madrigal, his position in the history of music exceeds in importance that of Ronsard; see Alfred Einstein, *The Italian Madrigal*, 3 vols. (Princeton,

1949), I, 109ff. See also Dean T. Mace, "Pietro Bembo and the Literary Origins of the Italian Madrigal," *The Musical Quarterly*, LV (1969), 65–86. The brilliance of Mace's article is not diminished but slightly flawed by his yielding to the temptation to judge Alfred Einstein's view on the genesis of the Italian madrigal on the basis of a marginal speculation: "One may consider sixteenth-century secular music as an aberration, a deviation from the natural course of development initiated by the frottola . . . " (*Madrigal*, I, 153). To deduce from this passing remark, never further developed, that "the idea of evolution . . . has caused a great historian of music to believe that the entire art of the Italian madrigal is an inexplicable aberration" (p. 86) is absurd.

79. For an excellent account of the Pléiade and the role played there by Tyard and Ronsard, see Yates, *French Academies*, pp. 48–52, and chapter IV on "Poetry and Music and the Encyclopaedia."

80. See Muret's setting of Ronsard's ode *Ma petite colombelle*, the first of "Quatre chansons de Pierre de Ronsard" appended to G. Thibault and Louis Perceau, *Bibliographie des Poésies de P. de Ronsard mises en musique au XVIᶜ siècle* (Paris, 1941).

81. *Harmonice Musices Odhecaton A*, ed. Helen Hewitt (Cambridge, Mass., 1942).

82. *Ottaviano Petrucci, Canti B*, ed. Helen Hewitt, *Monuments of Renaissance Music*, Gen. Ed., Edward E. Lowinsky, II (Chicago, 1967).

83. Modern edition by Henry Expert, *Les Maîtres Musiciens de la Renaissance Française* (Paris, 1897), nos. 11 and 21.

84. *Jacobi Arcadelt Opera Omnia*, VIII, ed. Albertus Seay (American Institute of Musicology, 1968), 14–15.

85. "Vaudeville, vers mesurés et airs de cour," *Musique et poésie au XVIᶜ siècle* (Paris, 1954), pp. 185–201. The same Arcadelt wrote a number of settings of verses of Horace, Virgil, and Martial in homophonic texture slightly loosened by occasional melismas, in a syllabic declamation in which word accent replaces metric accent. No doubt, he followed here Adrian Willaert's example which we shall deal with below. Compare his setting of Virgil's scene of Dido's death, *At trepida et coeptis immanibus effera Dido*, which contains Dido's famous last words (Le Roy et Ballard, *Sixiesme livre de chansons*, Paris, 1556; *Arcadelt Opera Omnia*, VIII, 80–83) with Willaert's *Dulces exuviae* (Ex. 15 below). For settings of Martial and Horace, see *ibid.*, pp. 84–86, and vol. IX, nos. 65, 66, 67, the latter three pieces set for three voices.

86. See André Verchaly's edition, *Airs de Cour pour voix et luth (1603–1643), Publications de la Société française de Musicologie*, 16 (Paris, 1961).

87. "Non toutefois, que je croye estre impossible d'acommoder proprement la Musique figurée aus paroles, ni que je desespere de ce tems: mais la dificulté de notre langage non encores mesuré en certeines longeurs ou brievetez de sillabes, et le peu d'égard que je voy y estre pris par les Musiciens, qui tous, ou la plus part, sont sans lettres, et connoissance de Poësie: comme aussi le plus grand nombre des Poëtes mesprise, et, si j'ose dire, ne connoit la Musique, me fait creindre que tard, ou rarement, nous en puissions voir de bons et naturels exemples" (*Solitaire second*, p. 133).

88. *Biographisch-Bibliographisches Quellen-Lexikon der Musiker und Musikgelehrten*, 10 vols. (Leipzig, 1900–1904), III, 419.

89. See Knud Jeppesen, "A Forgotten Master of the Early Sixteenth Century: Gaspar de Albertis," *The Musical Quarterly*, XLIV (1958), 311–328, esp. 311.

90. Modern edition in *Adriani Willaert Opera Omnia*, ed. Hermann Zenck, II (American Institute of Musicology, 1950), 59–62. Since the work does not appear in the first edition of 1539, we may reasonably suppose that it was written between 1540 and 1545.

91. It is possible that he was influenced by his Venetian fellow-citizen Trifone Gabrieli (see section VII, last paragraph).

92. See chapter 33 of book IV of his *Istitutioni harmoniche* (Venice, 1558), entitled: "Il modo, che si hà da tenere, nel porre le Figure cantabili sotto le Parole."

93. See Lowinsky, "A Treatise on Text Underlay by a German Disciple of Francisco de Salinas," *Festschrift Heinrich Besseler* (Leipzig, 1961), pp. 231–251; for a comparison between the rules of Zarlino and those of Stocker, see pp. 244–245. For further information on the identity of Stoquerus, see *idem*, "Gasparus Stoquerus and Francisco de Salinas," *Journal of*

the American Musicological Society, XVI (1963), 241–243. For the rules of text underlay given by Giovanni Maria Lanfranco and by Nicola Vicentino, see Don Harrán, "New Light on the Question of Text Underlay Prior to Zarlino," *Acta musicologica*, XLV (1973), 24–56, and *idem*, "Vicentino and His Rules of Text Underlay," *The Musical Quarterly*, LIX (1973), 620–632.

94. Modern edition in *Cipriani Rore Opera Omnia*, VI, 6–15. Rore was not the first composer to set this text to music. A Venetian frottolist, Filippo de Luprano, preceded him (Petrucci, *Frottole libro VIII*, Venice, RISM 1507¹, no. 12). For a modern edition, see Benvenuto Disertori, *Le Frottole per canto e liuto intabulate da Franciscus Bossinensis* (*Istituzioni e Monumenti dell'arte musicale Italiana*, n.s., III; Milan, 1964), no. 13, pp. 164–166. Here we have an accompanied monody, the soprano singing the text, the three lower voices entrusted to the lute. It is not much of an exaggeration to say that Luprano's setting compares to Rore's as a child's stammering to the dramatic rendering by a mature woman.

Solo performance of frottole as well as of odes—Italian and German—is well documented in the literature (see for instance Walter Rubsamen's article on "Frottola" in *MGG*, IV, under XI: *Lateinische Gedichte*, cols. 1026–1027).

95. In the two hundred thirty-six measures of the three *partes* of *Dissimulare* we find only one (incomplete) intermediate cadence (two, if we count the repeat) in the *secunda pars* (mm. 80–81 and 83–84), none at the final cadences or elsewhere. Rore's shunning the cadence differs essentially from the *fuggir la cadenza* that Zarlino speaks of in chapter 52 of the third book of his *Istitutioni*. To "evade the cadence" means only to evade the last part of the cadence, not the cadence formula itself. A deceptive cadence, for example, belongs to the concept of *fuggir la cadenza*. On the other hand, the humanistic ode, by virtue of its strictly homophonic style, evades the rhythmic and melodic-melismatic aspects of the sixteenth-century clausula, but not its harmonic character. Tritonius' *Jam satis terris* (Ex. 3) closes with a clearly articulated cadence V–I–IV–V–I; Sebastian Forster's *Arma virumque cano* (Ex. 4), closing likewise with a strong authentic cadence, is organized in distinct phrases rendered audible by use of cadences of various kinds. This is of course already foreshadowed in Tritonius' much shorter example. Rore has not one single complete authentic cadence in his large homophonic structure; indeed, the harmonic progressions steer clear of tonal implications and give even this chromatically moderate work a decidedly manneristic physiognomy.

96. *Italian Madrigal*, I, 419–420.

97. See the preface to Claudio Monteverdi's fifth book of madrigals, *Scherzi musicali* (1607), the famous *Dichiaratione* written in his name by Claudio's brother, Giulio Cesare. The preface is published in a collection of all prefaces, dedications, and letters of the master by G. Francesco Malipiero, *Claudio Monteverdi* (Milan, 1929), pp. 72–85; see p. 78. For an English translation, see Strunk, *Source Readings*, pp. 405–412; p. 408.

98. A reduction of the open score to solo and four-part accompaniment will be instructive. To indicate the emotional character of the music, I take the liberty to suggest some marks for tempo and expression. In connection with *Se ben il duol*, Einstein, too, is reminded "of the monodic attempts which, forty or fifty years later, look almost like arrangements of such pieces for voice and lute" (*Italian Madrigal*, I, 421).

99. *Cipriani Rore Opera Omnia*, VI, 16–22.

100. For a discussion of the ideological and theoretical difficulties, see Lowinsky, "Music of the Renaissance as Viewed by Renaissance Musicians" (see note 3), pp. 156–161.

101. Henry W. Kaufmann, *The Life and Works of Nicola Vicentino (1511–c. 1576)* (American Institute of Musicology, 1966), p. 22.

102. See the facsimile edition by Lowinsky (*Documenta Musicologica*, XVII; Kassel, 1959).

103. To obtain these, it took no great learning. Indeed, Vicentino has been rightly faulted for his "small Latin"—see Bertha A. Wallner, "Urkunden zu den Musikbestrebungen Herzog Wilhelms V. von Bayern," *Gedenkboek aangeboden aan Dr. D. F. Scheurleer* (The Hague, 1925), pp. 369–377—and "less Greek"; Giovanni Battista Doni accused him of "having boldly rushed into this field without having read the classical authors" (see Postface to the facsimile edition of Vicentino's treatise).

104. Ed. by Henry W. Kaufmann (American Institute of Musicology, 1963).

105. *Italian Madrigal*, I, 423.

106. See Guglielmo Barblan and Agostina Zecca Laterza, "The Tarasconi Codex in the Library of the Milan Conservatory," *The Musical Quarterly*, LX (1974), 195–221.

107. See Lowinsky, "Early Scores in Manuscript," *Journal of the American Musicological Society*, XIII (1960), 126–173.

108. See N. Bridgman and F. Lesure, "Une anthologie 'historique' de la fin du XVIᵉ siècle: le manuscrit Bourdeney," *Miscelánea en homenaje a Monseñor Higinio Anglés*, 2 vols. (Barcelona, 1958–61), I, 161–172, and Oscar Mischiati, "Un'antologia manoscritta in partitura del secolo XVI," *Rivista Italiana di Musicologia*, X (1975), 265–328.

109. The piece is particularly valuable because it stands stylistically midway between the composer's first book of madrigals of 1546 and the fifth (1572), the books in between having been lost. It gives us an idea of Vicentino's madrigal style in, I venture to guess, the time span between 1555 and 1560, for reasons that cannot be discussed here, but can be deduced from my recent study on "The Problem of Mannerism in Music: An Attempt at a Definition," *Studi Musicali*, III (1974 [publ. 1977]), 131–218. There Vicentino's treatise is characterized as "the manifesto of mannerism" (pp. 160–167; esp. p. 165).

110. For a definition of mannerism in music, see the article cited in the preceding footnote.

111. See Lowinsky, *Secret Chromatic Art in the Netherlands Motet* (New York, 1946; repr., 1967), p. 90. This interpretation has been rejected by Leo Schrade on grammatical grounds ("A Secret Chromatic Art," *Journal of Renaissance and Baroque Music*, I [1946], 156–167, esp. 165–166), a rejection emphatically endorsed by Claude Palisca ("A Clarification of 'Musica Reservata' in Jean Taisnier's 'Astrologiae,' 1559," *Acta Musicologica*, XXXI [1959], 133–161, esp. 151–152). It has been accepted by Charles van den Borren ("Y avait-il une pratique musicale ésotérique au temps de Roland de Lassus?" *Revue Belge de Musicologie*, II [1948], 38–43, esp. 42), Alfred Einstein (*Italian Madrigal*, I, 228), Hellmut Federhofer ("Eine neue Quelle der musica reservata," *Acta Musicologica*, XXIV [1952], 32–45, esp. 32 and 42), Gustave Reese (*Music in the Renaissance* [New York, 1954], p. 513), Knud Jeppesen (review of Reese's book in *The Musical Quarterly*, XLI [1955], 378–391, esp. 390), Wolfgang Boetticher (*Orlando di Lasso und seine Zeit* [Kassel, 1958], p. 73, n. 18; p. 213, n. 10; p. 845), and Bernhard Meier (articles on "Musica reservata" in *MGG*, IX, cols. 946–949, esp. 946, and *Handwörterbuch der musikalischen Terminologie*, ed. H. H. Eggebrecht [1976]), p. 2. Moreover, Jeppesen, Boetticher, and Meier furnish new documentation in support of my interpretation.

112. Ernst R. Curtius, *European Literature and the Latin Middle Ages*, trans. Willard R. Trask, Bollingen Series, XXXVI (New York, 1953), pp. 190–191, from which the following translation is taken.

113. Except for using a note of double length for a long syllable at the caesura of the third foot, (*patu-*)*lae*, and a pause after the sixth foot. This is in accord with classical scansion, but not with the metrical system used by Celtis-Tritonius who confine themselves to two different lengths, although the fermata used at the end of a line indicates a rest. At one point we encounter a four-fold length of a long syllable, a liberty taken in accord with the meaning of the text, (*tu, Tityre*), *len-*(*tus in umbra*) (p. 70, m. 3), ("you, Tityrus, lazy in the shade").

114. In 1559 by the Imperial Vicechancellor Dr. Seld; see W. Boetticher, "Neue Lasso-Funde," *Die Musikforschung*, VIII (1955), 385–397, esp. 396. On Dr. Seld and *musica reservata*, see Lowinsky, *Secret Chromatic Art*, pp. 91ff.

115. See Orlando di Lasso, *Sämtliche Werke, Neue Reihe*, I, ed. W. Boetticher (Kassel, 1956), no. 1.

116. *Ibid.*, no. 13; Boetticher has shown that the *Magnum opus musicum* of 1604, on which the Gesamtausgabe is based, offers the work with the text *Bestia stultus homo* (vol. XI, no. 444). The original is preserved in a number of French chanson prints by Adrian le Roy, for the first time in the twenty-first book of chansons, 1577 (see Boetticher, *Orlando di Lasso*, p. 451).

117. Text, German translation, and commentary, *ibid.*, p. xxxii; music, no. 13, pp. 67–70.

118. Boetticher's emendation; orig.: *passim*. In the same line I emend the *per similes* to *persimilis* (with no change of meaning, but with grammatical construction improved), since all words, save for the refrain, begin with "p"—undoubtedly an onomatopoetic device.

119. See note 117.

120. See Lowinsky, "Music in the Culture of the Renaissance," *Journal of the History of Ideas*, XV (1954), 509–553, esp. 526–528; also in *Renaissance Essays from the Journal of the History of Ideas*, ed. P. O. Kristeller and Philip P. Wiener (Harper Torchbooks: New York, 1968), pp. 337–381, esp. 354–356.

121. "...qui quidem adeo apposite lamentabili et querula voce, ubi opus fuit, ad res et verba accommodando, singulorum affectuum vim exprimendo rem quasi actam ante oculos ponendo, expressit. . . . Hoc quidem musicae genus musicam reservatam vocant. . . ." (For the complete text, see Marcus van Crevel, *Adrianus Petit Coclico* [The Hague, 1940], p. 300.)

122. See Leo Schrade, *La représentation d'Edipo Tiranno au Teatro Olimpico (Vicence 1585)* (Paris, 1960).

123. Schrade attributes these unusual "colors" to Gabrieli's daring use of *musica ficta*. Speaking of the juxtaposition of chords without mutual relationships, he remarks: "l'accord revête sa 'couleur' insolite grâce à l'emploi de la *musica ficta* que Gabrieli utilise avec beaucoup d'audace" (p. 74). One must distinguish between *musica ficta* and chromaticism. The "sudden chord changes and the introduction of quite unexpected sounds" that Schrade correctly observes have nothing to do with *musica ficta*, which operates within the medieval system of modes and its diatonicism. Even the boldest application of *musica ficta* rules cannot produce the sudden changes found in Gabrieli's score; they are due to the use of direct chromaticism called forth by precise and daring use of accidentals which is not only beyond anything *musica ficta* can accomplish, but also entirely beyond the confines of traditional theory. The frequent chromatic steps (from C to C#, D to D#, etc.) cannot be conceptualized within the system of the modes, of solmization, and of *musica ficta*.

Nor is it correct to say that "la variété que réalise Gabrieli . . . et les effets vraiment extraordinaires qu'il obtient dans un domaine inexploré, n'ont pas d'équivalents dans la musique du XVIᵉ siècle" (*ibid.*). Gabrieli's chromatic harmony is entirely within the tradition of the Italian chromatic movement. Precisely thirty years before *Edipo tiranno*, Nicola Vicentino published his epoch-making treatise, *L'antica musica ridotta alla moderna prattica*, the same year in which Orlando di Lasso brought out his opus I in Antwerp with astonishing chromatic works of his own as well as of Cipriano de Rore (the famous chromatic ode *Calami sonum*, written for four bass parts). The language of chromatic harmony that Gabrieli speaks was created a generation before *Edipo tiranno*; it can be studied in the chromatic compositions illustrating Vicentino's treatise and in the cycle of Sibylline compositions of the young Lasso (see the edition by H. J. Therstappen in *Das Chorwerk*, 48 [1937]).

For further discussion of the "nouvelle manière d'aulcuns d'Italie" (as Lasso called it in his *Libro primo dove si contengono Madrigali, vilanesche, canzon francesi e motetti a quattro voci . . .*, Antwerp, 1555), see Lowinsky, *Das Antwerpener Motettenbuch Orlando di Lasso's und seine Beziehungen zum Motettenschaffen der niederländischen Zeitgenossen* (The Hague, 1937), p. 23, n. 4, and *idem*, "The Problem of Mannerism in Music," pp. 143–158.

124. "Ueber den Kontrapunkt. Eine kurze Anweisung aus dem XVI. Jahrhundert," *Monatshefte für Musikgeschichte*, X (1878), 63–65.

125. *Die Niederländer und das deutsche Lied (1400–1640)* (Berlin, 1938), p. 275, n. 54 (see also reprint, Tutzing, 1967).

126. I shall deal more fully with the treatise and its position in the theory of *musica reservata* in a larger context.

127. See its ironic use by Lasso for the words "ogni agro stile" in his madrigal *Gia mi fu co'l desir* or "antichi desir" in *Hor qui son, lasso* (Examples 10 and 11 of Lowinsky, "The Problem of Mannerism in Music," pp. 211–212).

128. One might wonder whether Schrade is not speaking of *falsobordone* rather than fauxbourdon, inasmuch as the French use the term for both the three- and the four-part forms of psalmody. This is not the case. Schrade speaks explicitly of "le parallélisme des accords avec consonances imparfaites du fauxbourdon, employé constamment depuis le

XVe siècle dans les compositions sur les tons psalmodiques . . . " (p. 76). To reinforce his point, Schrade attributes to Gabrieli's work "another characteristic phenomenon": "la fréquence des mouvements parallèles dans les successions d'accords. Ce parallélisme entraîne la présence dans les accords non seulement d'intervalles de sixte et quarte mais aussi des consonances parfaites telles que l'unisson, la quinte et l'octave, et le mouvement parallèle en consonances parfaites n'est nullement l'exception" (p. 75). Indeed, he claims that such parallel movements are found in long passages from one end of the work to the other and create the misleading impression that this practice comes from improvisation.

Two points should be made here: when Gabrieli uses parallel fifths or octaves, he takes great care to avoid them on paper through the device of voice-crossing. This speaks against even the assumption of improvisation. The second point has been made in a review of his edition by Hans Engel (*Die Musikforschung*, XVIII [1965], 465–467) when he says: "An Parallelismen kann ich nichts finden." Neither can the present writer.

129. The personal relations between Lasso and Andrea Gabrieli are well documented. When Duke Albrecht of Bavaria, in 1562, traveled to Prague for the coronation of Maximilian as King of Bohemia, he took with him Orlando di Lasso and his best musicians, among them Andrea Gabrieli as organist; see Horst Leuchtmann, *Orlando di Lasso*, 2 vols. (Wiesbaden, 1976–77), I, 122. That the court of Munich remained in touch with Andrea may be seen from the mention of his name in Lasso's letter of 26 February 1574 from Mantua (*ibid.*, II, *Briefe*, no. 10). It seems that Duke Wilhelm of Bavaria, Albrecht's son, had asked Lasso to persuade Andrea to come as "capo della musica" for Wilhelm's private musical establishment in Landshut (*ibid.*, II, 65).

130. See the facsimile editions of the two works in *Bibliotheca Musica Bononiensis*, ed. Giuseppe Vecchi, Sezione IV. N. 2, 1968 (Peri), N. 3, 1969 (Caccini).

131. See Girolamo Mei, *Letters on Ancient and Modern Music to Vincenzo Galilei and Giovanni Bardi*, ed. Claude V. Palisca (*Musicological Studies and Documents*, III; American Institute of Musicology, 1960), and Nino Pirrotta, "Temperaments and Tendencies in the Florentine Camerata," *The Musical Quarterly*, XL (1954), 169–89.

132. *La Poetica di Bernardino Daniello Lucchese* (Venice, 1536). I have had a copy of the work in my library for over twenty-five years. It is now available in *Trattati di poetica e retorica del Cinquecento*, ed. by Bernard Weinberg, 4 vols. (Bari, 1970–74), I, 229–318. All references will be made to this edition, which gives the original pagination in the margin.

133. My friend, Dr. Ursula Kirkendale, has independently made the same discovery.

134. Daniello, *La Poetica*, pp. 231 and 232. The uncertainty of Andrea Gabrieli's birthdate, still given as "between 1510 and 1520" in the article of *MGG* following Einstein (*Italian Madrigal*, II, 521), can be removed by this date. Andrea is the older of the two nephews (see Daniello, p. 264) and appears throughout the dialogue as the more mature, well read, and intelligent of the two; his opinions are usually well received by Trifone (see in particular pp. 277 and 291). A birthdate of 1520 would make Andrea a thirteen-year-old at the time of the conversation, a date between 1510 and 1512 would present him as 23 or 21 years of age—very much more in keeping with his role in the dialogue and with Daniello's calling him "Messer Andrea."

135. Emanuele Antonio Cicogna, *Delle Inscrizioni Veneziane*, III (Venice, 1830), 208–223.

136. *Ibid.*, p. 209.

137. See Felix Gilbert, "The Date of the Composition of Contarini's and Giannotti's Books on Venice," *Studies in the Renaissance*, XIV (1967), 172–184, esp. 177–182.

138. On Trifone's role in Giannotti's work, see William J. Bouwsma, *Venice and the Defense of Republican Liberty* (Berkeley and Los Angeles, 1968), pp. 155–159.

139. See Alessandro Luzio-Rodolfo Renier, "La coltura e le relazioni letterarie di Isabella d'Este Gonzaga," *Giornale storico della letteratura italiana*, XXXVII (1901), 201–245, esp. 215. Bembo frequently requested Trifone to revise now a poem of his composition, now his most important literary work in prose, *Prose della volgar lingua* (see his letters to Trifone of 11 Dec. 1507 and 1 April 1512 in Pietro Bembo, *Opere in volgare*, ed. Mario Marti [Florence, 1961], pp. 712 and 713).

140. *In Epistolam Q. Horatii Flacci de Arte Poetica Iasonis de Nores Ciprij ex quotidiano Tryphonis Gabrieli sermonibus interpretatio. Eiusdem Brevis, Et Distincta summa praeceptorum de arte*

dicendi ex tribus Ciceronis de oratore collecta (Venice, 1553*).* Thirty-six years later, the same author published an astronomical treatise, *Sphera* (Padua, 1589), in which he translated Trifone Gabrieli's treatise *Spheretta* from Latin into Italian with the latter's revisions and additions (fols. 28ff). Girolamo Tiraboschi, in his *Storia della letteratura italiana,* VII, 2 (Florence, 1810), p. 484, reports about the *Dialogo sopra il discorso del Cielo* by "Jacopo Gabrielli, nipote di Trifone," published in Venice in 1554 and dedicated to Bembo, who thanked the author for his gift, praising him for having become not only an excellent astronomer but also "*maestro della Toscana lingua,* which we Venetians learn not without difficulty" (*ibid.*)—a double compliment to the memory of Jacopo's uncle as a teacher of astronomy and of the vernacular.

141. See his letter to Bernardino Daniello of 22 Dec. 1536 in Pietro Aretino, *Il primo libro delle lettere,* ed. Fausto Nicolini (Bari, 1913), pp. 100–101; also in *Lettere sull'arte di Pietro Aretino commentate da Fidenzio Pertile,* ed. Ettore Camesasca, 4 vols. (Milan, 1957–60), I, 35–36. Here Aretino calls Trifone "the father of the pure, learned and sublime style."

142. See the moving tribute to his recently deceased uncle in the dedication to the *Concerti di Andrea, et di Gio. Gabrieli . . .* (Venice, 1587), in Emil Vogel, Alfred Einstein, François Lesure, Claudio Sartori, *Bibliografia della musica italiana vocale profana pubblicata dal 1500 al 1700,* 3 vols. (Pomezia, 1977), I, no. 1046.

143. *Italian Madrigal,* II, 534.

144. Daniello, pp. 276–277.

145. Petrarch, *Canzoniere,* 365 and 353.

146. *Ibid.,* 125.

147. *Ibid.,* 126. The two *canzoni* had been objects of careful analysis by Pietro Bembo in his *Prose della volgar lingua* published in 1525, but written much earlier; see Pietro Bembo, *Opere in volgare,* pp. 328–329. Both poems, and particularly "Chiare, fresche, e dolci acque," attracted the attention of Italian and Italianate Netherlandish madrigalists throughout the sixteenth century.

148. *Di Andrea Gabrieli organista della illustrissima S. di Venetia in S. Marco il Primo Libro di Madrigali a cinque voci . . .* (Venice, 1566).

149. ". . .la dimostrazione, che si fa quasi dinanzi agli occhi degli ascoltanti ponendo quella cosa della qual si ragiona, sì fattamente dipignendola che paia a quei cotali vederlasi rappresentare davanti tale quale ella si finge, o quale stata veramente et avenuta sia" (p. 300). Daniello uses here (and elsewhere) a definition that has a long pedigree and eventually goes back to Aristotle's poetics. I intend to deal also with this question in a wider context.

150. ". . .quanto egli sia stato singulare nell'imitatione in ritrovar suoni esprimenti l'Energia delle parole, e de' concetti." The translation offered in Einstein's *Italian Madrigal,* II, 521, is slightly ambiguous: "how unique an imitator he was in finding sounds to express the force of words and of ideas." It might be better to say "how unique he was in imitating [the affects and] in finding the sounds expressing the 'energy' of the words and the concepts." Already earlier Giovanni had extolled Andrea's music, saying that "he who has tasted the sound of his compositions and the harmony of his counterpoints can attest to having experienced the true motions of the affects . . . " (my translation). The theory of "imitation" was a *topos* of both literary and musical poetics; it related chiefly to the representation of human passions, whether in drama, epic, fable, poetry or in Lied, chanson, motet, madrigal, madrigal comedy, and eventually in the musical drama (see Armen Carapetyan, "The Concept of *Imitazione della Natura* in the Sixteenth Century," *Journal of Renaissance and Baroque Music,* I [1946], pp. 47–67).

151. Daniello, *Poetica,* p. 233.

152. Horace, *Ars poetica,* 396–397: ". . .fuit haec sapientia quondam, publica privatis secernere. . . ."

153. Daniello, *Poetica,* p. 234.

154. *Ibid.,* p. 229.

155. See the discussion in V, p. 122.

156. Einstein, *Italian Madrigal,* II, 521.

157. *Ibid.,* I, 384.

158. "La qual cosa potrete per voi medesimo vedere ciascuna volta che voi farete a qual si voglia eccellente musico, la voce insieme col suono sciogliendo et accordando, una delle canzoni d'Orazio prima e dopo una di quelle del Petrarca cantare. Conciò sia cosa che vie più (senz'alcun dubbio) di soave armonia empierà ciascun giudicioso orecchio questa seconda, che fatto non avrà la prima. E ciò solamente avverà per la rima, la quale tanto più s'accorderà col suono e più renderà di dolcezza, quanto meno sarà dall'altra sua compagna rima lontana" (Daniello, *Poetica*, p. 317).

159. See Bernardo Pisano, *Collected Works*, vol. I of *Music of the Florentine Renaissance*, ed. Frank A. D'Accone (American Institute of Musicology, 1966); see also Alfred Einstein, *Italian Madrigal*, I, 128ff.

160. Einstein, *Italian Madrigal*, II, 523.

161. *Ibid.*, II, 525ff. Professor Warren Kirkendale had the kindness to communicate to me, in a letter of 6 Aug. 1980, his discovery of the testament of an Andrea Gabrieli, not the composer, in the Venetian Archivio di Stato. "The testament," he writes, "was made on Oct. 16, 1568, and probated in mid-November, 1571, surely soon after Andrea's death." Kirkendale is convinced (a) that this Andrea is the nephew of Trifone Gabrieli since the will mentions clearly identifiable members of Trifone's family; (b) that it is very unlikely that two brothers would give their sons identical Christian names so that their names would be indistinguishable; (c) that Andrea, the composer, could hardly have been Trifone's nephew, because it is unlikely that a nobleman would have practiced music professionally. Andrea's position at St. Mark's, Kirkendale states, was that of an organist, not a composer. In sixteenth-century Italy, musical performance was clearly classified among the "mechanical" occupations, and sixteenth-century Venetian law specifically excludes not only persons with such occupations, but also their children from the *libro d'oro* and the *maggior consiglio*, which included all members of patrician families. Moreover, Kirkendale did not find a second Andrea of the generation of Trifone's nephews in the Venetian manuscript genealogies of Trifone's family nor in the *libro d'oro*, the register of the patrician families of Venice.

As for my own preliminary position: the relationships between Trifone and Andrea Gabrieli, the composer, that I have been able to develop in the present study are too numerous and too weighty to be lightly dismissed. To replace the Andrea in Daniello's dialogue, whom I took to be the composer, with the newly discovered Andrea would require to fit the new Andrea into the role of Trifone's chief interlocutor. The composer Andrea fits so well into this role that it would seem to be more difficult to displace him than to hypothesize that Daniello was misled by the name and by the relationship of uncle and nephew between Trifone and the second interlocutor, Jacopo, to believe that Andrea, too, was a nephew. Nor do I share the view that a nobleman could not easily have become a professional musician.

Finally, one cannot rule out the possibility that Andrea Gabrieli, even were he not a nephew of Trifone's nor the interlocutor Andrea of the treatise, had read the book and adopted both its teachings and the person of the "Venetian Socrates," whom he either knew in person or by reputation, as models to follow in his art and in his life.

162. "Tenghino i cori nelle tragedie (quando più nelle comedie non s'usano, ma in lor vece fra l'un atto e l'altro, affine che vota non rimanga la scena, e suoni e canti e moresche e buffoni mescolatamente si sogliono introdurre) . . . " (Daniello, *Poetica*, p. 252). Since the fifteenth century, the *moresca* was a ballet danced between the acts of a comedy.

163. "Problems in Adrian Willaert's Iconography," *Aspects of Medieval and Renaissance Music. A Birthday Offering to Gustave Reese*, ed. Jan LaRue (New York, 1966), pp. 576–594; esp. 588–589.

164. Eric W. White, *Stravinsky* (Berkeley and Los Angeles, 1969), p. 24.

V

Humanism as a Mode of Perception: The Case of England

Arthur B. Ferguson
Duke University

Humanism remains an elusive concept, its morphology at best debatable, at worst subject to willful distortion, yet it is a concept we seem unable to do without. If we are to understand that complex transition from medieval culture to early modern that, for lack of any better term, we have become accustomed to call the Renaissance, we must make up our minds about what was in fact its most vital intellectual force. Like Romanticism, with which, incidentally, it has much else in common, Renaissance humanism had the chameleon's ability to take on the color of its surroundings. But there, precisely, lies the problem: to what extent, if at all, is it possible to discover a common factor, other than a common education and a common methodology, linking those varying, and at times mutually contradictory, manifestations we think of as humanist? Must Renaissance humanism be defined only in terms of method, not of substance? The question is simple enough, the answer is not. It must be sought below the intractably variegated surface of explicitly expressed ideas and specific interests. Moreover, the humanist impulse moved and changed with the circumstances of Renaissance life. I am confining myself to the curiously idiosyncratic case of England whose soil had a way of altering the chemistry of all imported plants, while capable of fostering peculiarly native growths. What applies to sixteenth-century England may not, however, be wholly irrelevant elsewhere. In any case, the answer must, I believe, be sought not in any particular idea or pattern of ideas nor in any special interests, still less in a systematic philosophy, but in a way of looking at things, in a mode of perception.

Efforts to identify humanism more substantively have always tended to limit or even to confuse. The idea of "civic humanism," for example, though applicable enough to England, provided the changeables are changed, remains restricted to a particular kind of humanist and a particular situation. "Christian humanism," even more applicable to England, is still a concept likely to be either equally restrictive or merely redundant. English humanism reveals a deep tincture of Platonism; yet to identify it that way is to minimize the strong Aristotelian strain remaining in it and the continuing tendency to revert to scholastic habits. Even to identify English humanism exclusively with the study of classical antiquity is to ignore the part that Christian antiquity also came to play in humanist thought as Renaissance disciplines were brought to bear on Reformation issues—just as identifying it with an optimistic confidence in the efficacy of human reason ignores the pessimistic strain that stems from a continuing consciousness of man's fallen nature on the part of scholars possessing all the other attributes commonly thought of as humanist. Confusing also, has been the tendency to treat English humanism almost exclusively in the context of belles lettres, a tendency natural enough for literary scholars, though less marked than it used to be before Douglas Bush took a longer look at the subject some forty years ago, and before English historians themselves decided to take intellectual history seriously. With a few notable exceptions, the writers who set the tone for English humanism were not creative artists.

Convinced that humanism could not be defined in terms of any consistent body of ideas or any special interests, Professor Kristeller undertook some years ago to find a definition that would stand up among the varying, sometimes contradictory expressions of humanist thought.[1] In what has become the starting point for most subsequent discussion of the subject, he argued that humanists must be considered primarily as professional practitioners within the strict limits of the *studia humanitatis*, essentially grammarians and rhetoricians, who took as their subject matter the literature, history, and moral philosophy of ancient Greece and Rome and who, in the process of their studies, developed certain characteristic techniques of textual criticism. Kristeller admitted, however, that, in their reinterpretation of classical culture, humanists assumed certain characteristic attitudes and accepted certain typical values: "an unbounded admiration for classical antiquity, an often unfair contempt for the middle ages," and "an emphatic and genuine concern with man, and with human, that is, primarily moral considerations." One may quibble at the "unbounded" part, and even at the scorn for things medieval. Still, this definition was, and remains, basic as far as it went; and it provided the important service of forestalling futile attempts to create a distinctively humanist philosophy. But it also remained severely restrictive. It defined humanism in terms rather of method than of content. It left out humanism, as it were, in action, humanism as it was applied to the varying concerns of learned men in a period of more than rapid change.

Such a disjunction between method and application becomes especially troublesome in the case of England where the interests of humanists tended to be practical rather than academic and the *studia humanitatis* to be considered a means rather than an end in itself—a means, that is, to the right ordering of "the very and true commonweal of this realm of England." By the same token, any attempt to restrict the definition of a humanist to those professionally engaged in the core curriculum of humane studies is likely to fail in the case of England where professionals and nonprofessionals alike applied a common learning and the inspiration it provided to ends outside the limits of classical scholarship.

A look at representative examples of those who, by virtue of their grounding in the *studia humanitatis* and their ability to put the scholarly techniques associated with them to practical use, can hardly be denied membership in the goodly company of humanists, will show both how diverse their interests could be and how futile it is to distinguish between professionals and amateurs when dealing with the English Renaissance. To begin with, take the four well-known Thomases who moved so obviously in the mainstream of English humanism: Sir Thomas More, lawyer by profession, humanist by avocation, translator of Lucian, yet ready to devote his skills to the causes of his generation, and, in a moment of inspired insight, to subject contemporary society to an analysis of unprecedented realism; Sir Thomas Elyot, landowner, sometime member of parliament, busily engaged in compiling a much-needed English-Latin dictionary, yet concerned primarily with educating the governing class for a life of active citizenship;

Thomas Starkey, recently returned from Italy, full of his Paduan studies, yet ready to rent out his literary skill and legal expertise to Cromwell's propaganda campaign and to compose, on his own, what is certainly the second most penetrating analysis of English society made in early Tudor England; Sir Thomas Smith, professor, academic administrator, diplomat, and Renaissance man at large, capable of turning from arguments over the pronunciation of Greek vowels and the spelling of English and from arcane researches into the wages of a Roman footsoldier to what became the standard treatise in his time on English government and, in the brilliant *Discourse*, now usually attributed to him, to what amounted to a pioneer work in mercantilist theory.[2] We find even professional teachers like Sir John Cheke, "who taught Cambridge and King Edward Greek," becoming embroiled in the royal administration and turning his talents to the task of explaining the king's policy to his fellow countrymen in their own language.[3] Others deserve to be mentioned, at least, if only to emphasize the diversity of ends to which scholars, thoroughly trained in the disciplines of humanism, applied their training. Take the churchmen, for example. The fact that the Reformation virtually coincided with humanism's ultimate domestication in England meant that many of the best-trained humanists were drawn away from pure scholarship to ecclesiastical controversy: Colet, Fisher, Gardiner, and the noble army of English recusant scholars, Tyndale and Cranmer among the several founders of English Protestantism, Jewel, Whitgift, and Hooker, among the architects of the Anglican Settlement. Then, of course, there were the men of letters more conventionally considered: Ascham and Mulcaster, both as interested as Elyot had been to educate English gentlemen for a life of virtuous service; literary critics and linguistic reformers like Puttenham and Wills and Daniel, to say nothing of Smith and Mulcaster again, all concerned to make the vernacular a fit medium for the socially useful purposes of translation and public discussion as well as for those of purely literary expression. Nor should we forget the antiquaries, scholars like Camden, lawyers like Selden and Spelman, alike effectively, if somewhat belatedly, overtaking the historical and legal scholarship of Continental humanists. English humanism was thus essentially an applied humanism; and English humanists can best be known by their fruits.

While they did not lack a proper concern for grammar and rhetoric or for *bonae literae*, events tended to press them into the service of issues where their essentially humanist learning could be employed to advantage, and their classically inspired sense of citizenship made them see to it that it was so employed. They were by no means deaf to the virtues of eloquence. They knew as well as any of their Continental predecessors that rhetoric, by making wisdom articulate, could move the will to action. For them, however, it was the action that counted. They were more concerned with directing the tradition of Cicero and Quintilian to practical ends than with debating more academic questions such as the relation of rhetoric to philosophy. To them, the lives of action and contemplation were by no means mutually exclusive alternatives. They saw their own reflection in those archetypal orators and poets who, according to ancient myth, had brought mankind in the youth of the world from a caveman existence to civility; and with remarkable consistency, they resorted to that very myth as a quasi-anthropological foundation for their favorite programs of reform.[4]

Pure scholarship, indeed, lagged in Tudor England. Elizabethan humanists to some extent made up for its deficiencies by the socially useful labor of translation. Second hand or not, however, the fact remains that the methods and inspiration associated with humanism continued to be very much alive well into the seventeenth century and in the work of scholars to whom the designation of humanist can hardly be denied.

If, however, we are to identify English humanists by the way they applied their learning, we run into certain difficulties. For one thing, where do we stop? The names I have just recalled indicate that English humanism, so far from perishing on the scaffold with Thomas More, as some otherwise respectable scholars at one time would have had us believe, had in fact a long life.[5] The trouble is that by the end of the Tudor century it had entered so completely into the bloodstream of English intellectual life that singling out any one writer affected by it as a humanist becomes almost redundant.

By then, therefore, a distinction becomes necessary, one which differentiates between card-carrying humanists and those men of letters who were simply heirs to the humanist tradition, those who, in other words, had been taught to accept *literae humaniores* as models to be emulated rather than imitated, and who had come to hold as an article of faith that the best way to approach contemporary problems was by way of sources, preferably, but not exclusively, those derived from ancient Greece and Rome. Although they were themselves heirs to an already developed tradition, the men who set the tone for English humanism, from the generation of More to that of Smith and Ascham, stood out clearly in a society as yet barely ready to assimilate them. A generation or so later, Camden and Hooker still bore the same insignia. Yet so, in their way, did most of the writers of late Elizabethan England—Spenser and Sidney, for example, or Daniel and Davies. However, unless they are all to be considered humanists, which would be merely to reiterate the obvious fact that humanism was by that time the constant current in English intellectual life, we should restrict the designation of humanist to those directly engaged in the *studia humanitatis* or who applied that learning and its derivatives in some form of scholarly discussion. Spenser and Sidney surely shared the learning of humanism and were as devoted as Elyot had been to the education of the governing class for a life of active citizenship, but they were primarily poets, though Spenser's reflections on the place of Irish culture in the history of civilization and Sidney's excursus into literary criticism tend to make them both borderline cases.[6] Daniel and Davies, on the other hand, applied their basically humanist learning, the former to the history of England, and of Western civilization for that matter, the latter to the study of law.[7] Both accordingly might lay legitimate claim to inclusion among the ranks of practicing humanists. So, necessary as it may be in the interests of definition, the distinction between humanists and heirs to the humanist tradition, between humanists proper and humanists, as it were, by courtesy, must remain imprecise.

The point at which the history of the humanist tradition itself may be considered complete becomes similarly imprecise. Nor is it perhaps critical: in a sense the humanist tradition never really died. Still, a change did take place, a change which, while by no means obliterating the marks of humanist scholarship, introduced a new and distinctive ingredient, one essential to modern thought. The end of the story comes, then, not with the demise of the tradition, but with the emergence of that new synthesis which humanism itself had never managed to achieve, when, in other words, the new philosophy which, for John Donne, had called all in doubt, had become sufficiently accepted to serve as the basis for a new assurance. Bacon stands as a massive landmark at that very point. More of an heir to the humanist tradition than he might have been willing to admit—in his own classical learning, in his historically oriented scholarship, in his sense of the learned man's responsibility to the society in which he lived, and in his residual respect for the ancients—he was nevertheless clearly the prophet of a new dispensation.

If we are willing to consider humanists as more than professional practitioners in the prescribed *studia humanitatis*—as in the case of England we must do or have little to talk about—we are still faced with the fact that humanists of both the sixteenth and seventeenth centuries applied their learning in disconcertingly diverse ways. Their interests, as we have seen, led them in widely divergent directions. Moreover, they could be either secular in their outlook or religious, rationalistic or profoundly fideistic, optimistic or pessimistic, scornful of the Middle Ages or nostalgically drawn to them, depending, in any case, on the circumstances. They were, in short, too eclectic, too responsive to contemporary issues to be fitted into any single model constructed out of specific interests or explicitly expressed ideas.

Does this, then, mean that we are driven back to something like Professor Kristeller's astringent definition? Must we choose between the irreducible common factor of a methodology (including a common education) and no common factor at all? I think not. Kristeller himself had to make allowances for certain common attitudes and values. We must, however, look for it well beneath the surface—so far, admittedly, as seemingly to raise a new problem rather than to provide a solution. Yet the intractability of the surface leaves us no choice but to look below it. Accordingly, I am suggesting that the essence of English humanism, that which characterizes both the humanist, proper, and the more pervasive tradition of humanism, lies not in formal ideas or particular interests, but in a mode of perception, specifically in a new acuity in the way the humanist mind looked at things.

Actually, this clarity of vision may be better expressed as a function of two closely related modes of perception, the one involving a sharpness of focus in the perception of contemporary life, the other a clarity of perspective in historical perception. To be more specific, I mean by the former a habit of viewing things human in terms of what is actually observable, ponderable, even to some extent manageable, and of distinguishing them for the many practical purposes of human existence from things divine, even in ecclesiastical issues. By perspective, I mean a tendency to look to the past for light on present problems and to view it in the context of an evolving human history rather than in that of *historia sacra*. Both involved a respect for experience.

Both, moreover, involved a willingness to consider experience in relation to the fact of social change, a fact increasingly borne in upon observers of Renaissance society. Societies had, of course, always changed, and the fact could hardly have escaped observation hitherto. The difference lay partly in the actual speed of change and in its radical character. Sixteenth-century England was experiencing changes, all in varying degrees revolutionary, in many areas, agrarian, commercial, administrative, religious, and, most dramatically, in the relation of church and monarchy. The difference lay also, however, in attitudes toward the issues involved. Maladjustments within the body politic obviously required remedy, and remedy presupposed a search for causes, a search that depended on a realistic catechism of experience. The result in early Tudor England was the beginnings of a new era in the history of social analysis, one in which humanists took a conspicuous lead.[8]

This sensitivity to change becomes especially helpful in explaining the emergence of the newly acute historical vision.[9] The humanists' commitment to classical antiquity obviously committed them also to a historical interpretaion of sorts. But until they were able to see that the antique world itself had changed and that it was separated from their own by a process of change as well as by a chasm of time, their perception remained incomplete. Fortunately, by the time humanism reached England, that step had already been taken, however hesitantly. By then, too, English humanists were prepared to seek both understanding and psychological assurance in the extended experience provided by his-

tory. In monotonous iteration, they cited Cicero's famous definition of history. That definition could mean very much—that
history was the very source of all wisdom—or precious little—that
it was merely a record of exemplary deeds—depending on the
outlook of the person repeating it; but in any case it attested to a
vague but profound faith in the efficacy of historical knowledge.
It was this hope of bringing in the past in order to redress the
balance of the present that had set Renaissance scholars, in the
first place, to reexamining the remains of a culture they were
coming to think had more to say to their own than that of the
immediately preceding age. In the process, they developed something that became more and more like the modern sense of history. But it is important to recognize that it resembled the modern
sense of history not because it looked to the past for enlightening
examples, examples by which moral philosophy might be taught.
There was nothing new about that. Indeed, since the exemplary
view of history presumed an essentially static past that could provide as useful examples from one age as from another, it harked
back to older assumptions more than it foreshadowed the modern
social scientists' search for uniformities. The novelty arose instead
out of a dawning awareness of process in the affairs of this world
and of the relativity of things to the changing circumstances of
time and place, and out of the related ability to view the past from
a fixed point in time which Panofsky taught us to think of as
analogous to the Renaissance painter's perception of the distance
between the eye and the object.

Ironically, perspective of this sort is to be found in England not
in how history was written (the Tudor chronicles, in particular,
perpetuated thoroughly traditional approaches) but in how history was used, how the past, especially the social and cultural past,
which conventional histories tended to ignore, might cast light on
contemporary issues, most of which were, after all, social and cultural in character or implication. Whether they were dealing with
matters of learning, religion, government, or the nature of man
himself, Tudor humanists sought authority and stability in a past
that sometimes stretched before their eyes with the deceptive fix-
ity of a landscape, but sometimes, and increasingly, took on the
aspect of a moving picture. In this perspective, religious and secu-

lar interests and ideas that at times seem mutually incompatible converge in a common search for fountainheads located within the range of man's documented memory.

What I am trying to say may become clearer if we take a closer look at the strange case of England and the conditions actually affecting the origins and growth of humanism there.

But first let me reassure the medievalists that I mean to imply no sharp break between a humanist and a prehumanist era, or to deny that a special kind of humanism flourished in the Middle Ages. On the contrary, Renaissance thinkers were still willing, depending on context, to view human problems under the aspect of eternity or against the fixed backdrop of a presumably changeless nature; and, again depending on the context, they remained willing enough to view the past in the perspective of redemptive history. The Reformation, in fact, gave new life to both of these traditional modes of perception. I wish, instead, to point out that new modes of perception did, in fact, begin gradually to become apparent in English thought as those problems matured that characterize the transition from medieval society and culture to early modern. The blend of the new and the old remains admittedly unstable, like the blend of the old and the new in the preceding era. Much, in either case, depends on the context. Words that sound traditional may, as we shall see, take on a new meaning when perceived in a new environment, just as words that, by themselves, sound new may sink easily into the landscape of an earlier day. The new, moreover, is often new more in degree than in kind. Still, by the early sixteenth century, a fresh atmosphere was becoming unmistakably and increasingly apparent in English intellectual life; and it was an atmosphere so deeply tinctured with humanism as to become all but identifiable with it.

It is important to recognize, however, that the new mode or modes of perception which characterize that climate of thought were not necessarily a product of humanism alone. Humanism came late to England—as to a last frontier—and from abroad, from Italy initially, though increasingly filtered through the pietistic and reformist strata of northern scholarship. Despite the slender succession of scholars who followed Duke Humphrey's lead to Italy in the preceding century, and the occasional Italian scholar who found his way to England (and more than likely wished he had not) the new scholarship did not really thrive in England until the Tudor era,[10] not in fact until it was energized by the mounting crisis in religion. It did not have deep native roots, as the humanism of Italy had in the late medieval rhetorical tradition. Nor were Englishmen in the later Middle Ages inspired, as were their neighbors, to take a new look at classical antiquity by the obvious relevance of Roman Law to an increasingly secular society.[11] They already had a secular government that worked, in a raffish sort of way, and that had made an advantageous peace with the church; and their common law had already absorbed a great deal of the civil law during the great medieval renaissance— just enough in fact to make them feel no need to adopt any more of it even to secure a necessary efficiency. England may thus have escaped the trauma of absolutism, but she also missed an important stimulus to humanist scholarship. But late medieval England did have a tradition, a habit might be the better term, of realistic observation and criticism, something not unlike that penchant for treating human problems in human terms which became so marked a characteristic of a mature humanism. Late medieval England was facing many of the same problems as were then besetting the rest of Europe, and they were similar to those that came later to preoccupy English humanists. Not surprisingly, similar problems tended to elicit similar responses. So, by the time the new scholarship became really domesticated, an atmosphere had been created that was especially congenial to the peculiarly utilitarian kind of humanism later to flourish there.

Two examples come to mind. Bishop Pecock turned a mind shaped apparently exclusively by scholasticism to the increasingly pressing problem of authority in the church, and, in the course of his efforts to counteract the fundamentalist biblicism of the later Lollards, undertook to treat the problem, not on grounds of accepted authority, but on those of reason, and managed in the process to interpret the history of the church in human, even more or less developmental terms. However faintly, he foreshadowed the rational, historically oriented approach made to a roughly similar problem by Richard Hooker nearly a century and a half later. More than that, apparently entirely on his own, he subjected the Donation of Constantine to a critique comparable in its sense of anachronism to Lorenzo Valla's better-known work.[12] Sir John

Fortescue, equally conventional in his formal background, made nevertheless a freshly realistic and essentially secular approach to the crisis he appears to have thought impending should a badly needed efficiency in English government be bought at the expense of the subjects's rights and English kings be induced to follow the despotic example of their French brothers by adopting the civil law of Rome. By prescribing for the ills of English government in terms of a specific time and place and of the impersonal mechanism of administration rather than in those of the personal worthiness of the persons in charge, he foreshadowed the approach made to similar problems by the pamphleteers of the mid-sixteenth century; and, by sensing, however dimly, the value of a comparative approach to the law, he moved in the general direction, not of Tudor legal scholarship—that remained stubbornly insular—but in that taken by the legal humanists of Renaissance France.[13]

When the newer, classically oriented learning finally came to England to stay, it flourished more in response to the kind of problems that concerned Pecock and Fortescue than to the demands of pure scholarship, elemental as the latter clearly remained. Moreover, and the point is important, the learning of humanism came in a form already relatively mature, its theoretical problems well aired, if not solved, its scholarly techniques well tested. Above all, it came already possessed of the idea that a person trained in the *studia humanitatis* had the key to a special wisdom and a special duty to employ it in the common interest. As the dialogues of More and Starkey and Smith bear eloquent witness, the humanist scholar had constantly to bear in mind his role, indeed his primary role, as a citizen. It was in this spirit that Tudor humanists turned from a pure to an applied scholarship and to the study of antiquity as a means rather than an end in itself.

It is here, in their practical objectives, that the humanists of Tudor England most clearly demonstrated their clarity of social vision. Their service to the monarchy and / or the church and their frequent efforts, freelance, in the service of what they liked to call the "commonwealth" are by now too well known to need extensive illustration. Perhaps the best example is to be found in the literature of public discussion that appeared during the early and middle decades of the sixteenth century.[14] The authors, mostly humanists either by profession or training, men like our four Thomases, undertook to diagnose the ills of the commonwealth and, where possible, to prescribe remedies. They wanted to know what actually caused the maladjustments they detected in the social organism, the secondary causes, that is, those discernible well to this side of Divine Providence and within range of man's unaided capabilities. This mode of perception permitted them to reconcile the old and the new. It allowed them to refurbish the typically medieval notion of a Christian commonwealth, with all that it implied of a static organism whose health depended on the moral fibre of its members, and made it fit the more dynamic and impersonal context of Renaissance life. True, much of the resulting analysis is still set in the conventional language of a universal morality. For many, the covetousness of "greedy cormorants" still provides a shortcut to the causes of, for example, poverty and inflation. And, as in Thomas Starkey's otherwise penetrating *Dialogue*, the analogy of the body politic retains its almost exclusive domination over the language of political discussion. But the important thing is that it now receives fresh interpretation in consonance with the dawning perception that society is a complex of moving forces rather than an organism capable of change only insofar as its health had its ups and downs. Sir Thomas Smith's decision to abandon the organic analogy at one point in favor of the more impersonal one of the mechanical clock is no doubt a rare example, but it fits his cast of mind, and it symbolizes a changing perception of social reality.[15] Generally, however, what we see here is a new clarity of focus rather than a new idea.

Though at first glance less likely than social analysis to exemplify the ability of the humanist mind to focus with clarity on things human, ecclesiastical discussion was in fact fully as likely to do so. Protagonists in those interminable controversies, most of whom shared a common background of humanist scholarship, were as concerned as their more secularly oriented contemporaries to keep discussion within the bounds of human experience— up to the point, that is, where it impinged on matters of faith; but, to a degree surprising in what was still an age of faith, discussion in sixteenth-century England turned on the church as an institution and on the quality of religious life. William Tyndale's insistence on viewing ceremonies, for example, in a human context reveals a perception quite in keeping with his Erasmian background, with its tendency to demystify religious observances.[16] That it also supported his own covenant theology does not detract from this fact. Those reformers who shared a similar concern for human values would have been quite prepared to second Erasmus himself when he remarked that, if all the fragments of the Lord's Cross exhibited as relics were to be gathered together, they could fill a freighter.[17] It would be wrong, of course, to assume that the human dimension of the humanist literature devoted to ecclesiastical controversy was determined by Protestant reformism. For a while, at any rate, the Erasmian spirit animated Catholic reform as well as Protestant; and, insofar as the arguments turned on questions of discipline, ceremony, and church polity, all but the most extreme elements shared roughly the same, essentially humanist rules of the game.

A similar willingness to distinguish between things human and things divine, and a similar respect for the data of experience marks the historical sense. Nowhere, indeed, has Renaissance humanism, considered as a mode of perception, left clearer traces than in its uses of the past. Here, as in so many respects, English humanism owed much to Erasmus, who spent many of his most innovative and productive years in England, and at a time when both he and his friends among the English humanists were most flexible in their thinking. But it may well be that they owed as much in this respect to that other visitor to Henrician England, Juan Luis Vives, who stayed among them even longer. Erasmus, by far the more brilliant writer, though not the more profound thinker, was ideally equipped to inspire and crystallize the mood of English humanists who hoped to reform their society in both soul and body. And by his respect for original sources, by his ability to interpret the church fathers in the context of their age, and by the sense of anachronism he brought to his critique of Ciceronianism, he undoubtedly provided English humanists with lessons in historical perspective that remained with them and their descendants unto the third and fourth generations. But he had little feeling for the continuity of history, or, for that matter, for history as such. "He who trusts history," he wrote at one point, "does not sin, but what does it profit him?"[18] Vives, on the other hand, like Bacon almost a century later, felt it necessary to subject the learning of the past to a historical critique in order to set the cultural needs of the present in perspective. In the course of his critique, moreover, he came closer to a developmental, not to say a progressivist interpretation of cultural history than anyone before Bacon himself.[19] How much of this rubbed off on English scholars is hard to estimate, so little had been done to investigate it, but, from then to the end of the century, Vives crops up in scholarly citations with suggestive frequency.

The kind of historical sense that Vives represents does not, however, make any significant appearance in the formal writing of history, not at any rate until near the end of the Tudor century. Except for More's innovative treatment of Richard III, and Polydore Vergil's workmanlike arrangement of English political history, Tudor historiography added little to the medieval chronicle tradition until Camden, Hayward, and Bacon pioneered in a new kind of political history that could be considered a belated reflection of that same mode of perception which English humanists had long since brought to the analysis of contemporary society.[20] By then, too, Bacon, and even Ralegh (in a sense the last of the Renaissance historians) were able to rationalize the search for secondary causes in history on much the same grounds as those on which Smith and the "commonwealth men" of the mid-century had based their analysis of society.[21]

As a matter of fact, the historical perspective of humanism achieved a measure of maturity in a social and cultural context more than in that of past politics, of *res gestae*, ordinarily considered by Renaissance theorists to be the primary, indeed virtually the sole responsibility of the historian. Pioneer work was being done in this respect by the Elizabethan and Jacobean antiquaries who, without dignifying themselves as "historians," were busy unearthing (sometimes literally) the remains—the "footsteps" they like to call them—of earlier ages and in particular the origins of the national customs and institutions, the very things formal historiography had largely ignored.[22]

Meanwhile, however, it was public discussion of one sort or another that stimulated insights into the social and cultural past with all the implications of process and development that tended to accompany such investigation. Ecclesiastical discussion, in particular, elicited the most penetrating use of humanist source criticism made during the period. Here, as in its appeal to the culture of antiquity, the humanist mind preferred to seek both authority and psychological assurance in a return to the sources: *ad fontes!*— any *fontes*, depending upon the point at issue. So, when the crisis in the church and in its relation to the monarchy came upon them, English humanists turned once more to antiquity, now, however, to Christian antiquity and to patristic authority. A succession of churchmen, all well versed in the scholarly techniques of humanism—Cranmer, Jewel, Whitgift, Hooker, to say nothing of their recusant and, to some extent even their Puritan opponents—chose to defend their respective positions to a remarkable extent on historical grounds. By distinguishing between those things essential to salvation and things indifferent, matters, that is, of ceremony, discipline, and church polity, all of which were of human origin and therefore historically conditioned, they opened to the best techniques of historical scholarship the long-drawn-out debates concerning the shape of the visible church.[23]

That so many of the humanistically trained minds of Renaissance England were drawn into ecclesiastical controversy explains a good deal about the peculiar history of English humanism. Whereas in France the problem of government, in an era of political instability and civil war, tended to draw humanists to the study of law and politics, in England, similarly trained scholars were drawn into the service of the national church. In both instances, circumstances made special demands on historical scholarship. But why were English humanists not also drawn to the study of law or English lawyers, as a profession, to the comparative, historically oriented legal humanism pioneered on the Continent by Budé, Alciat, Cujas, and Zasius? Thereby hangs a long tale and one which space will not permit me to tell as it should be told.[24] But it has an important, if curiously reverse, bearing on the problem of perception. English common lawyers, having only one law to deal with, and that already effectively inoculated against further outside influence by the partial acceptance of Roman law principles in its early formative years, were able to resist any temptation to indulge in the comparative, historical study of law which Continental lawyers had been forced to undertake as a result of the constant interaction in their society of Roman law and native customary laws. The result was that, with a few notable exceptions, English common lawyers tended to become hopelessly insular and uncritical in their historical sense, willing until well into the seventeenth century to accept the wildest of myths about the origin of English laws and institutions. Sir Edward Coke, perhaps the foremost legal mind of that later period is a classic and shocking example.[25] By the same token, most English humanists found little to attract them in legal studies except when, like Starkey and Smith, they were trained primarily in the civil law. It was not that English lawyers were, as individuals, untouched by humanism. Many, fortunate enough to have the time, indulged in various scholarly activities such as translation and antiquarian research, but seldom connected with the study, especially the comparative historical study, of law. As a profession, English common lawyers (most of the civilians were not much different) remained blind to the possibilities inherent in humanist historical scholarship as an aid to legal studies. May we not conclude, then, that where humanism was *not* encouraged, the sense of history lagged?

Be that as it may, the impression seems inescapable that the historical mode of perception constituted an essential element of English humanist thought.

The problem, however, appears again to become complicated by the fact that historical perception was itself undergoing certain changes. But that is merely to say that humanism, as the moving spirit in a more than ordinarily transitional age, was itself moving. For example, the controversial and antiquarian literature of the sixteenth century shows an increasing tendency to reach beyond the morally responsible individual, hitherto the central object of social comment, Renaissance as well as medieval, to the impersonal and collective factors in social change, to the problems Bacon once referred to as those of "man congregate" as distinct from "man segregate."[26] Just as Sir Thomas Smith, for one, could see that the cause of mid-century inflation lay not so much in the greed of those in the market-place as in the operation of an impersonal economic mechanism, so those heirs to the humanist tradition who debated the relative merits of nature and custom in the history of language,[27] or the issues involving the church, considered as an institution, or those antiquaries who were investigating the customs, institutions, and beliefs of past ages, ultimately and notably including Sir Henry Spelman who has been credited with "discovering"[28] feudalism, all found themselves tracing the "footsteps" not of individuals, but of peoples and societies.

This kind of investigation, unlike the investigation of *res gestae*, had of necessity to deal, however superficially, with process in history. The story of deeds done could readily enough be seen unfolding against the fixed backdrop of an ordained social order. In contrast, any investigation of customs, institutions, and beliefs could hardly avoid the fact of change and the relativity it implied. No such researches would have been undertaken in the first place had not questions arisen involving either continuity or discontinuity, either the fear of change or the hope it might evoke, or perhaps merely a simple curiosity about origins, about roots. It was this sensitivity to change, borne in upon the Tudor humanists by the circumstances of their own age, that no doubt helped, as much as the study of antiquity, whether classical or Christian, to get scholars to see that antiquity itself had undergone processes of change.

That humanism involved a peculiar mode of perception should be clear enough. It might be enlightening, however, to notice in addition some examples of how interpreting English humanism in this light helps to clarify certain confusions about it.

Perhaps the best example may be found in questions concerning the relation between Renaissance humanism and the Middle Ages. Those who would find the culture of Tudor England, including Tudor humanism, still essentially medieval have no trouble making their point: habits more typical of medieval than of modern thought unquestionably continued throughout the Renaissance—especially the English Renaissance. But the fact remains that, despite their obvious links with the past, Renaissance humanists looked at things differently than their predecessors did. The commonwealth, which so many English humanists nurtured as a social ideal, was a profoundly Christian commonwealth, and the ends of humanist learning were profoundly ethical. Yet, as we have seen, those same writers were able to bring to bear on the issues of their day a realism, a clarity of focus, rare in medieval social comment. As a result, they were in some instances able eventually to bridge the gap between the morally responsible individual and the impersonal forces at work in society, between private morality and public policy. Then, too, those who applied the learning of humanism to religious issues, as so many of the humanistically trained minds of Tudor England had had to do, admittedly brought to their task attitudes toward human nature which are not supposed to be charactristic of humanism—John Colet's low opinion of his own species, for example,[29] or the residual Calvinism that clung to the minds of the most scholarly spokesmen for the Anglican establishment. Yet their ability to place religious issues in a historical context marks them as humanists more surely than their attitude toward human nature would mark them as medieval. Or take the example of Richard Hooker who undoubtedly proclaimed his kinship with the scholastics by adapting the Thomist-Aristotelian interpretation of natural law as the philosophical groundwork for the Anglican Settlement, but who developed the historical relativism inherent in his Thomism in a way Aquinas would have found both strange and unnecessary.[30]

The historical perspective of humanist thought in particular, made it possible for scholars, no matter how devoted they might be to the classics, to take a new and more accurate look at the Middle Ages as a whole. Humanists, we are told, nourished a settled antipathy toward the Middle Ages. Many of them certainly did: that, after all, is how those ages got to be called "middle" in the first place. Those who, like Ascham, looked to classical antiquity for guidance, or, like Cranmer or Jewel, sought authority in Christian antiquity, came naturally to feel that the Middle Ages were a dark time between two eras of enlightenment. Erroneous as the judgment may have been in either case, it did represent a legitimately historical vision. Yet a similar sense of history, differing only in point of view and scholarly sophistication, moved Hooker to resort to the Thomist tradition, and allowed Samuel Daniel (either the most historical of English poets or the most poetical of English historians, depending on one's point of view) not only to see good in medieval culture but to discern lines of continuity running between that era and his own.[31] Although Spenser revealed, in his penchant for the chivalric theme, an apparent medievalism which Ascham would probably have deplored, and which seems to run counter to his own classical education, that same attitude attests, by its deliberate archaism,[32] to a new and typically humanist ability to view the cultural past in a relativistic perspective. Indeed, it is this sense of the temporal distance separating the present from the truly chivalric past that distinguished the Elizabethan revival of chivalric forms from the revival of its very essence hopefully envisioned by Caxton a century earlier.[33] The reassessment of the Middle Ages by these Elizabethans—humanists by virtue of that very reassessment—serves even more than the analogous reassessment their predecessors had made of classical antiquity to foreshadow the romantic historicism of a later age.

To examine humanism as a mode of perception makes it possible also to make certain qualitative distinctions within the tradition itself—distinctions which, insofar as they may serve to clarify the subject, serve also to validate the method of identifying it. For example, few scholars of Tudor England demonstrated a greater zeal in philological scholarship than those like Humphrey Llwyd or Sir John Price who employed it in support of the legends about the origins of the British people handed down as part of Geoffrey of Monmouth's mischievous legacy.[34] Yet their fanciful disregard for historical perspective or for the evidence of historical experience and plain common sense makes it questionable to consider them humanists at all. As a matter of fact, the dark area where history shades off into legend and legend into myth remained a blind spot in the perception of otherwise respectable humanistically trained scholars until well into the next century. By then, however, Camden and his kind had achieved enough historical sense to recognize just how dark that area really was and to nourish a healthy skepticism about anything not capable of documentary illumination.[35] The case of John Foxe is similar, though in this one respect only. Despite the truly monumental scholarship of his *Acts and Monuments*, and a regard for documentary sources second to none, his insistence on a time scheme taken straight out of the Book of Revelation renders suspect any claim on his behalf to the status of humanist. Useful as they may be for purposes of definition, such judgments are, of course, those of modern scholarship, and they reflect the questionable tendency of historians to create their ideal humanist in their own image.

More important, a criterion based on the quality of historical perception serves to illuminate significant shadings in the attitude of learned minds toward the course of civilization itself.[36] There was plenty in late Renaissance life to justify either a pessimistic or an optimistic outlook, depending on the author's point of view. Both presumed a theory of history. Yet it becomes increasingly clear as the confrontation between the exponents of these points of view developed, that, insofar as the optimists grounded their arguments on documented experience, they spoke more nearly the language of humanism than did their opponents. I have already mentioned the near unanimity with which reform-minded humanists resorted to the progressivist myth of man's more or less successful struggle to achieve civility. They had other alternatives—cyclical notions, or the various Golden Age myths, or the peculiarly paralyzing myth of the decay of all nature; and, such was the tolerance of Renaissance thought for adopting contradictory ideas with little sense of incongruity, they were quite capable on occasion of embracing any or all of them. The optimistic anthropology clearly predominated, however, in the discussion of substantive social and cultural issues, whereas the pessimistic continued to appeal more to the elegiac sense of poets and to the moral sense of preachers. Scholars, for example, who hoped to place the English language under some kind of discipline found themselves inquiring with some degree of objectivity into the processes by which language and letters had evolved; and the Elizabethan antiquaries, employing typically humanist methods of investigation, were coming to the truly revolutionary conclusion that, not only had mankind arisen by slow stages from a cave-man existence, but their own ancestors, the early Britons, represented an early stage in that process and were, in fact, little different from the half-naked and painted savages of the New World. George Hakewill's confrontation with Godfrey Goodman[37] and Bacon's call to creative mastery of man's environment marked only the opening engagements in the long conflict between the Ancients and Moderns; but those engagements ensured that it would be a climactic one in the history of the Renaissance by ensuring also that the progressivist side had the more effective weaponry.

Finally, the realistic and historically oriented mode of perception serves to link the humanism of the earlier sixteenth century with that of the late century and the early seventeenth. In either period, humanists were responding, as was their wont, to the logic of circumstances. The very same mode of perception which had allowed them to "rediscover" the culture of classical antiquity now made it possible for some of them to "rediscover" the Middle Ages. The same also facilitated that partial reorientation of humanist learning from moral philosophy to natural philosophy for which Bacon and the considerable group of pre-Baconians stood.[38] This reorientation was what ultimately supplied that element of ideological consistency which humanism had always lacked. After Bacon, English learning entered a new phase, one in which the temporal vision of humanism can safely be taken for granted as part of a newly evolving synthesis, and which, for that reason, relieves us at last from the responsibility of definition.

To conclude, we can easily agree on a minimum definition of humanism, but it is likely to reflect little more than a firm grasp of the obvious. We can agree that Renaissance humanism was grounded on what the humanists themselves called the *studia humanitatis*. The literature, history, and moral philosophy of ancient Greece and Rome, the *litera humaniores*, constituted its basic sources, and philology its primary technique of source criticism. But its materials remained self-limited unless used, and its methods mere machinery. What energized these studies, what set the machinery in motion, indeed what had drawn scholars to the humane studies in the first place, were the circumstances, social, cultural, and political, of a period of more than ordinarily radical transition. In that process of transition, humanism itself became both cause and effect. So the humanist tradition must be considered to involve not merely the standard studies but their reinterpretation in the light of contemporary life. This becomes especially apparent in northern humanism. By the sixteenth century, by the time the new scholarship became domesticated in England, much of its basic work had been done. The culture of classical antiquity had been initially explored, or, more accurately, reinterpreted, and the study of Greek was no longer the prestigious novelty it had once been. By then, too, the crisis in the church was requiring that its sources be supplemented by those of Christian antiquity. It is consequently as an applied scholarship that English humanism entered its most vigorous period. But it is this very fact that has made any really useful, that is to say any functional, definition of humanism so teasingly frustrating. Humanists applied their learning in such diverse areas and in such divergent directions that as Professor Kristeller wisely warned, it becomes difficult, if not impossible, to find in their thinking any common bond of ideas or interests.

For this reason, I have suggested that, if any common factor is to be found, if, in other words, humanism is to become more than a capriciously self-defining concept and capable of serving more than ad hoc purposes, that factor must be sought in an underlying mode, or related modes, of perception. It may, I believe, be found in a fresh way of looking at the world and man, a way more typical of modern than of medieval thought. More specifically, it may be found in a tendency to focus with clarity on things human and to separate them, for the purposes of this world, from things divine, and, above all, to view the present in the perspective of history and history in relation to the circumstances of time and place. I do not mean that this mode of perception precludes the operation of others more traditional: in the Renaissance, the old and the new coexisted in a variety of mutually convenient relationships. Nor do I mean that it characterizes all humanists in the same way or to the same extent: humanism, like romanticism, wore many masks. I mean only that it became an especially pervasive aspect of the English Renaissance, and that, although not discovered by the humanists, it became broadly characteristic of their mentality and may properly be used to "identify" them.

Notes

1. Paul O. Kristeller, "Studies on Renaissance Humanism during the last Twenty Years," *Studies in the Renaissance*, IX (1962), 7–30. See also W. J. Bouwsma, *The Interpretation of Renaissance Humanism*, 2nd ed., Service Center for Teachers of History, Publication No. 18 (Washington, D.C., 1966) for a survey of the development of scholarly work on the subject, and the same author's *The Culture of Renaissance Humanism*, AHA Pamphlet No. 401 (Washington, D.C., 1973); see also G. M. Logan, "Substance and form in Renaissance humanism," *Journal of Medieval and Renaissance Studies*, VII (1977), 1–34.

2. Sir Thomas More, *Translations of Lucian*, ed. Craig R. Thompson (New Haven, 1974), and *Utopia*, ed. Edward Surtz and J. H. Hexter (New Haven, 1965); Sir Thomas Elyot, *The Dictionary of Syr Thomas Eliot knyght* (London, 1538) [later editions entitled *Bibliotheca Eliota*], and *The Boke named the Gouernour*, ed. H. H. S. Croft, 2 vols. (London, 1880); Thomas Starkey, *A Dialogue between Cardinal Pole and Thomas Lupset*, ed. K. M. Burton (London, 1948); Sir Thomas Smith, *De recta et emendata Linguae Anglicae scriptione, Dialogus*, ed. Otto Deibel (Halle, 1913), *De Republica Anglorum, A Discourse on the Commonwealth of England*, ed. L. Alston (Cambridge, 1906), *A Discourse of the Commonweal of This Realm of England* [attributed], ed. Mary Dewar (Charlottesville, 1969). The arguments for Smith's authorship are summarized in *ibid.*, introduction.

3. Sir John Cheke, *The hurt of sedicion howe greuous it is to a communewelth* (London, 1549).

4. Arthur B. Ferguson, "'By little and little': The early Tudor humanists on the development of man," *Florilegium Historiale: Essays . . .* , ed. J. G. Rowe and W. H. Stockdale (Toronto, 1971), pp. 125–150.

5. The idea was first put forth by J. S. Phillimore, "The Arrest of Humanism in England," *Dublin Review* (1913), and was given an air of scholarly respectability by R. W. Chambers, *Thomas More* (New York, 1935).

6. See Fritz Caspari, *Humanism and the Social Order in Tudor England* (Cambridge, 1956), chaps. 7 and 8. Notice also Edmund Spenser's *A View of the Present State of Ireland*, ed. W. L. Renwick (Oxford, 1970), and Sir Philip Sidney's *Defence of Poesie*, ed. Lewis Soens (Lincoln, Neb., 1970).

7. See Samuel Daniel, *The Collection of the History of England*, ed. A. B. Grosart, *Works*, 5 vols. (London, 1885–96), IV and V, and the animadversions on Western culture in *Musophilus*, ed. Raymond Himelick (University of Purdue Studies, 1965); Sir John Davies, *Irish Reports (Les Reports des Cases et Mattres en Ley . . .)* (1615, trans. Dublin, 1762), and *A Discovery of the True Causes why Ireland was never entirely subdued*, in *Historical Tracts by Sir John Davies* (Dublin, 1787).

8. Arthur B. Ferguson, *The Articulate Citizen and the English Renaissance* (Durham, N.C., 1965), Part II.

9. Most of the material on historical consciousness, here and throughout the rest of this paper, is based on my *Clio Unbound: Perception of the Social and Cultural Past in Renaissance England* (Durham, N.C., 1979). See also F. J. Levy, *Tudor Historical Thought* (San Marino, 1967), and F. S. Fussner, *The Historical Revolution: English Historical Writing and Thought, 1580–1640* (New York, 1962).

10. See Roberto Weiss, *Humanism in England during the Fifteenth Century* (Oxford, 1941).

11. Walter Ullmann has suggested that this fact helps to explain the relatively late advent of a fully developed humanism in England. *Medieval Foundations of Renaissance Humanism* (Ithaca, 1977), pp. 185ff.

12. Reginald Pecock, *The Repressor of Over Much Blaming of the Clergy*, ed. C. Babington (Rolls Series, 1890).

13. See especially Sir John Fortescue's *Governance of England*, ed. C. Plummer (Oxford, 1885), reprinted in *Complaint and Reform in England*, ed. W. H. Dunham and Stanley Pargellis (New York, 1928), but see also *De Laudibus Legum Angliae*, ed. and trans. S. B. Chrimes (Cambridge, 1942); Ferguson, *Articulate Citizen*, chap. 5.

14. Ferguson, *Articulate Citizen*, Part II, for an extended discussion of this literature.

15. Smith, *Discourse*, p. 96.

16. *The Obedience of a Christian Man* . . . , ed. Henry Walter, Parker Society, No. 42 (Cambridge, 1848), pp. 274–275, *The Practyse of Prelates* . . . , ed. Walter, Parker Society No. 43 (Cambridge, 1849), pp. 324–328.

17. *Ten Colloquies*, ed. and trans. Craig Thompson (New York, 1957), p. 68.

18. Quoted by P. G. Bietenholz, *History and Biography in the Work of Erasmus of Rotterdam* (Geneva, 1966), p. 13.

19. *De causis corruptarum artium*, in *Opera Omnia* (Valentia, 1784), VI. Cf. especially Bacon's earlier writings, edited and translated by Benjamin Farrington (Liverpool, 1964), but a historical critique underlies much of his later work as well.

20. More's *Richard III*, Polydore's *Anglica Historia*, Camden's *History of Elizabeth*, Hayward's *Henry IIII*, and Bacon's *Henry VII* are fully discussed by Levy.

21. See, for example, *The Works of Sir Walter Ralegh*, ed. Oldys and Birch, 8 vols. (Oxford, 1829), book II, chap. xix, and Bacon, *Works*, ed. J. Spedding and R. L. Ellis, 14 vols. (London, 1857–74), VIII, 155.

22. The contribution of the antiquaries to the theory and practice of social and cultural history is discussed in Ferguson, *Clio Unbound*, chaps. 2 and 4.

23. Ferguson, *Clio Unbound*, chaps. 5 and 6.

24. See D. R. Kelley, "History, English Law, and the Renaissance," *Past and Present*, no. 65 (1974), 24–51. Cf. Christopher Brooks and Kevin Sharpe, "Debate: History, English Law, and the Renaissance," *ibid.*, no. 72 (1976), 133–142. See also J. G. A. Pocock, *The Ancient Constitution and the Feudal Law* (Cambridge, 1957).

25. E.g., *The Reports of Sir Edward Coke*, ed. J. H. Thomas and J. F. Fraser (London, 1826), *III Reports*, preface, xiv-xviii, *IV Reports*, preface, iii-iv.

26. *Works*, IX, 60–61.

27. E.g., Puttenham, Hart, Wills, Mulcaster, and Smith himself.

28. F. W. Maitland, *The Constitutional History of England* (London, 1908), pp. 142–143.

29. *Exposition of St. Paul's Epistle to the Romans*, in *Opuscula quaedam theologica*, ed. and trans. J. H. Lupton (London, 1876), p. 162.

30. See Arthus B. Ferguson, "The Historical Perspective of Richard Hooker; a Renaissance Paradox," *Journal of Medieval and Renaissance Studies*, III (1973), 17–50.

31. See Arthur B. Ferguson, "The Historical Thought of Samuel Daniel," *Journal of the History of Ideas*, XXXII (1971), 185–202.

32. *The Poetical Works of Edmund Spenser*, ed. J. C. Smith, 3 vols. (Oxford, 1909), III, 485–487. Cf. Rogar Ascham, *The Scholemaster*, in *English Works*, ed. W. A. Wright (Cambridge, 1904), pp. 281–292.

33. See Ferguson, *The Indian Summer of English Chivalry* (Durham, N.C., 1960).

34. Humphrey Llwyd (or Lloyd), *Commentarioli descriptionis Britannicae fragmentum* (Cologne, 1572), trans. T. Twyne as *The Breviary of Britain* (London, 1573); Sir John Price, *Historiae Brytannicae defensio* (London 1573).

35. William Camden, *Britannia*, trans. Richard Gough, 3 vols. (London, 1789), I, liv, lxix; see also preface.

36. See Arthur B. Ferguson, *Clio Unbound* (Durham, N.C., 1979), chap. 11, for a fuller discussion.

37. See Goodman's *The Fall of Man, or the Corruption of Nature* (London, 1616), and Hakewill's *An Apologie of the Power and Providence of God in the Government of the World* (London, 1627). Both books were the product of much earlier thought.

38. Gabriel Harvey, one of the newer humanists who appreciated the significance of science and invention, spoke enthusiastically of these men—Digges, Hariot, and Dee among the theorists, Boroughs, Bourne, Shute, Baker, Norman, and Hester among the articulate technicians who had done much to add a practical dimension to the work of the mathematicians, and Hakluyt, the prophet of empire and pioneer in economic history. *The Works of Gabriel Harvey*, ed. A. B. Grosart, 2 vols. (London, 1884), II, 289–290.

Appendix

*Lecture and Seminars of the Ninth Session
of the Southeastern Institute
of Medieval and Renaissance Studies
3 July—11 August 1978*

AN APOCALYPSE PANEL ON THE RUTHWELL CROSS

Guest Lecturer: Paul J. Meyvaert, Executive Secretary, The Mediaeval Academy of America. Supplementary Sessions: Palaeography, Image and Text, and Medieval Manuscript Problems.

I. ENGLISH HUMANISM: THE PROBLEM OF DEFINITION

Senior Fellow: Dr. Arthur B. Ferguson, Professor of History, Duke University; Associate Editor, *Journal of Medieval and Renaissance Studies*; Consulting Editor, *Journal of the History of Ideas*; Ford Foundation grantee, 1954–55; Senior Fellow, Southeastern Institute of Medieval and Renaissance Studies, 1967; Guggenheim Fellow, 1971–72; Fellow of the Royal Historical Society. Author: *The Indian Summer of English Chivalry: Studies in the Decline and Transformation of Chivalric Idealism* (1960); *The Articulate Citizen and the English Renaissance* (1965); *Clio Unbound: Perception of the social and cultural past in Renaissance England* (1979). "Renaissance Realism in the 'Commonwealth' Literature of Early Tudor England," *Journal of the History of Ideas*, XVI (1955); "The Problem of Counsel in *Mum and the Sothsegger*," *Studies in the Renaissance*, II (1955); "Fortescue and the Renaissance: A Study in Transition," *Studies in the Renaissance*, VI (1959); "The Tudor Commonweal and the Sense of Change," *The Journal of British Studies*, III (1963); "Reginal Pecock and the Renaissance Sense of History," *Studies in the Renaissance*, XIII (1966); "The Complete Works of St. Thomas More," vol. 4, *Utopia*, ed. E. Surtz, S.J., and J. H. Hexter (review article), *Journal of the History of Ideas*, XXIX (1968); "Circumstances and the Sense of History in Tudor England: the Coming of the Historical Revolution," *Medieval and Renaissance Studies*, III, ed. John M. Headley (1968); "John Twyne: a Tudor Humanist and the Problem of Legend," *The Journal of British Studies*, IX (1969); "The Early Tudor Humanists on the Development of Man," *Florilegium Historiale, Essays pre-*

sented to W. K. Ferguson, ed. J. G. Rowe and W. H. Stockdale (1971); "The Historical Thought of Samuel Daniel," *Journal of the History of Ideas*, XXXII (1971); "The Historical Perspective of Richard Hooker: a Paradox," *Journal of Medieval and Renaissance Studies*, III (1973).

Description: The seminar focused on the problems involving English humanism, but the main source for discussion was the projects undertaken or forwarded by the members of the seminar themselves.

Fellows: Carl Galliher Estabrook (Brown University); Walter Martin Gordon (University of Georgia); Ian Thompson (Indiana University); Alvin P. Vos (State University of New York at Binghamton); Warren Walter Wooden (Marshall University).

II. FORM IN MIDDLE ENGLISH LITERATURE

Senior Fellow: Dr. George Joseph Kane, William Rand Kenan, Jr., Professor of English, University of North Carolina, Chapel Hill; Fellow of the British Academy (1968); Fellow of University College, London (1971); Corresponding Fellow of the Mediæval Academy of America (1975); Fellow of King's College, London (1976); Fellow of the American Academy of Arts and Sciences (1977). Author: *Middle English Literature* (1951); *Piers Plowman: The A Version* (1960); *Piers Plowman: The Evidence of Authorship* (1965); *The Autobiographical Fallacy in Chaucer and Langland Studies* (Chambers Memorial Lecture for 1965); *Piers Plowman: The B Version* (1975); "'Piers Plowman': Problems and Methods of Editing the B-Text," *Modern Language Review*, XLIII (1948); "The Middle English Verse in MS Wellcome 1493," *London Mediaeval Studies*, II, i (1951); "Conjectural Emendation," in *Medieval Literature and Civilization: Studies in Memory of G. N. Garmonsway* (1969); "A Short Essay on the Middle English Secular Lyric," *Neuphilologische Mitteilungen*, LXXIII (1972); "Some Reflections on Critical Method," in *Essays and Studies by Members of the English Association* (1976); "Chaucer and the Idea of a Poet," publ. of the *Accademia Nazionale dei Lincei* (1978).

Description: A study of the implications of form, in the several senses of the term, for both the history of Middle English literature and the meaning of individual literary works.

Fellows: Denise N. Baker (University of North Carolina at Greensboro); John W. Conlee (William and Mary); David Earl Faris (University of Texas at Dallas); David E. Lampe (State University of New York College at Buffalo); Esther Casier Quinn (Hunter College); Arnold Francis Soucy (Cedar Crest College).

III. FROM DUFAY TO JOSQUIN: STYLISTIC DEVELOPMENTS IN FIFTEENTH-CENTURY MUSIC

Senior Fellow: Dr. Edward Elias Lowinsky, Ferdinand Schevill Distinguished Service Professor, Emeritus, University of Chicago; Guggenheim Fellow (1947–48) and (1976–77); Director, International Josquin Festival-Conference, Lincoln Center, N.Y.C. (1971); Fellow, Institute of Advanced Study, Princeton (1952–54); Bollingen Fellow (1953–54) and (1956–58); Fellow, American Academy of Arts and Sciences. Author: *Das Antwerpener Motettenbuch Orlando di Lassos und seine Beziehungen zum Motettenschaffen der niederländischen Zeitgenossen* (1937); *Secret Chromatic Art in the Netherlands Motet* (1946); *Tonality and Atonality in Sixteenth-Century Music* (1961); *The Medici Codex of 1518,* 3 vols., in *Monuments of Renaissance Music,* vols. 3–5 (1968); *Josquin des Prez: Proceedings of the International Josquin Festival-Conference,* ed. (1976); "The Function of Conflicting Signatures in Early Polyphonic Music," *The Musical Quarterly,* XXXI (1945); "The Concept of Physical and Musical Space in the Renaissance," *Papers of the American Musicological Society* (1946); "A Newly Discovered Sixteenth-Century Motet Manuscript at the Biblioteca Vallicelliana in Rome," *Journal of the American Musicological Society,* III (1950); "Music in the Culture of the Renaissance," *Journal of the History of Ideas* (1954); "Adrian Willaert's Chromatic 'Duo' Re-Examined," *Tijdschrift voor Muziekwetenschap,* XVIII (1956); "A Treatise on Text Underlay by a German Disciple of Francisco de Salinas," *Festschrift Heinrich Besseler* (1961); "Musical Genius—Evolution and Origins of a Concept," *The Musical Quarterly,* L (1964); "Renaissance Writings on Music Theory," *Renaissance News,* XVIII (1965); "Music of the Renaissance as Viewed by Renaissance Musicians," *The Renaissance Image of Man and the World* (1966); "Ockeghem's Canon for Thirty-six Voices: An Essay in Musical Iconography," *Essays in Music in Honor of Dragan Plamenac on his 70th Birthday* (1969); "Josquin des Prez and Ascanio Sforza," *Il Duomo di Milano, Congresso Internazionale: Atti II* (1969); "A Music Book for Anne Boleyn," *Florelegium Historiale: Essays Presented to Wallace K. Ferguson* (1970); "Secret Chromatic Art Re-Examined," *Perspectives in Musicology* (1972).

Description: The seminar focused on selected works of Dufay, Ockeghem, and Josquin des Prez in an attempt to understand the profound changes that occurred in fifteenth-century music: from successive to simultaneous conception of the voices in a polyphonic complex; from an intervallic to a harmonic approach to counterpoint; from neglect of the text, serving as vehicle for art-ful polyphony to concentration on clear declamation and expressive setting of the words and the stylistic means used to achieve this goal; thematic imitation, homophony, extension of the tone repertory, a more colorful harmonic palette, development of modulation and dissonance as a means for symbolic presentation and poetic expression. Attention was given to the influence of humanism on this whole evolution.

Fellows: William Dillard Gudger (University of California at Davis); Patricia Ann Myers (Eastman School of Music); Martin Picker (Rutgers University); Richard Wexler (University of Maryland); Jane Ozenberger Whang (University of North Carolina at Chapel Hill); Laura Seale Youens (University of Georgia).

IV. GENRE EXPECTATION AND INDIVIDUAL VOICE IN SEVENTEENTH-
CENTURY ENGLISH VERSE

Senior Fellow: Dr. Dale B. J. Randall, Professor of English, Duke University; Guggenheim Fellow (1970–71); Folger Shakespeare Library Senior Fellowship (National Endowment Research Fellowship) (1978); Cochairman, Southeastern Institute of Medieval and Renaissance Studies (1968–69) and (1974–75); Chairman, Southeastern Institute of Medieval and Renaissance Studies (1969–74) and (1975–77). Author: *The Golden Tapestry: A Critical Survey of Non-Chivalric Spanish Fiction in English Translation* (1543–1657) (1963); *Joseph Conrad and Warrington Dawson: The Record of a Friendship* (1968); *Jonson's Gypsies Unmasked: Background and Theme of "The Gypsies Metamorphos'd"* (1975); *Medieval and Renaissance Studies*, ed., vol. VI of the Proceedings of the Southeastern Institute of Medieval and Renaissance Studies (1976); *Studies in the Continental Background of Renaissance English Literature: Essays Presented to John L. Lievsay*, ed. with George Williams (1977); "A Note on Structure in *Sir Gawain and the Green Knight*," *Modern Language Notes*, LXXII (1957); "Dodsley's Preceptor—A Window into the Eighteenth Century," *Journal of the Rutgers University Library*, XXII (1958); "A 1613 Chaucer Allusion," *Philological Quarterly*, XXXIX (1960); "*Axa and the Prince*: A Rediscovered *Novela* and Its English Translator," *Journal of English and Germanic Philology*, LX (1961); "*The Troublesome and Hard Adventures in Love*: An English Contribution to the Bibliography of *Diana*," *Bulletin of Spanish Studies*, XXXVIII (1961); "Andrew Borde's Spanish Lesson (1542)," *Romance Notes*, IV (1962); "The Classical Ending of Quevedo's *Buscón*," *Hispanic Review*, XXXII (1964); "The 'Seer' and 'Seen' Themes in *Gatsby* and Some of Their Parallels in Eliot and Wright," *Twentieth Century Literature*, X (1964); Coeditor, "Literature of the Renaissance," *Studies in Philology*, LIX (1962), LX (1963), LXI (1964); "*Ecce Signum!* Hamlet's Handsaw Again," in George W. Williams, ed., *Renaissance Papers* 1965 (1966).

Description: This seminar explored the relationship between genre and writer, taking cognizance of the impact of the times upon both. Emphases in discussion reflected particular interests of participants, but the general aim was to consider early and late works, minor and great ones, from Donne to Dryden.

Fellows: Jeanie Renee Brink (Arizona State University); Jay A. Gertzman (Mansfield State College); Marvin Thomas Hester (North Carolina State University); Naomi Conn Liebler (Montclair State College); Frances M. Malpezzi (Arkansas State University); Anna Karen Nardo (Louisiana State University); Robert V. Young, Jr. (North Carolina State University).

V. THE NOVELLA FROM BOCCACCIO TO CERVANTES

Senior Fellow: Dr. Karl-Ludwig Selig, Professor of Spanish Literature, Columbia University; Fellow, Folger Shakespeare Library (1959) and (1963); Special Fellow, Belgian American Educational Foundation (1960) and (1961); Member of Editorial Board, *Yale Italian Studies*, (1976–); General Editor, *Revista Hispanica Moderna*, (1971–); Mark van Doren Award, Columbia University (1974). Author: *The Library of Juan Vincencio de Lastanosa, Patron of Gracián* (1960); ed., Thomas Blundeville, *Of Councils and Counselors* (1963); ed., (with A. G. Hatcher), *Studia Philologica et Litteraria in Honorem L. Spitzer* (1958); ed., (with J. E. Keller), *Hispanic Studies in Honor of Nicholson B. Adams* (1966); "Góngora and Numismatics," *Modern Language Notes*, LXVII (1952); "Concerning Solórzano Pereyra's *Emblemata regio-politica* and Andrés Mendo's *Príncipe perfecto*," *Modern Language Notes*, LXXI (1956); "Zu Valdés Erasmischem *Diálogo de Mercurio y Carón, Bibliothèque d'Humanisme et Renaissance*, XX (1957); "The *Blemata* of Luis Tribaldos de Toledo," *Hispanic Review*, XXIX (1961); "Emblem Literature: Directions in Recent Scholarship," *Yearbook of Comparative and General Literature*, XII (1963); "Three Spanish Libraries of Emblemata and Compendia," *Essays in History and Literature Presented to Stanley Pargellis* . . . (1965); "A Volume of 'Comedias de Ingenios,'" *Bulletin of the Comediantes*, XVIII (1966); "Cervantes y su arte de la novela," *Actas del Segundo Congreso de la Aso. Int. de Hispanistas* (1967); "Notes on Ronsard in the Netherlands," *Studi Francesi*, No. 38 (1969); "The Interplay of Form and Point of View in *El casamiento engañoso*," *Spanische Literatur im Goldenen Zeitalter* (1973); "The Battle of the Sheep (*Don Quixote*, I, 18)," *RHM*, XXXVIII (1976); "The Ricote Episode in *Don Quixote*: Observations on Literary Refractions," *RHM*, XXXVIII (1976); "Concerning the Structure of Cervantes' *La Gitanilla*," rev. version, *Die romanische Novelle* (1976).

Description: A critical examination of the genre and form with particular emphasis on problems of structure and form as well as on narrative technique and devices. Principal texts: *Decameron, Heptameron, Exemplary Novels*. A special supplementary session of six meetings was offered by Professor Karl-Ludwig Selig, "*Ut pictura poësis* and the Interrelationship of the Arts." Six one-hour sessions were devoted to the tools of research (emblemata, mythographies, iconologies, and related works). They were open, by permission, to fellows from all disciplines.

Fellows: Margaret Egan (Yale University); Frances Exum (Winthrop College); Eduardo Gonzalez (Bennington College); Salvador Jimenez-Fajardo (New England College); Emilie Pauline Kostoroski-Kadish (Case-Western Reserve University); Colbert I. Nepaulsingh (State University of New York at Albany).

Index

Index prepared by J. Samuel Hammond, Duke University